Building a
Web Site

FOR

DUMMIES®

4TH EDITION

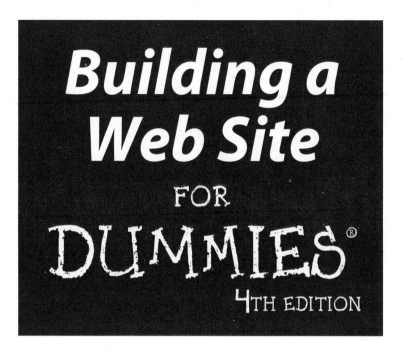

Building a Web Site

FOR DUMMIES®

4TH EDITION

by David A. Crowder

WILEY

Wiley Publishing, Inc.

Building a Web Site For Dummies® 4th Edition

Published by
Wiley Publishing, Inc.
111 River Street
Hoboken, NJ 07030-5774

www.wiley.com

Copyright © 2010 by Wiley Publishing, Inc., Indianapolis, Indiana

Published by Wiley Publishing, Inc., Indianapolis, Indiana

Published simultaneously in Canada

For general information on our other products and services, please contact our Customer Care Department within the U.S. at 877-762-2974, outside the U.S. at 317-572-3993, or fax 317-572-4002.

For technical support, please visit www.wiley.com/techsupport.

Wiley also publishes its books in a variety of electronic formats. Some content that appears in print may not be available in electronic books.

Library of Congress Control Number: 2010926852

ISBN: 978-0-470-56093-8

Manufactured in the United States of America

10 9 8 7 6 5 4 3 2

WILEY

About the Author

David A. Crowder has authored or coauthored nearly 30 books on subjects ranging from computers to historical mysteries, including popular bestsellers such as *Sherlock Holmes For Dummies, Building a Web Site For Dummies* and *CliffsNotes Getting on the Internet.* He was selling hypertext systems back in the days when you had to explain to people what the word meant. He's been involved in the online community since its inception and is the recipient of several awards for his work, including *NetGuide Magazine*'s Gold Site Award.

He is the son of a teacher and a college president, and his dedication to spreading knowledge, especially about the computer revolution, goes beyond his writing. He also founded three Internet mailing lists (discussion groups), JavaScript Talk, Java Talk, and Delphi Talk, all of which were sold to Ziff-Davis. One of his most treasured memories is the message he received from an old-timer on one of those lists who said that he had never seen such a free and open exchange of information since the days when computers were built by hobbyists in home workshops.

When he isn't writing, he spends his time with his wife Angela, wandering through villages in the Andes or frolicking in the Caribbean surf.

Dedication

For Angela. *Eres mi sol, nena, eres mi luna.*

Author's Acknowledgments

Thanks are due to Steven Hayes, Christopher Morris, Barry Childs-Helton, and James Russell, my fine editors, who were there for me every step of the way. Sometimes the relationship between writers and editors is smooth as silk, and sometimes it's tempestuous, but it always results in a better book through the give-and-take of the writing/editing process — and I'm grateful for the critiques and contributions of all the members of the Wiley team. All helped to make this the best book we could put together for you. And they're just the tip of the iceberg: About a zillion people work their tails off anonymously and behind the scenes at Wiley to bring you the finest books they can possibly produce. My hat is off to all of them, from the top editors to the humblest laborer on the loading dock. Last, but by no means least, I'd like to say how much I appreciate all the hard work done by my literary agent, Robert G. Diforio, without whose help I would be lost in the intricacies of the publishing world.

Publisher's Acknowledgments

We're proud of this book; please send us your comments through our online registration form located at `http://dummies.custhelp.com`. For other comments, please contact our Customer Care Department within the U.S. at 877-762-2974, outside the U.S. at 317-572-3993, or fax 317-572-4002.

Some of the people who helped bring this book to market include the following:

Acquisitions, Editorial, and Media Development

Senior Project Editor: Christopher Morris

(Previous Edition: Jean Rogers)

Executive Editor: Steven Hayes

Senior Copy Editor: Barry Childs-Helton

Technical Editor: James Russell

Editorial Manager: Kevin Kirschner

Media Development Project Manager: Laura Moss-Hollister

Media Development Assistant Project Manager: Jenny Swisher

Media Development Associate Producers: Angela Denny, Josh Frank, Marilyn Hummel, Shawn Patrick

Editorial Assistant: Amanda Graham

Sr. Editorial Assistant: Cherie Case

Cartoons: Rich Tennant (www.the5thwave.com)

Composition Services

Project Coordinator: Katherine Crocker

Layout and Graphics: Claudia Bell, Ashley Chamberlain, Christin Swinford

Proofreaders: Laura Bowman, Lindsay Littrell

Indexer: Steve Rath

Special Help: Anne Sullivan

Publishing and Editorial for Technology Dummies

Richard Swadley, Vice President and Executive Group Publisher

Andy Cummings, Vice President and Publisher

Mary Bednarek, Executive Acquisitions Director

Mary C. Corder, Editorial Director

Publishing for Consumer Dummies

Diane Graves Steele, Vice President and Publisher

Composition Services

Debbie Stailey, Director of Composition Services

Contents at a Glance

Table of Contents

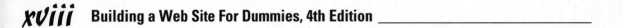

Introduction

Maybe you already have your own Web site and you're not quite satisfied with it. Or perhaps you're still in the planning stages and want to know what you can do to make your site as good as it can be. You've been to Web sites that have all the bells and whistles, and you wouldn't be human if you weren't just a wee bit envious. Well, now you can have it all too. In *Building a Web Site For Dummies,* 4th Edition, I show you some of the best stuff around, and I tell you just how to go about putting it on your site.

About This Book

This isn't just another Web design book. It's special. Really. I set out to write the one book I'd want by my side if I were looking to set up a really fancy Web site and not break the bank doing it. I tracked down and tested zillions of Web-site enhancements and selected the top of the line to share with you. And I'm honestly proud of the results. I've authored or coauthored more than 20 books on computers and the Internet, and this one is my hands-down favorite.

It's full of things you're sure to love. It's packed with fun stuff, but it's got plenty of serious stuff, too, like how to get past the hype and really make money through your Web site. You'll wonder how in the world you ever got along without having these features on your Web site.

How to Use This Book

Keep this book next to your computer and never lend it to anybody. It's far too precious for that. Make your friends buy their own copies. If you need to make space on your bookshelf, throw away anything else you own to make room for it. When you travel, take it with you. Hold it in your arms at night and tell it how much you love it.

Each chapter is a stand-alone entity. (Don't you just love that word?) You don't have to read the whole thing, and it's a rare person who will read the book from cover to cover right off the bat. Go ahead — hit the table of contents or the index and jump to the parts you're most interested in. But don't forget to explore the rest of the book after you're done with the parts that excite you most. You won't regret spending the time — you'll find wonders in every chapter.

Foolish Assumptions

I assume that you have a favorite Web-page creation program — whether it's Dreamweaver, plain old Notepad, or the UNIX-based text editor vi — and you know how to use it. So when I say to copy and paste text or save your file, you know what you need to do. Just in case you don't have a good Web-authoring program, I include sources for some good HTML editors in this book.

Conventions Used in This Book

It's all organized; I promise. Even though it's rather plebeian compared with finding free content for your site, lots of people worked very hard to make sure that this book follows some straightforward rules and typographical conventions.

Code listings, of which there are plenty, look like this:

```
<HTML>
<HEAD>
<SCRIPT>
...
</SCRIPT>
<TITLE>
...
</TITLE>
</HEAD>
...
```

HTML elements in this book are in uppercase, and their attributes are in lowercase, as in this example:

```
<INPUT type="hidden" name="answer" value="yes">
```

If the value of an attribute is in normal type, you enter it exactly as shown. If it's in italics, it's only a placeholder value, and you need to replace it with a real value. In the following example, you replace *myownimage* with the name of the image file you intend to use:

```
<IMG src="myownimage">
```

Whenever you see the URL for one of the top sites I've tracked down, it appears in a special typeface within the paragraph, like this: www.dummies. com. Or it may appear on a separate line, like this:

```
www.dummies.com
```

How This Book Is Organized

This book is divided into six parts. I organized it that way, with a little help from the folks you see in the Acknowledgments. You did read the Acknowledgments, didn't you? Don't tell me that you're the kind of person who reads the Introduction but doesn't read the Acknowledgments. Please tell me that you didn't miss the Dedication, too?

Each part has chapters in it. And each chapter has headings and subheadings. All the sections under these headings and subheadings have text that enlightens the heart and soul. Here, take a look.

Part I: Building Your First Web Site

Part I spills the secrets of how to plan a successful site from the ground up. It tosses in a quick refresher course in basic HTML, then goes into more depth with some of the more advanced approaches such as tables and frames. Toss in a look at WYSIWYG site creation and some advice on getting your material on the Net, and you're ready to transform a bunch of Web pages into a coherent Web site.

Part II: Building Better Web Pages

Part II introduces you to Cascading Style Sheets, and different ways to add images and forms to your site.

Part III: Adding Frills and Fancy Stuff

Part III gives you a ton of ways to make your site work, look, and sound great. This part demystifies JavaScript and DHTML (Dynamic HTML), then it covers the different ways that you add new features like blogs to your Web site and shows you where to get great multimedia.

Part IV: Making Money

Part IV takes a look at making money from your site. It explodes the myths about Internet income and shows you how to really make a profit, how to get a credit card merchant account, and how to work both ends of the affiliates game.

Part V: The Part of Tens

Part V is The Part of Tens. Well, it just wouldn't be a *For Dummies* book without The Part of Tens at the end, right? This part comprises three chapters, so you've got 30 extra bits here that tell you all sorts of wonderful things, like where to go for Web-site design advice and ways to add value to your site.

Finally, at the end of the book is a glossary of all the tech terms that might otherwise leave you baffled.

Icons Used in This Book

The icons in the margins of this book point out items of special interest. Keep an eye out for them — they're important.

Psst! Listen, pal, I wouldn't tell just anybody about this, but here's a way to make things a bit easier or get a little bit more out of it.

Time to tiptoe on eggshells. Make one false step, and things can get pretty messy.

You don't really need to know this stuff, but I just like to show off sometimes. Humor me.

Well, of course, it's all memorable material. But these bits are ones you'll especially want to keep in mind.

Where to Go from Here

Well, keep turning pages, of course. And use the material to make your own Web site the hottest thing there ever was.

One of the hardest parts about getting this book together was categorizing the material in it. Many times, a Web site add-in could've been slotted into a different chapter than the one it ended up in because it had multiple features or attributes. So when you're visiting any of the sites that I mention in this book, be sure to take a good look around. A site that has a great chat room might also have a fine affiliates program. One that offers a good series of Java applets could have some solid tutorials on Web design. A site that has good information on dedicated servers may have the best e-commerce solution for you. I encourage you to browse up a storm.

Additionally, you can go to this book's companion Web site, at `www.dummies.com/go/buildingawebsite4efd`, where you can find links to many of the sites discussed in the book.

Part I
Building Your First Web Site

The 5th Wave   By Rich Tennant

VISUAL WEB DEVELOPMENT TEAM

" Give him air! Give him air! He'll be okay. He's just been
exposed to some raw HTML code. It must have
accidentally flashed across his screen from the server."

In this part . . .

1 start off by covering all the things you need to know to put together a Web site. Chapter 1 shows you the differences between a random bunch of Web pages and a coherent Web site, while Chapter 2 is a quick refresher course in basic HTML. Chapter 3 goes into some more advanced areas like tables. Chapter 4 shows you how to use a WYSIWYG editor to visually design your pages. Finally, Chapter 5 gives you everything you need to know about different Web-hosting options.

Chapter 1

Planning for Good Site Design

*P*eople argue about what the number-one factor in quality Web site design is, and they probably always will. Some say great graphics are the key. Others say worthwhile information is everything. Still others think that ease of use is the most important factor. I'm not so sure that there's such a thing as a linear ranking for these kinds of things. After all, a good-looking site that doesn't work well is useless. A site with a combination of good content and lousy graphics is nothing to crow about either. This book shows you how to do it all and how it all fits together to make a Web site that's actually worth visiting. If you want to get the basics of Web page structure down pat, check out Chapters 2 and 3 on HTML; for the lowdown on graphic design, make sure you spend some time with Chapter 7.

In this chapter, I walk you through the fundamental things you should consider as you create your Web site. And at the end of the chapter, I give you four basic rules for creating Web sites that work. Take 'em with a grain of salt — remember, you're the ultimate judge.

Drafting a Plan

Are you publicizing a political candidate? Trumpeting your favorite cause? Looking for a job? Selling shoe polish? Notice the verbs in each example. They're the key factors in determining your site's *purpose,* as opposed to its *topic.*

What do you want to accomplish?

Just having a topic isn't enough — you need a purpose, too. The *topic* is merely what the site is about; the *purpose* is what the site does. Say, for example, that you want to create a site about penguins. Okay, that's a nice starting point. You like penguins — they're cute, unusual, and pretty interesting; many people share your interest in them. But why do you want to create a Web site about them? Do you have something to say? Do you have information to give, an opinion to share, or a particular point of view that you want to put across?

You don't need to have a PhD in aquatic ornithology to create such a site. Maybe you just like funny-looking birds that swim. But you still need a purpose, or the site just won't work out in the long run. Perhaps you spent ages plowing through the search engines, and you've gathered together the world's greatest collection of penguin links. But why did you go to all that trouble? What's your purpose?

If the purpose for creating a penguin site is for your own personal enjoyment, you really don't need to do much with the site. In fact, you can just create a Web page on your own hard drive or even settle for leaving the links in your Web browser's bookmarks. If you do want your page on the World Wide Web, however, you need to take into account the needs of your potential visitors, as well as your own needs for creating such a site.

Suppose you're putting your penguin page on the Web for the purpose of sharing everything you know about these birds with the world. How does that purpose change your approach to site design? You need to include more on the Web site than a bare list of links, for one thing. Everything you do with the site must help people understand its purpose. If you're setting up your own domain name, for example, you want to pick one that clearly describes your site's content — such as `www.penguinfacts.com`. (Grab it quick — it still wasn't taken at press time.)

The purpose of your site trickles down through each step you take in creating it. You want the title of each page in the site to specify how it supports the site's purpose. The textual content of each page needs to lead naturally into some specific aspect of the topic that furthers your goal. Each graphical image must be just the right one to drive home or emphasize a critical point.

Who do you want to reach?

Who are the people you expect to visit your site? What geographical or cultural groups do you want the site to appeal to? Without at least a general idea of your potential audience, you can't have much of an idea about what type of site to create.

If data is available about the audience for similar sites, you want to track it down. But where do you find it? Surprisingly, most of it's available from the people you're competing with. (Even if you're not running a commercial site, similar sites are your competitors.) Anyone who's been involved in any type of corporate intelligence work would be shocked at the way people on the World Wide Web casually throw around valuable information, instead of keeping it under lock and key.

Many sites offer links to their visitor data. Even a quick perusal of the server logs (which automatically record information about visitors) can provide you with priceless insights into the sort of people who visit sites similar to the one you're creating. If the sites you want information on don't list links to their log data, send an e-mail message to the Webmaster asking how to access it. Most Webmasters aren't the slightest bit security-conscious about their customer data, and you may be surprised at how many of them are more than willing to spill the beans about their visitors.

Keeping your site fresh

If your material never changes, the odds are pretty good that most people won't come back to it very often, if ever. Unless your sole topic is a rock-solid reference subject, you can't get away with anything less than constant updating. Sure, the *Oxford English Dictionary* can come out with a new edition only every few generations. (The first edition came out in 1928 and the second one in 1989, with only two supplements in between.) But such cases are very rare. Even if you deal with a modern high-tech equivalent, such as a site on the Java programming language or the current HTML standard, you need to stay on your toes.

 If your core material is something that doesn't change often, you need to add some peripheral material that you can replace more frequently. Consider adding a Tip of the Day, fresh links, a Did You Know? column, or something along those lines so you can avoid offering only stale content to your return visitors.

How often you need to update your site depends partially on your topic and partially on your site policy. With sites that deal with volatile topics such as breaking international news, you need to update on an hourly basis at a minimum. On the other hand, sites that analyze the news can stand a more leisurely pace — daily, weekly, or even monthly — because their scope is considerably wider.

Even if your topic doesn't absolutely demand a certain update schedule, you should still establish a regular policy for how often you add fresh material to your site. Whatever schedule you establish, make sure you stick with it.

Remember the comfort factor and bear in mind that your site's visitors will be less comfortable if they don't know what to expect from you. Consistency on your side helps build trust on theirs.

A Web site must change at least once a month to keep visitors interested in coming back to it.

User-generated content

When the World Wide Web first got started, it was pretty much a one-way street — Webmasters like you always made the decisions about what would appear and how it could be used. As the Web has evolved, however, it has taken on some important new characteristics.

Today, some of the Web's most popular sites aren't so much controlled by their Webmasters as they are by their users. Places like YouTube and MySpace are hotbeds for the users' self-expression — and, indeed, that is their reason for existence. The new trend that has led to the phrase "Web 2.0" is user-generated content, supplemented by social networking.

Of course, the majority of Web sites are still generated almost totally by either individuals or small teams working together, but the public's hunger for its own chance to shine is seemingly insatiable — and it's something you might want to keep in mind as you design your own Web site. Wikipedia and the other wikis are collaborative efforts, and the old personal home page has largely given way to *blogs* — Web logs, or personalized diaries that can be syndicated and sent to others automatically. (See Chapter 12 for more information on blogs.)

Designing the Look of Your Site

All great art depends on having every necessary component in place and nothing — not one thing — that you don't need there. Great literature doesn't add extraneous characters or pad its plot lines. Great paintings don't have extra brush strokes or colors thrown in for no particular reason. When you're practicing the art of Web design, strive for that kind of purity.

Appealing to your audience

The audience — which is made up of the visitors you hope to attract to your site — determines the content. To set some basic limits, think of these visitors as being at a beginning, an intermediate, or an advanced level, and gauge your content accordingly. If you're aiming advanced content at a beginning audience or vice versa, you're looking at failure from the word go.

Not only does your audience determine your content, but its preferences influence your visual-design requirements as well. If your audience consists of high-school students whose interests revolve mainly around the latest musical sensations, you need a far different look from what you'd shoot for if it consists of retired naval officers who want to know about international events.

For the young music lovers, for example, you need to strike a tone that's lighthearted and exciting, both in your words and graphics. Brighter colors and a more relaxed and informal tone for the text are the call here. For the old salts, though, you need to take a heavier approach, with darker, duller colors and a middling-formal approach to language.

Whatever the group you're aiming for, ask yourself the following questions:

- ✔ **How do they communicate with one another?** Roller-hockey players don't communicate quite the same way as cartographers do. What are the level and style of language usage in the group? Do its members have a particular jargon, slang, or regional dialect? If so, can you use it comfortably and correctly?

- ✔ **What kind and color of clothes do they wear?** This kind of information tells you volumes about their preferences. People who are willing to wear suits and ties in midsummer don't think the same way as those who prefer casual clothing. The colors they wear also indicate the color ranges they're likely to feel comfortable with on your site.

- ✔ **What's their worldview?** For many people, the world consists of their apartment or house; the road between it and their workplace; their cubicle, office, or factory floor; and a couple of restaurants somewhere along that pathway. For others, the world consists only of Wall Street and the Asian financial markets. For some, the world is a series of airports, cell phones, and e-mail messages. Anything that exists outside your audience's worldview is invisible to them and probably doesn't belong on your Web site.

Find out all that you can — from what kind of cars your visitors drive to the hours they wake and sleep. Any kind of information you can nail down about your visitors and their lives helps you to understand them — and that understanding can't help but improve your site's appeal.

Avoiding clutter

If you're one of those people who keeps a perfectly clean desk where your speakers line up exactly perpendicular to the edge of your monitor, whose laundry basket is more than occasionally empty, and who always knows where to find everything you own, I probably can't tell you much about organization. If you're like the rest of us, however, read on.

Far too many Webmasters seem to think that the best kind of Web page is one that has everything in the world crammed into it. It's like a novel that introduces 27 characters in the first two pages — the overkill ruins it, and your mind is left swimming.

Perhaps you absolutely must put together a Web page containing a dozen frames, several JavaScript pop-ups, numerous Java applets running in the background, and a bunch of animated GIFs that move around the screen by using Cascading Style Sheets (CSS) positioning. If so, please, please, *don't* put in an image map, too.

The line between losing and winning is very fine if you're considering using Web gadgetry. Without it, most sites seem a bit on the dull side, and Web designers exhibit a really strong keep-up-with-the-Joneses streak that usually results in a frenzy of site changes whenever some new technique becomes popular. Too much of a good thing — or too many good things in one place — can, however, become a real problem.

The key is to remember your site's purpose as you're designing any page. If anything you're considering adding to the page doesn't serve that purpose, don't add it. If you discover some fun or glitzy gizmo that you simply *must* put on a page — and I show you plenty in this book to tempt you — first determine if you can make it fit in with what you already have on that page. If you absolutely can't fit it in, but you still want to add it, maybe you can take something else out to make room for it.

This doesn't mean you can't have more than one unusual feature on a page — just make sure that you follow a path of moderation.

Achieving Usability

Usability is an important word for Web designers. It means just what it says — making a site usable. Without usability, nothing else you do matters. What good is it to have wonderful content if nobody can find it? What good is it to have beautiful graphics on a page that is inaccessible except by dumb luck?

Fortunately, designing a usable Web site isn't difficult, and following a few simple rules can set you on your way. As with any set of rules, you may want to break these from time to time, but you do so at your own peril:

- ✔ **Keep your navigation system consistent on all the pages in your Web site.** If you have a link to your home page at the top of half your pages and you put that link at the bottom of the rest, you'll confuse your visitors.

- ✔ **Put links to your home page and your search function on both the top and bottom of every page.** Too many Web designers put them on only the top or the bottom, forcing users to scroll to find them. Don't make your visitors do extra work.

 ✔ **Never use blue, underlined text for anything but a link.** In fact, try to avoid underlining at all. Use bold or italics for emphasis instead; otherwise you'll fool a lot of people into clicking underlined text to no effect.

 ✔ **Don't use too many links in a navigation bar.** Half a dozen is about the most you should add. Remember that a navigation bar is not a site map, but a guide to the major sections within your site.

 ✔ **Use words!** Using graphical icons may make your pages prettier, but you should design your navigation bar (or whatever alternative you use) to instantly communicate what it means to someone who has never been to your site before. In this case, a picture is *not* worth a thousand words.

 ✔ **If your site is composed of hierarchical pages (and most of them are), consider using *breadcrumb navigation*.** The term comes from the idea of leaving a trail of breadcrumbs as you walk so you can easily retrace your steps. When applied to a Web site, the metaphor refers to a listing at the top of the page showing the current page's relationship to the hierarchy; most often, these breadcrumbs are links that you can click to go directly back to any place along the trail.

The Big Rules for Planning Your Site

Here are some short rules to condense the information in this chapter down to a few rules that I think are pretty good guidelines, going by my own experience as both designer and visitor. Make these rules a part of your very being. Do them in calligraphy and hang them on your wall. Use a wood-burning kit to engrave them on your dcsk. Tattoo them backward on your forehead so you see them in the mirror every morning.

 ✔ **Rule #1:** The Web is for reaching out to people.

 ✔ **Rule #2:** Keep your Web pages lean and clean.

 ✔ **Rule #3:** Know who your visitors are and what they want.

 Remember that design and content are more a matter of art than science, which means that your own gut feelings count more than anything else. If someone tells you that your design decisions are wrong, and that person is someone whose input you respect, you certainly want to give that opinion some consideration. But if you're firmly convinced that you're right, never let anyone else's concepts override your own. This brings me to The Big Rule:

 ✔ **Rule #4:** It's your Web site. It's your vision. Do it your way.

Online Sources for Web Design

Table 1-1 lists some places on the World Wide Web where you can find more information on the topics covered in this chapter.

Table 1-1	Online Resources for Web Design
Web Site Name	**Web Address**
Beginners Web Design Tutorial	www.how-to-build-websites.com
useit.com	www.useit.com
Web Pages That Suck	www.webpagesthatsuck.com
Web Style Guide	www.webstyleguide.com/index.html?/contents.html

Chapter 2

Creating a Web Page with Basic HTML Tags

In This Chapter

▶ Taking a look at tags

▶ Using HTML tags to format text

▶ Getting the lowdown on links

▶ Adding graphics to your Web site

*T*his chapter's here just in case you need a refresher on basic Web page building before plunging ahead into all the wonderful stuff that's covered in the rest of the book. Here I touch on how you use HTML to create Web pages — and populate those pages with text and images. I show you how to format text, set the colors on your Web page, and set up links between pages with both text and images.

Even if you already know all about these things, you may want to browse through the chapter and check out some of the Web sites listed in the tables.

Tagging Along with HTML

Web pages are built primarily by writing instructions in *HyperText Markup Language* (HTML). HTML is a simple language that tells a computer how to create a document; its main aim is to tell a Web browser, such as Firefox or Microsoft Internet Explorer, how a Web page should look on-screen. Happily, there's nothing really complex about HTML: The files you create are just plain old text files and you don't need anything more complex than Notepad or any other simple text editor to create them. What I cover in this chapter is the bare minimum that you need to know to create Web pages and link them to make a Web site. If you're interested in going deeper into HTML, check out *HTML, XHTML & CSS For Dummies* by Ed Tittel and Jeff Noble (Wiley Publishing).

You can find the HTML 4.01 specification at `www.w3.org/TR/html401`.

HTML is composed of *elements.* A paragraph or an image, for example, is an element. Elements, in turn, are composed of tags, attributes, and — sometimes — content. Here's a little more information about each of those:

- ✔ **Tags:** A tag is a simple descriptive term that tells a Web browser what element it's dealing with.

  - • *Start tag:* The beginning of each element is shown by the name of that element within angle braces; this is called a *start tag.* The start tag for a paragraph, for example, is `<P>`; for an image, it's `<IMG>`.

  - • *End tag:* The end of an element is shown by the *end tag,* which is just like the start tag except that the end tag has a slash before the element's name. The end tag for a paragraph, therefore, is `</P>`. Some elements, such as `IMG`, don't have end tags.

- ✔ **Attributes:** An *attribute* is a modification of the basic element. You specify the width and height of an image, for example, by adding attributes to the tag, as in the following example:

  ```
  <IMG width="100" height="30">
  ```

- ✔ **Content:** Content is anything that goes between the start tag and the end tag, as in the following example:

  ```
  <P>This is the content of this paragraph.</P>
  ```

The tags and attributes you need most often are covered in more depth in the rest of this chapter, but the basics I just covered help you to understand the choices you face among different Web page-building programs.

A typical Web page features a basic structure of three elements: `HTML`, `HEAD`, and `BODY`. The `HTML` element contains both the `HEAD` and `BODY` elements, as the following example demonstrates:

```
<HTML>

<HEAD>
</HEAD>

<BODY>
</BODY>

</HTML>
```

You can make a Web page without using the `HTML`, `HEAD`, and `BODY` tags, but I don't recommend it. It's technically possible, and even legitimate under the HTML standard. But leaving them out can't help anything, and putting them in helps you to keep the other elements in their proper places.

All the code for everything that's visible on the Web page goes into the BODY element. The HEAD element contains information such as the page's title, which goes between the <TITLE> and </TITLE> tags like this:

```
<HEAD>
<TITLE>This is the page title.</TITLE>
</HEAD>
```

The title doesn't appear on the actual Web page — it's displayed in the title bar at the top of the visitor's Web browser.

Getting Wordy

Words are the foremost method of communication on the World Wide Web, and it's a rare Web page indeed that hasn't got a passel of 'em scattered all over it.

In the examples provided in the following sections, I show the basic code necessary for creating the particular elements (all made of words) that I talk about (using a few more words).

Paragraphs

Paragraph elements are what you normally use to place text on a Web page. You put the text between the <P> and </P> tags, as in the following example:

```
<P>This is where the textual content goes.</P>
```

Technically, the end tag for a P element is optional in HTML. You don't need to include it, although most Web-page creation programs add it automatically.

Web browsers add a bit of space between paragraphs automatically. If you want some extra space, you can add it by using the line break, or BR, element, as the following example shows:

```
<P>This is the first paragraph.</P>
<BR>
<P>This paragraph has a space above it.</P>
```

Figure 2-1 shows the results of using the BR element.

You can usually get away with using an empty P element — one with no content between the start and end tags — to create a blank line between paragraphs instead of using a BR element. Unfortunately, this technique doesn't work for all Web browsers. Because empty P elements aren't allowed under the HTML standard, browsers that strictly follow the standard ignore them and don't insert a blank line.

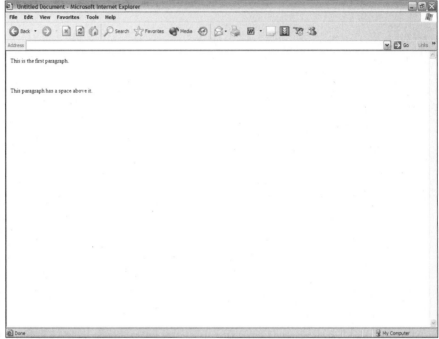

Figure 2-1:
Paragraphs
with line
breaks
add more
white space
to your
Web page.

The standard solution to this problem is to put some invisible content into the P element. Because Web browsers ignore plain white space, you can't just press your spacebar. Just put in a nonbreaking space with a special code . Here's how you do it:

```
<P>This is the first paragraph.</P>
<P> </P>
<P>This paragraph has a space above it.</P>
```

If you use a nonbreaking space, make sure that you include the semicolon at the end. If you don't, you end up with the characters   on-screen rather than a blank space.

Headings

Headings are also elements that contain text. Different headings create different sizes of text and make that text bold. HTML uses half a dozen heading elements, ranging from the humongous H1 size all the way down to the teeny-weeny H6. (You can probably guess that H2, H3, H4, and H5 are between H1 and H6 in size, so I won't bother to explain that.)

You use headings to differentiate one section of text from another. Smaller headings designate subsections under larger headings. Say, for example, that you're running a news Web site. You use H1 for the main headline and follow it with the text in P elements. Any subheads in the article use H2 headings, any subheads under those headings use H3, and so on, as the following example demonstrates:

```
<H1>Clown Runs Amok</H1>
    <P>In a surprising development today, Clown of the Year
    Toby O'Dell-Gonzalez went on a rampage through the
    Hideyoshi Circus, spraying at least 17 elephants with
    whipped cream.</P>
<H2>Echoes Earlier Incident</H2>
    <P>Highly placed sources within the circus confirm that
    this is not the first time the famed performer has
    committed such an act. "Toby just kind of has a thing
    about dairy products," said one of the co-owners of the
    circus.</P>
```

Figure 2-2 shows how the preceding code listing looks on your Web page.

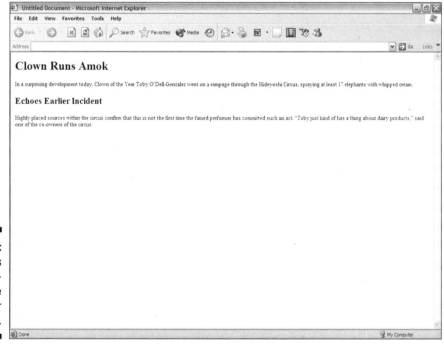

Figure 2-2:
Headings help organize the text on your Web page.

Fonts

Font is a fancy term that describes the way a letter is shaped. **This** word is in a font that's different from the font **this** word is in. You can just go with the default fonts — those fonts that are set automatically in the Web browser — or you can specify which fonts you want. For casual Web-page development, the default fonts work just fine, but you may prefer to make your own choices to get just the right look.

Two elements that you use most often for altering fonts are B and I. These elements set the enclosed lettering to bold or italic print, respectively, as in the following example:

```
<P>This is normal print. <B>This is bold print.</B>
          <I>This is italicized print.</I></P>
```

You can also use the FONT element to set the *face* of the text, which is the basic appearance of the lettering (whether it's Arial, Times New Roman, and so on), as well as the size and color. (See the section "Using Color," later in this chapter, for more information on setting color.) The following example shows how to use the FONT element to set face, size, and color:

```
<P><FONT face="Arial, Helvetica, sans-serif" size="5"
   color="blue">This is blue-colored Helvetica in
   size 5.</FONT>
<FONT face="Times New Roman, Times, serif" size="3"
   color="red">This is red-colored Times Roman in
   size 3.</FONT>
<FONT face="Courier New, Courier, mono" size="7"
   color="black">This is black-colored Courier in
   size 7.</FONT></P>
```

Figure 2-3 shows the results of the two preceding code examples.

Although I used the FONT element on whole sentences in the code example, you can also apply it to smaller stretches of text — even to a single character.

The reason for the face attribute's several choices is that many different computer systems are hooked up to the Internet, and Windows doesn't offer the same options that Macs or Unix systemsdo. If the font you specify isn't available, the visitor's Web browser makes its best guess about what font to substitute. By offering a series of font options for the browser to use, you improve the chances of a visitor seeing just what you intended. The preceding code example includes all you need to cover the three main types of font faces common on the World Wide Web.

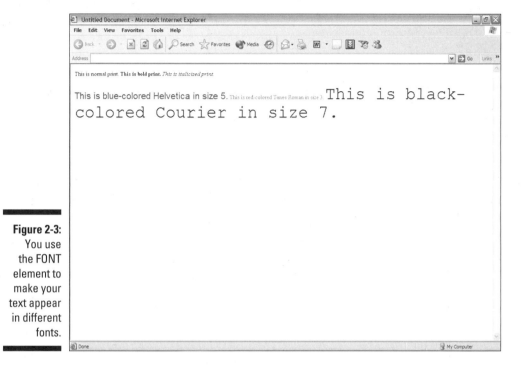

Figure 2-3:
You use
the FONT
element to
make your
text appear
in different
fonts.

Lines

Okay, a horizontal line isn't really a word, but this part of the book is the least unlikely place I can think of to discuss this element. In HTML, these lines are technically known as *horizontal rules,* so the element that represents them is called HR. Horizontal rules separate one section of a page from another visually, underline an image, and do just about anything you normally do with lines.

You can set the width of horizontal rules as either a percentage of the width of the screen or as an exact pixel value. The default width value of a horizontal line is 100 percent of the screen width, so if you don't specify the value of the width attribute, that's what you get. To specify a width of 50 percent, for example, use the following code:

```
<HR width="50%">
```

To specify a width of 400 pixels, you do it like this instead:

```
<HR width="400">
```

You use the `size` attribute to set the height, or thickness, of the line, as the following example shows:

```
<HR size="6">
```

By default, the line is hollow, or _shaded_. (The hollow line is called _shaded_ because back in the days when Web pages weren't so colorful and all you had to work with was black text on a medium-gray background, hollow horizontal lines appeared to sink into the page, creating a shaded, or 2-D, effect. Against most other background colors, the effect isn't apparent.) To make a line solid, you need to add the `noshade` attribute, as in the following example:

```
<HR noshade>
```

The following code creates the Web page shown in Figure 2-4:

```
<HR>
<HR width="100%">
<HR width="50%">
<HR width="200">
<HR width="400">
<HR size="10">
<HR size="6" noshade>
```

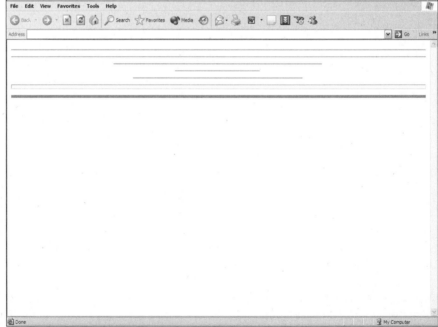

Figure 2-4:
Different width and size values change the appearance of horizontal rules.

Many Web designers use graphics (such as GIF files) to create horizontal lines instead of relying on HTML. See the clip-art sources in the section "Picturing It: Using Images," later in this chapter, for some examples.

Using Color

Unless you're really into television reruns or artsy photography, you probably don't see much of anything in black and white these days. The world's a colorful place, and you may disappoint your visitors if you don't use color on your Web site.

I touch on color in the earlier section "Fonts," but you can use color in many places. As time goes by, you will doubtlessly be able to color every element in HTML.

If you use *Cascading Style Sheets* (CSS), you have much more control over color than you do with normal HTML. There's an introduction to CSS in Chapter 6 of this book, and you can find out even more in the book *Creating Web Sites Bible,* by Philip Crowder and yours truly (Wiley Publishing).

If you read the "Fonts" section earlier in this chapter, you already know that you can set the color of a particular set of letters, but you can also set the base color for all the text — as well as for a page's background and its links. The links use three different colors: one for links a visitor hasn't clicked, one for links that he or she is clicking, and one for links already visited.

You can accomplish all these color changes by setting the values for various attributes of the BODY element:

- ✔ text — Text color
- ✔ bgcolor — Background color
- ✔ link — Unvisited link color
- ✔ vlink — Visited link color
- ✔ alink — Color for a link that someone's clicking (the *active link*)

Setting all these attributes at once looks like this:

```
<BODY text="black" bgcolor="white" link="blue" vlink="red"
       alink="purple">
```

Creating Links

When it comes to the World Wide Web, *links* (which connect different files) are everything. Without them, the Web wouldn't exist. You create links with the A (anchor) element. That element's href (hypertext reference) attribute gives the Web address of the file you want to link to. This address is called a *URL,* which is short for uniform resource locator. Here's what a link looks like in HTML:

```
<A href="http://www.dummies.com/">content</A>
```

The part that reads *content* is where you put words or images that people can click to go to the linked file. This content appears by default as blue underlined letters (if it's a text link) or as a blue outlined image (if it's an image link).

Picturing It: Using Images

You can have a Web page with nothing but words on it, but most people think that's a bit dull. It's pretty rare to find a site that's not filled with images of one kind or another. When it comes to placing images on the World Wide Web, you need to use graphics files in one of three common formats: GIF, JPEG (also called JPG), or PNG. (Chapter 7 covers these file formats in more depth.)

Where do you get images? You can create them from scratch, or you can download ready-to-use files from some of the Web sites listed in Table 2-1. If you use other people's images — as most Web designers do — be sure first that you read all the fine print on their Web sites. Unless it states otherwise, the original artist owns the copyright on an image — which means you can't use it without permission. Fortunately, the vast majority of artists on the Web are eager to give that permission in exchange for nothing more than a link from your Web site back to theirs. This arrangement gives them free publicity and gives you free, high-quality artwork. Everybody's happy.

If the artist isn't willing to let you display copyrighted art in exchange for a link, you may have to pay to use the image. Sometimes, too, the image is free to use on noncommercial sites but costs money to use on commercial ones. To reemphasize the point, *make sure that you read the fine print.* Don't — I repeat, *don't* — just grab an image that's not free, use it, and figure that you can get away with it. It's possible, of course, to download any image you can see in a Web browser — *but* you're cheating the artist and running the risk of serious repercussions — which can include federal charges. Plenty of freely available art is out there. Stick with it, and you're a lot less likely to run into problems.

Table 2-1	Sources of Clip Art
Web Site Name	**Web Address**
Animation Arthouse	`www.animation.arthouse.org`
Barry's Clipart Server	`www.clipart.com/en`
Clipart Connection	`www.clipartconnection.com`
CoolArchive Free Clip Art	`www.coolarchive.com`
Graphic Maps	`www.worldatlas.com/clipart.htm`

Images

The most common item other than text on Web pages is the *image,* represented by the IMG element. The only absolutely required attribute for that element is the src attribute, which specifies the name and — if the file is located somewhere other than in the same directory as the HTML file that links to it — the location of the graphics file.

Thus, you code the simplest image on a Web page (see Figure 2-5) like this:

```
<IMG src="seated16.jpg">
```

To specify a graphics file in another folder, you add the path to the folder, as in the following example:

```
<IMG src="pets/seated16.jpg">
```

If the graphics file is on another Web server entirely, you add the full path to that URL, as follows:

```
<IMG src="http://www.anotherserver.com/seated16.jpg">
```

I mention in the section "Creating Links," earlier in this chapter, that you can use an image as a link just as you can use text for one. To do so, just put the IMG element right between the start and end tags for the A element, as the following example shows:

```
<A href="http://www.dummies.com/"><IMG src="seated16.jpg"></A>
```

IMG elements don't have an end tag.

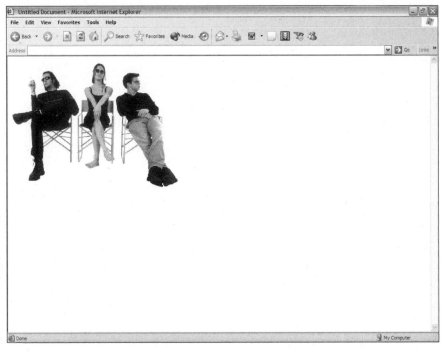

Figure 2-5:
This image
of some
bored
people is in
a JPEG file
format.

Background images

A background image follows the same rules as a regular image, except that you create it by using the background attribute of the BODY element rather than an IMG element, as shown in the following example:

```
<BODY background="guitar2.jpg">
```

Background images *tile,* which means they repeat themselves across the page until they reach the edge of the screen. Then they begin tiling again in the next available space below the first line of images, and so on, until they fill the entire page from side to side and top to bottom. Because of this characteristic, most people prefer to use small background images, such as the guitars shown in Figure 2-6.

Choose background images with care. Make sure they don't interfere with the other elements on the Web page. You want the color muted, the lines indistinct, and the content supportive of the overall theme.

Figure 2-6:
A page
with a tiled
background
image.

Putting It All Together

Okay, so you've seen the kinds of elements you use on a Web page. Now it's time to actually build a page from them. Of course, you'll probably never use every possibility, as some combinations would create design conflicts (if you use both a background color and a background image, for example, you'll never see the background color because the background image would cover it), but this example shows you how the elements fit together on a typical Web page:

```
<HTML>

<HEAD>
<TITLE>This is the page title.</TITLE>
</HEAD>

<BODY text="black" bgcolor="white" link="blue" vlink="red"
        alink="purple">

<H1>Clown Runs Amok</H1>
<HR width="50%">
```

```
    <P>In a <I>surprising development</I> today, Clown of
        the Year
    Toby O'Dell-Gonzalez went on a rampage through the
    Hideyoshi Circus, spraying at least 17 elephants with
    whipped cream.</P>
<IMG src="TODell.jpg">

<H2>Echoes Earlier Incident</H2>
    <P>Highly placed sources within the circus confirm that
    this is not the first time the famed performer has
    committed such an act. "Toby just kind of has a thing
    about dairy products," said one of the co-owners of the
    circus.</P>
<P>Click <A href="http://www.dummies.com/">here</A> for
        more info

</BODY>

</HTML>
```

Online Sources for Web Page Building

Table 2-2 lists some places on the World Wide Web where you can find more information about the topics covered in this chapter.

Table 2-2	Online Resources for Building Web Pages
Web Site Name	*Web Address*
HTML 4.01 Specification	`www.w3.org/TR/html401/`
HTML Goodies	`www.htmlgoodies.com`
HTML Writers Guild	`www.hwg.org`
Index DOT Html	`www.eskimo.com/~bloo/indexdot/html/index.html`
Introduction to HTML	`www.wdvl.com/Authoring/HTML/Intro/`

Chapter 3

Arranging Your Text with Tables and Other Advanced Tags

. . . .

In This Chapter

▶ Using rows and columns in your design

▶ Padding and spacing

▶ Spanning your table's rows and columns

▶ Working with framesets and frames

▶ Setting borders and margins

. . . .

A Web page doesn't have to be just a straightforward run of text and images from top to bottom. In this chapter, I show you some simple tricks you can use to add structure to your Web pages.

What you see on the screen isn't always what it looks like on the surface because savvy Web designers know that adding an internal skeleton adds strength to their efforts. The most common way to do that is to make your whole Web page into a table, a series of neatly aligned boxes into which you slot the components of your page. You can leave all the "bones" showing or, for a more elegant appearance, make them all invisible — that way, you get all the benefit of the underlying structure with none of the clutter usually associated with tables.

Frames can also be used for similar effect. Each frame is an entirely separate Web page with its own source code, yet, when you use frames, all these Web pages are displayed simultaneously on the same screen as if they were all from a single source.

Creating Tables

Over the course of your life you've seen tables used to structure information a zillion times. Usually they're nothing more than a blocky listing of some sort of data. On the Web, though, tables can be a whole lot more.

Defining rows and columns

Web tables, like normal ones, appear to be composed of rows and columns. In Web design, however, you only deal with the rows (horizontal areas). As you might expect, you start things off with a TABLE element. This contains a series of TR (table row) elements which contain some TD (table data) elements, or *cells*.

Here's an example of the coding for a simple table:

```
<TABLE border="1">
<TR>
<TD>Cell One</TD>
<TD>Cell Two</TD>
<TD>Cell Three</TD>
</TR>
<TR>
<TD>Cell Four</TD>
<TD>Cell Five</TD>
<TD>Cell Six</TD>
</TR>
<TR>
<TD>Cell Seven</TD>
<TD>Cell Eight</TD>
<TD>Cell Nine</TD>
</TR>
</TABLE>
```

Figure 3-1 shows how this looks in a Web browser.

In this example, the width of the border, or the lines surrounding it, is set to a single pixel.

If you set a value of "0" for the border, there won't be any lines around the table. This can be an important factor in your design because it enables you to use the structure of a table for formatting purposes without allowing the lines to intrude. Generally speaking, tables look best with border values between 1 and 4.

Setting table dimensions

You can set the size of a table by using the width and height attributes, specifying a measure either in pixels or as a percentage of the screen size. This example would set the size to 600 by 300 pixels:

```
<TABLE width="600" height="300">
```

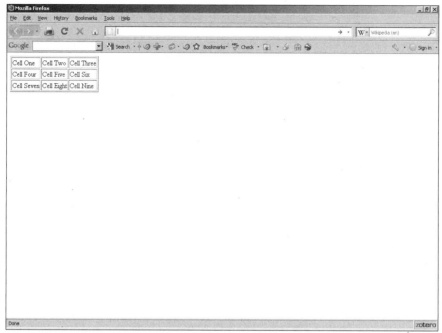

Figure 3-1:
A simple
table.

To specify that the table should take up all the available space on the screen, you'd use this code instead:

```
<TABLE width="100%" height="100%">
```

You also have the flexibility to mix the two approaches if your design requires you to do so. You could, for example, set a table so it would stretch across the entire screen from side to side, while restricting its height to 400 pixels, by using this code:

```
<TABLE width="100%" height="400">
```

You don't have to set both the width and the height. It's perfectly okay to specify one but not the other.

Defining cell sizes

Although the overall size of the table is an important consideration, of course, the greatest power for a Web designer comes from specifying the size of individual cells.

There are, as you might imagine, some tradeoffs you have to consider because the cells are contained within the table — therefore their settings can adversely affect the layout if handled incorrectly. The main thing to keep in mind is that setting height and width often affects more than one cell:

- ✔ If you set the height of one cell (TD), then every cell in that row (TR) will be set to that height. If you set heights for more than one cell in a row, the lower height values will be ignored and the greatest height will be applied to the entire row. With height, keep in mind that you're dealing with rows, not with columns — so the cells above and below the one whose height you set will remain unaffected.

- ✔ If you're setting width, all cells in the column will be set to the width you specify. Although there's no such thing as a "column element," this effect is intended to promote symmetry in the table. If you need varying cell widths in a single column, there's a way around this; see the "Spanning rows and columns" section later in this chapter for details.

Another potential "gotcha" when you're tinkering with cell sizes is the use of percentages. There's a big difference between setting cell size and setting table size: With a table, you're dealing with a percentage of the browser's screen size; with a cell, you're specifying a percentage of the table's size.

Let's say you have a table that has (as in the earlier example) a width of 600 pixels. When you specify a cell width that's 10% of that, you're setting that cell to be 60 pixels wide rather than 10% of the total screen width. If, on the other hand, you have a table set to be 80% of the screen width, then a cell set to 10% will be one tenth of that — 8% of the screen width.

Okay, so much for theory; let's get down to some actual coding. The following code sets the height of the first cell (TD element) to 100 pixels and the width of the fifth cell (the second one in the second row) to 200 pixels; the ninth one (the last one in the last row) has a width of 300 pixels:

```
<TABLE border="1" width="100%">
<TR>
<TD height="100">Cell One</TD>
<TD>Cell Two</TD>
<TD>Cell Three</TD>
</TR>
<TR>
<TD>Cell Four</TD>
<TD width="200">Cell Five</TD>
<TD>Cell Six</TD>
</TR>
<TR>
<TD>Cell Seven</TD>
<TD>Cell Eight</TD>
<TD width="300">Cell Nine</TD>
</TR>
</TABLE>
```

Figure 3-2 shows this in action.

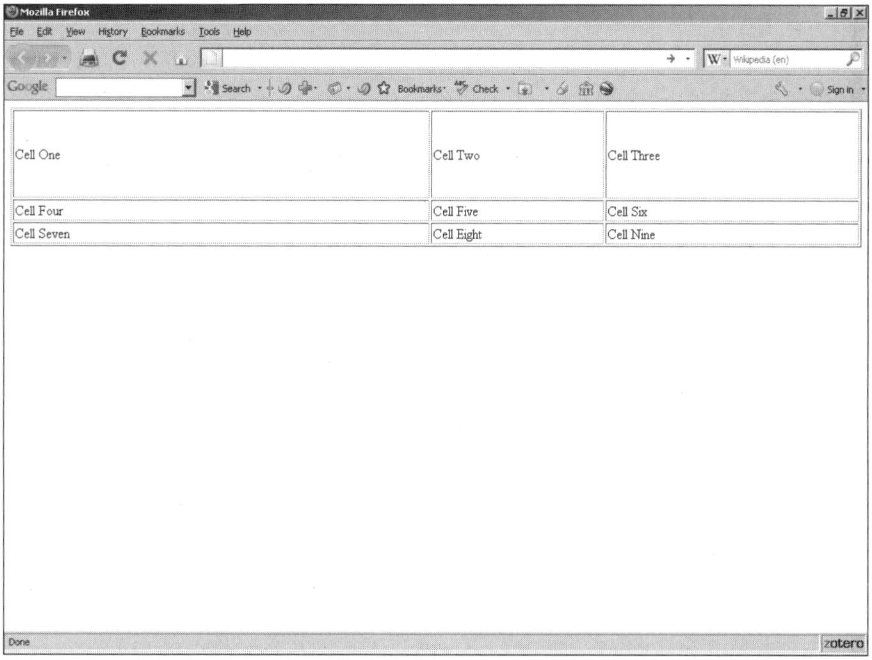

Figure 3-2:
Setting cell
sizes.

Padding and spacing cells

If you just go with default settings and don't specify any space adjustments, then every cell will be right up against its neighboring cells and any content you put in your cells will be flush with the edges of the cell. Depending upon your particular design requirements, this can be either good or bad.

You have control over these factors via the `cellspacing` and `cellpadding` attributes. *Cell spacing* refers to the amount of space between the cells themselves, whereas *cell padding* controls the space between the cell's edges and the cell's contents.

Cell padding can be especially important when you've set the table's border to `"0"` so that no lines show.

The following example creates three tables with cell-spacing values of 5, 10, and 20, respectively:

```
<TABLE border="1" cellspacing="5">
<TR>
<TD>Cell One</TD>
<TD>Cell Two</TD>
<TD>Cell Three</TD>
</TR>
<TR>
```

```
<TD>Cell Four</TD>
<TD>Cell Five</TD>
<TD>Cell Six</TD>
</TR>
<TR>
<TD>Cell Seven</TD>
<TD>Cell Eight</TD>
<TD>Cell Nine</TD>
</TR>
</TABLE>
```

```
<TABLE border="1" cellspacing="10">
<TR>
<TD>Cell One</TD>
<TD>Cell Two</TD>
<TD>Cell Three</TD>
</TR>
<TR>
<TD>Cell Four</TD>
<TD>Cell Five</TD>
<TD>Cell Six</TD>
</TR>
<TR>
<TD>Cell Seven</TD>
<TD>Cell Eight</TD>
<TD>Cell Nine</TD>
</TR>
</TABLE>
```

```
<TABLE border="1" cellspacing="20">
<TR>
<TD>Cell One</TD>
<TD>Cell Two</TD>
<TD>Cell Three</TD>
</TR>
<TR>
<TD>Cell Four</TD>
<TD>Cell Five</TD>
<TD>Cell Six</TD>
</TR>
<TR>
<TD>Cell Seven</TD>
<TD>Cell Eight</TD>
<TD>Cell Nine</TD>
</TR>
</TABLE>
```

Figure 3-3 shows the results.

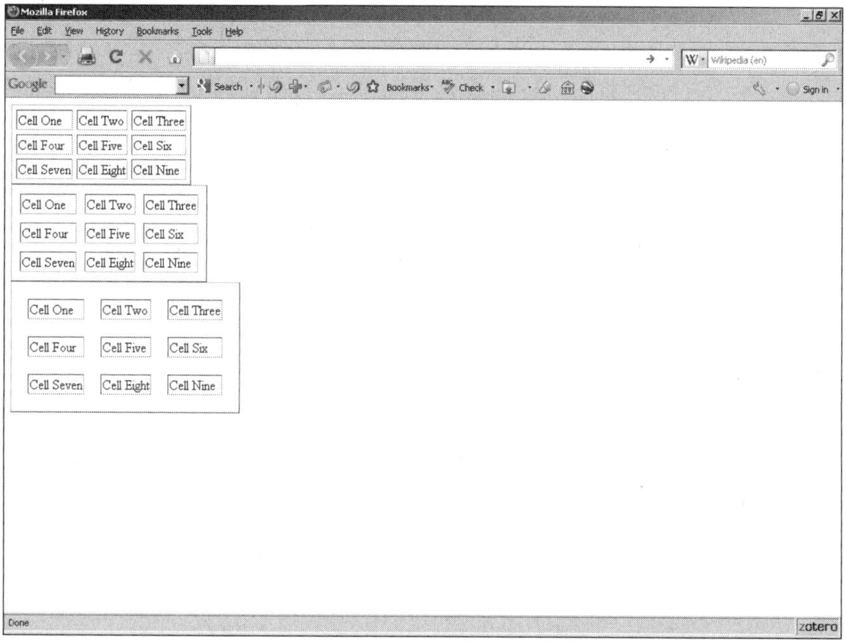

Figure 3-3:
Setting the spacing between cells.

Cell padding, as mentioned before, sets the distance between the content of a cell and the cell's border. This can be a very important factor, especially when you're dealing with text. Of course, other factors are involved as well; for details, see the "Playing with alignments" section later in this chapter.

To set the amount of space — again, in pixels — between a cell's content and its borders, you simply need to specify it via the cellpadding attribute. The following example creates three tables with cell padding settings of 5, 10, and 20, respectively:

```
<TABLE border="1" cellpadding="5">
<TR>
<TD>Cell One</TD>
<TD>Cell Two</TD>
<TD>Cell Three</TD>
</TR>
<TR>
<TD>Cell Four</TD>
<TD>Cell Five</TD>
<TD>Cell Six</TD>
</TR>
<TR>
<TD>Cell Seven</TD>
<TD>Cell Eight</TD>
<TD>Cell Nine</TD>
</TR>
</TABLE>
```

```
<TABLE border="1" cellpadding="10">
<TR>
<TD>Cell One</TD>
<TD>Cell Two</TD>
<TD>Cell Three</TD>
</TR>
<TR>
<TD>Cell Four</TD>
<TD>Cell Five</TD>
<TD>Cell Six</TD>
</TR>
<TR>
<TD>Cell Seven</TD>
<TD>Cell Eight</TD>
<TD>Cell Nine</TD>
</TR>
</TABLE>
```

```
<TABLE border="1" cellpadding="20">
<TR>
<TD>Cell One</TD>
<TD>Cell Two</TD>
<TD>Cell Three</TD>
</TR>
<TR>
<TD>Cell Four</TD>
<TD>Cell Five</TD>
<TD>Cell Six</TD>
</TR>
<TR>
<TD>Cell Seven</TD>
<TD>Cell Eight</TD>
<TD>Cell Nine</TD>
</TR>
</TABLE>
```

Figure 3-4 shows the results.

The cellspacing and cellpadding attributes affect the entire table; they cannot be set for individual rows.

Spanning rows and columns

Here's where things get really interesting. Your Web tables don't have to be just equal-size rectangles running up and down and right and left. With row and column spanning, you can alter the whole structure of a table to suit your needs.

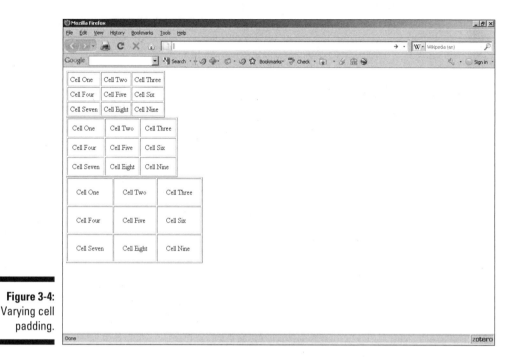

Figure 3-4:
Varying cell
padding.

The colspan and rowspan attributes are applied to individual cells (TD elements). In a data-presentation scenario, this technique is most commonly used for presenting category titles or headings, as shown in the following example:

```
<TABLE border="1">
<TR>
<TD rowspan="2"></TD>
<TD colspan="2">Title One</TD>
<TD colspan="2">Title Two</TD>
</TR>
<TR>
<TD>Subhead One</TD>
<TD>Subhead Two</TD>
<TD>Subhead Three</TD>
<TD>Subhead Four</TD>
</TR>
<TR>
<TD rowspan="2">
<P>Sidehead One<BR>
Sidehead Two</P>
<TD>Data One</TD>
<TD>Data Two</TD>
<TD>Data Three</TD>
<TD>Data Four</TD>
</TR>
<TR>
```

```
<TD>Data Five</TD>
<TD>Data Six</TD>
<TD>Data Seven</TD>
<TD>Data Eight</TD>
</TR>
</TABLE>
```

Figure 3-5 shows how this looks.

The <P> and <BR> tags in the preceding example illustrate a very important point. Cells are kind of like miniature Web pages — they can contain anything you can add via standard HTML — which means you can toss in links, images, videos, or whatever suits your fancy.

Playing with alignments

Aligning a table is a fairly simple matter; you simply set the TABLE element's align attribute to left, center, or right. Using the align attribute with the TR and TD elements, however, affects the contents of those elements rather than the elements themselves.

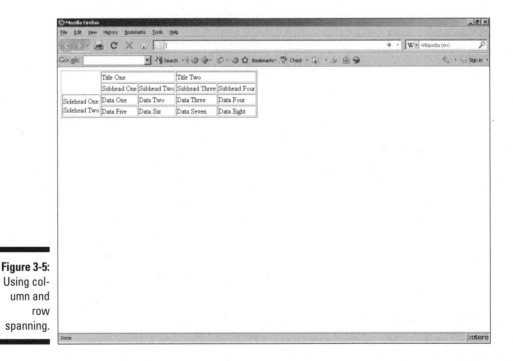

Figure 3-5:
Using col-
umn and
row
spanning.

If you set a row (TR) to center alignment, then all the contents of all the cells in that row are centered. If you set it to right alignment, then all the contents align with the right margin of the cells, and so on. However, you can specify different alignment values for each cell, and these override and value for the row as a whole.

The alignment of a row (TR) or cell (TD) depends upon two attributes: the align attribute for horizontal alignment (left, center, or right) and the valign attribute for vertical alignment (top, middle, or bottom).

By default, if no alignment is set for a row, all of its contents are horizontally left-aligned and vertically center-aligned.

The following example modifies the code from the previous example to specify different alignments:

```
<TABLE border="1">
<TR align="right">
<TD rowspan="2"></TD>
<TD colspan="2" align="center">Title One</TD>
<TD colspan="2">Title Two</TD>
</TR>
<TR height="60" valign="center">
<TD valign="top">Subhead One</TD>
<TD valign="bottom">Subhead Two</TD>
<TD>Subhead Three</TD>
<TD>Subhead Four</TD>
</TR>
<TR>
<TD rowspan="2">
<P>Sidehead One<BR>
Sidehead Two</P>
<TD>Data One</TD>
<TD>Data Two</TD>
<TD>Data Three</TD>
<TD>Data Four</TD>
</TR>
<TR>
<TD>Data Five</TD>
<TD>Data Six</TD>
<TD>Data Seven</TD>
<TD>Data Eight</TD>
</TR>
</TABLE>
```

Check out Figure 3-6 to see the resulting table.

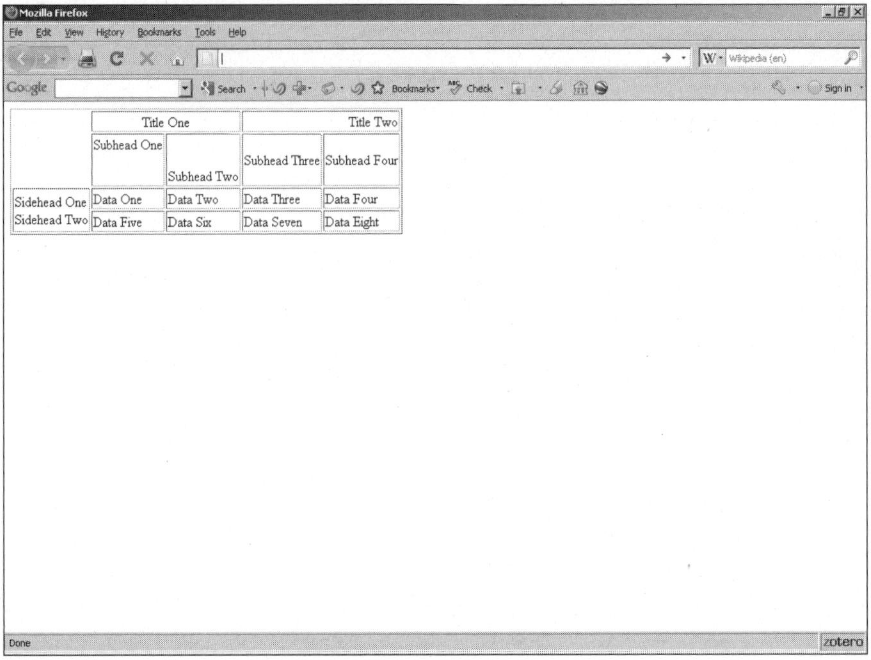

Figure 3-6:
Setting
alignments
in a table.

Using Frames and Framesets

The two basic kinds of Web page structures are *regular* and *framed.* Regular gets better mileage on highways, and framed looks nice on a wall. Wait, no, that's something else. . . . Okay: A regular Web page is a stand-alone structure. Frames, on the other hand, enable you to place more than one Web page on-screen at a time. To the visitor, a framed site appears as one coherent whole, no different from a regular page. Frames give you more capabilities, such as simultaneously showing many Web pages in a typical browser — and a few extra headaches (such as making them work with search engines as well).

Building pages with frames and framesets

As mentioned in Chapter 2, Web pages are built with *elements.* A typical Web page features a basic structure of three elements: HTML, HEAD, and BODY. The HTML element contains both the HEAD and BODY elements, as the following example demonstrates:

```
<HTML>

<HEAD>
</HEAD>

<BODY>
</BODY>

</HTML>
```

Framed sites work a bit differently from the way regular sites work: You build them out of *framesets,* which set off different areas of the screen. Each area contained within a frameset is known as a *frame,* and each frame contains its own Web page. The following HTML code sets up the pair of frames that you see in Figure 3-7:

```
<HTML>

<FRAMESET cols="80,*">
  <FRAME name="leftFrame" src="navigation.html">
  <FRAME name="mainFrame" src="main.html">
</FRAMESET>

</HTML>
```

Figure 3-7:
Framed
Web pages
enable you
to bring
content
from mul-
tiple files
onto one
screen.

The "`80,*`" in the preceding code listing means you're setting aside 80 pixels for the first frame, and the rest of the screen is available for the second frame. You can also specify a specific pixel amount for the second frame if you want. As with tables, you also have the option to specify a percentage of the screen for each frame rather than exact pixel sizes, as in the following example:

```
<FRAMESET cols="20%,*">
```

To create horizontal frames instead of vertical frames, you use the `rows` attribute instead of `cols` in the first frameset tag. Everything else works just the same way.

The `src` attribute works sort of like that attribute does with images: It specifies the source of the file that will be displayed inside the frame. Here, though, you're giving the location of an entire HTML file.

Adding borders and margins to frames

As with tables, you can play with the borders and margins in your frames in order to achieve your design goals.

By default, you have the kind of 3D borders between frames that appear in Figure 3-7. To change these, you use — you guessed it — the `border` attribute, as shown in this example that sets the width to 5 pixels:

```
<FRAMESET cols="80,*" border="5">
```

Figures 3-8 and 3-9 show the effect of border settings of a single pixel and 10 pixels.

Border colors (normally gray) can be specified using the `bordercolor` attribute. To modify the previous example so the borders are red, you'd do this:

```
<FRAMESET cols="20%,*" border="5" bordercolor="red">
```

You can set the amount of space between the edges of frames by specifying a value via the `marginheight` and `marginwidth` attributes of the `FRAME` element. Setting these values to "`0`" (zero) means that the contents of the frames are loaded with no space between them. If you wanted, on the other hand, to force an all-around margin of, say, 20 pixels, you'd do it like this:

```
<FRAME marginheight="20" marginwidth="20">
```

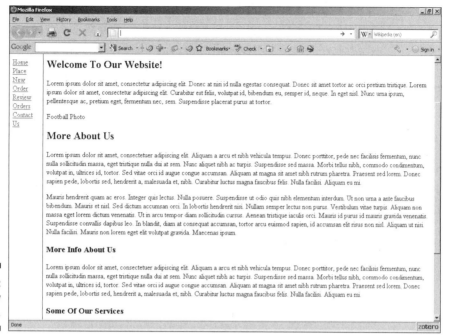

Figure 3-8:
Narrow
borders.

Figure 3-9:
Wide
borders.

Online Sources for Tables and Frames

Table 3-1 lists some places on the World Wide Web where you can find more information about the topics covered in this chapter.

Table 3-1	Online Resources for Tables and Frames
Web Site Name	**Web Address**
16 Frames	`www.w3.org/TR/REC-html40/present/frames.html`
HTML Frame Tags	`www.jqjacobs.net/web/frames/frame_tags.html`
HTML Frames	`www.w3schools.com/html/html_frames.asp`
HTML Table Basics	`www.pageresource.com/html/table1.htm`
HTML Tables	`www.w3schools.com/html/html_tables.asp`
HTML Tables: A very short introduction . . .	`www.cs.tut.fi/~jkorpela/html/tables.html`
Tables	`http://htmldog.com/guides/htmlbeginner/tables/`
Tables in HTML Documents	`www.w3.org/TR/html4/struct/tables.html`
The Layout of HTML Frames	`www.tufat.com/html_tutorials/HTMLFramesScreenLayout.php`

Chapter 4

Working with WYSIWYG

*W*YSIWYG (What You See Is What You Get) programs are easy for novices to use in the early stages of Web site creation, but they can quickly prove less than satisfactory. The reason for both factors is the same: The program makes a bunch of choices for you. Although this feature may seem like a comfort at first, it can quickly become a limitation. If you go for a WYSIWYG program, make sure that it's sophisticated enough that you can still use it as your skills advance.

Most WYSIWYG programs have at least some degree of depth beneath their surface simplicity. The CoffeeCup HTML Editor (the topic of this chapter), for example, lets you set the attributes for every element, in case you don't like the default choices. This gives you the best of both worlds, allowing you to create visually while working under the hood with the base code. That means you can enjoy both the quickness of WYSIWYG creation and the total control of text editing in the same page-creation session.

CoffeeCup, shown in Figure 4-1, is the main choice of many professional Web designers, though it isn't the only one. You can pick up a copy at www.coffee cup.com/html-editor (there's a 28-day trial version and the full version goes for $49). Table 4-1 lists several WYSIWYG programs you can use to build Web pages, along with the Web addresses where you can find them (or information about them).

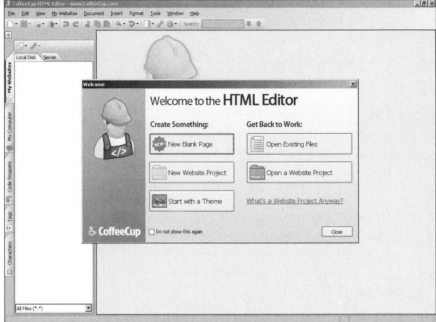

Figure 4-1:
CoffeeCup
is a full-
featured
WYSIWYG
environment
for building
Web pages.

Creating the Basic Page in CoffeeCup

After you understand what's going on under the hood of a Web page, as discussed in the previous chapters, it's time to sit back and let CoffeeCup do a little magic for you.

Don't worry about doing anything fancy here; I cover site design in other chapters. For now, just play around with CoffeeCup and experience the joy of working with a truly excellent program (one of my personal favorites, seriously). In the next few sections, I walk you through using it to set page properties and work with text and links. Of course, you should feel free to experiment with different values, colors, and so on, as you familiarize yourself with the program.

Setting the page properties

In Chapter 2, I explain how to set the page title and page background with the normal HTML approach. Here's how to set page properties with CoffeeCup:

1. **First, you need a page to work with. Click the New Blank Page button in the opening screen (refer to Figure 4-1).**

   The Quick Start dialog box appears.

2. **Enter a title in the Page Title text box.**

   This text will appear at the top of your visitors' Web browser screens when they visit your page.

3. **If you want to add a background image, click the Browse button (the little file folder with a green arrow) and then navigate to the image file and select it.**

4. **If you want to change the background color, click the arrow to the right of the Background color to open a drop-down palette, as shown in Figure 4-2. Choose a color from the palette by clicking it.**

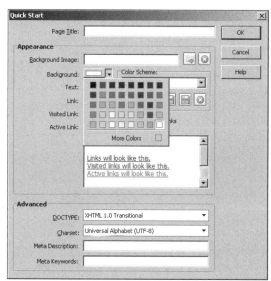

Figure 4-2:
Set the colors for your page in the Quick Start dialog box.

The color change is shown in the display area (see Figure 4-3).

If you have already set a background image, then the background color won't matter because the image covers it.

5. **Similarly, to change the colors of the text or links, click the arrow next to the appropriate color box and then choose a color from that palette.**

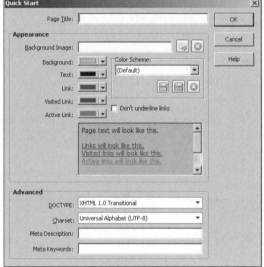

Figure 4-3:
CoffeeCup
shows the
effects of
different
color set-
tings as
you choose
them.

6. **Generally speaking, you shouldn't change the Advanced Settings such as Doctype unless your Web page has unusual requirements such as a need to use the Greek alphabet. However, you may want to enter your keywords in the Meta Keywords text box (see Chapter 13 for more on keywords).**

If you want to add keywords later on, choose Insert➪Meta Keywords from the menu.

7. **Click the OK button to complete the process.**

Working with text and links

A purely graphical Web page is, of course, something of an anomaly. Generally speaking, most of any given page is made up of text. Any text that leads to another Web page is said to be *linked* to the new page. (See Chapter 2 for more info on text and links.)

Modifying text

The Font button is the third one in the Code Editor's menu bar. It has several options that you can choose from, each of which changes the formatting of your text (see Figure 4-4).

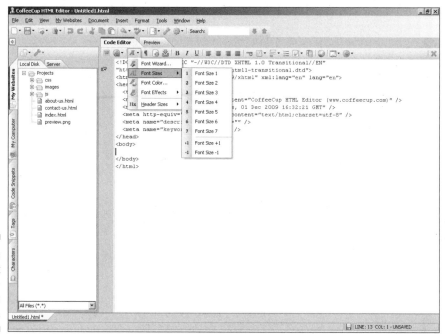

Figure 4-4:
The Font
button pres-
ents various
options.

When the Font button is clicked, these are the formatting options available:

- ✔ **Font Wizard:** To set the typeface (Arial, Courier, and so on), you need to click the Font Wizard option. In the resulting dialog box (see Figure 4-5), you can also specify the previously mentioned settings such as size.

- ✔ **Font Sizes:** Set the size of the font (1–7).

- ✔ **Font Color:** Select the text color.

- ✔ **Font Effects:** This option lets you choose options such as Bold and Italic.

- ✔ **Header Sizes:** Set the size of headers (H1–H6).

Adding links

To add a link, follow these steps:

1. **Select the text you want to make into a link.**

   You can skip this step and enter the text in Step 3 if you haven't typed it yet.

2. **Click the Link button (the second one in the Code Editor's menu bar) and select Link (or simply use the Ctrl+L key combination).**

   In the resulting dialog box (shown in Figure 4-6), the selected text is displayed.

3. **If no text was selected, you can enter it now in the Link Text box.**

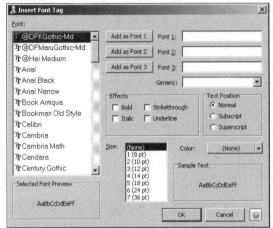

Figure 4-5:
The Font
Wizard
presents all
options in
one handy
location.

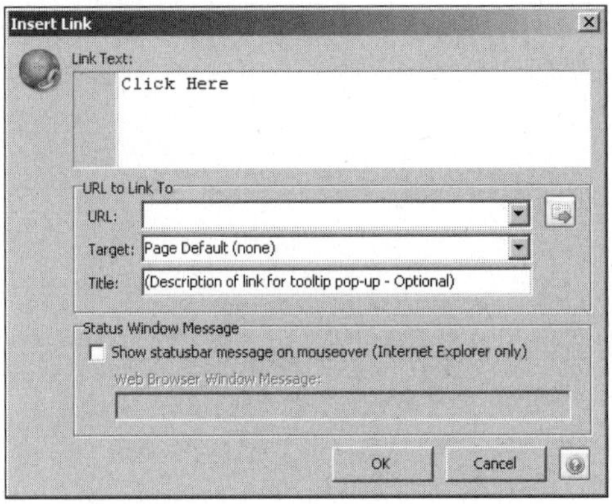

Insert Link dialog box image

Figure 4-6:
The Insert
Link dialog
box offers
several
options.

4. **Enter the URL of the page you want to link to.**

   If you've linked to this file before, you can click the arrow to the right to select it from a drop-down list. You can also click the Browse button to navigate to the file.

5. **If you don't want the linked page to open in place of your page, then choose the appropriate target (such as New Browser Window).**

6. **Optionally, enter text for a popup tooltip in the Title text box.**

7. **Optionally, enter text for a status-bar message (Internet Explorer only).**

8. **Click the OK button to complete the process.**

Adding images

Adding images in CoffeeCup is much easier than typing all the information in a text editor. Follow these steps to add images:

1. **Click the Image button (the first one in the Code Editor's menu bar) or use the Ctrl+M key combination.**

   The Insert Image dialog box (shown in Figure 4-7) appears.

2. **Navigate to the image.**

   The URL of the image file appears in the Image box.

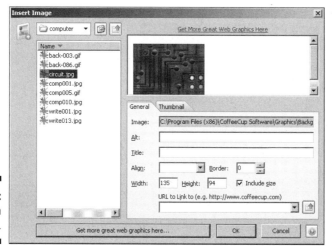

Figure 4-7:
Choosing an
image.

3. **Enter some alternate text (for non-visual browsers) in the Alt text box.**

   Alt text appears even if the image is unavailable.

4. **Optionally, enter a title for the image in the Title text box.**

5. **You can specify the alignment of the image so that (for example) text will flow around it.**

6. **If desired, set the width (in pixels) of a border that will appear around the image.**

7. **If you want to resize the image, type the new height and width in the appropriate text boxes.**

8. **If you want to make the image into a link, enter the URL or browse to locate the file.**

9. **Click the OK button to finalize the image insertion.**

Switching views

There are three ways to see the pages that you're creating in CoffeeCup: in the Code Editor (the actual HTML, XHTML, or whatever language you're using), in the Preview tab (the WYSIWYG view), or in a combination of the two.

It's an easy matter to switch among the views: In normal usage, simply click the Code Editor or Preview tabs. To see both the code and its effect without having to switch back and forth, press the F12 function key from within the Code Editor. To go back to the regular Code view, press it again. Figure 4-8 shows the Preview tab, and Figure 4-9 shows the Code and Preview option.

Figure 4-8:
Preview tab.

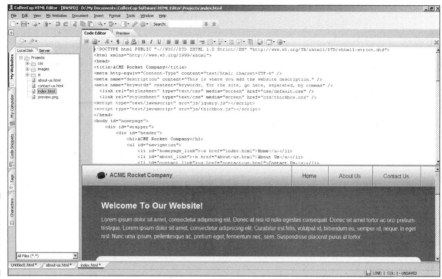

Figure 4-9:
Mixed
code and
Preview.

Working with Website Projects

Of course, unless your site is a minimal one, you don't just tinker with a page here and a page there, but with the site as a whole. That's where CoffeeCup's Website Project feature shines. Here's how to use it:

1. **Click the New Website Project button in the Welcome dialog box (see Figure 4-10) when you first launch CoffeeCup. To get a new project going if you're already working in CoffeeCup, select My Websites⇨New Website Project from the menu.**

Figure 4-10:
The
Welcome
dialog box.

2. **In the Website Project Settings dialog box (shown in Figure 4-11), enter a name for the new project.**

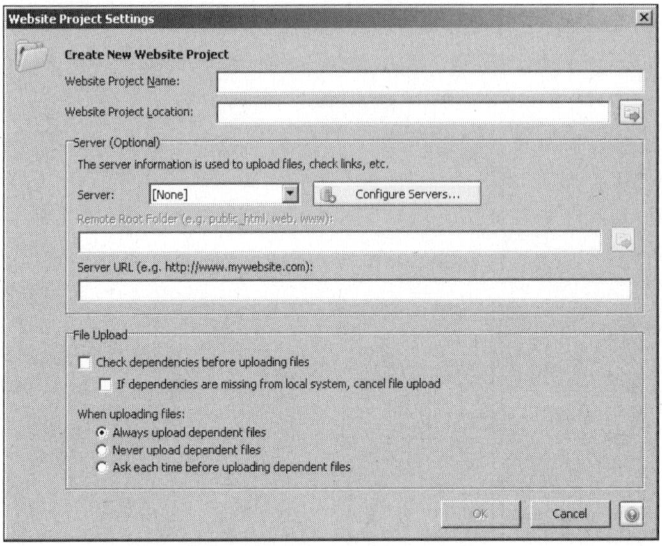

Figure 4-11:
Entering
project set-
tings.

3. **In the Website Project Location text box, click the Browse button to the right and navigate to the local folder you want to use as the root for your Web site.**

4. **If you have a Web server ready, check with your tech-support people to get the information you need to enter under the Server settings.**

   You can go ahead and build your site without having a Web server. When you're ready to go on the Web, just add this info.

5. **Under File Upload, choose how you want CoffeeCup to handle dependent files (for example, included images) during uploads.**

   If you don't select the Check Dependencies before Uploading Files check box, then you can upload a page without regard to any dependent files. You also have the option to specify whether to always upload dependent files (the default setting), never upload dependent files, or to have CoffeeCup ask you what you want to do at upload time.

6. **Click the OK button to finish.**

From now on, all pages you create in this project will go into the folder you selected, shown in the My Websites panel on the left side of the screen.

Online Sources for WYSIWYG

Table 4-1 lists some places on the World Wide Web where you can find more information about the topics covered in this chapter.

Table 4-1	WYSIWYG Programs
Program	*Web Address*
Microsoft Expression Web 3	`http://www.microsoft.com/Expression/products/overview.aspx?key=web`
Adobe Dreamweaver	`www.adobe.com/products/dreamweaver`
HotDog PageWiz 1.04	`http://download.cnet.com/HotDog-PageWiz/3000-10247_4-10032809.html`
Web Studio 5.0	`www.webstudio.com`

Chapter 5

Letting the World In: Choosing a Host and Domain Name

In This Chapter

▶ Choosing a host

▶ Finding free Web site providers

▶ Picking and registering domain names

*I*f you don't already have a Web site or if you're unhappy with your current Web space provider, you have several options. You can run your own Web server, of course. With any type of broadband connection and Linux, it's even possible to put together a creditable setup in your own home. But that's a lot of work — ask network administrators just how much leisure time they have. And many broadband providers have policies forbidding you from doing that sort of thing, anyway.

If you want to focus on developing and maintaining your site, your best bet is to leave the day-to-day grunge work of keeping the server up and running to someone else.

Practically every Web-hosting provider offers all sorts of extended services in addition to plain Web space. These often include some form of e-commerce hosting, ranging from simply supplying the software to setting up a complete turnkey solution ("here's your system — turn the key and you're good to go") for you.

Going Live: Choosing a Host

You have three basic options when it comes to Web hosting:

- ✔ ISPs
- ✔ Virtual servers
- ✔ Dedicated servers

ISPs

The same people who provide you with Internet access can also be your Web space provider. Almost certainly, you have at least some room for Web pages as part of your basic service. If you're not interested in a very extensive site or in one that has tons of glitzy features, the basic setup the ISP gives you will probably suffice. Even if you don't have any kind of CGI access (see Chapter 8 for more on the Common Gateway Interface), you can probably still use remotely hosted services, like the ones described in this book, to enhance your site.

Many domain name registrars (described in "Finding a registrar," later in this chapter) also provide various amounts of Web site space as a part of their services.

Virtual servers

Virtual servers are nothing more than directories on a hard drive. If that hard drive is on an existing Web server that supports virtual server capabilities, however, the Webmaster can make each one of those directories seem as though it's a fully functional Web server.

Other than being a really clever example of how you can use computer technology, does this have a practical application for you? It depends on your budget and your site's traffic expectations. It's certainly one of the cheapest ways to get your site up and running. You could pay for a couple of months' worth of a typical virtual server by skipping one good dinner at a decent restaurant. Some virtual servers are so cheap that you could pay for them just by skipping dessert.

On the other hand, you're sharing one physical server with lots of other virtual servers. Any physical server's performance degrades as it gets busier, with more and more people connecting to it and placing demands on it. But if you're on a virtual server, that scenario has a slightly different meaning. People visiting a Web site on one of the other virtual servers hosted on the same physical server as yours are putting a drain on your resources, too, because those resources are shared. Basically, if someone else's site gets too busy, yours can slow down till it looks like a turtle in molasses. And vice versa.

Dedicated servers

Nearly every company that handles virtual servers also leases dedicated ones. A *dedicated server* is a step up from a virtual server: Although it costs a bit more, it's your very own physical computer holding your Web site, with nobody else on it.

Both virtual and dedicated servers offer more than just Web hosting. For example, they also handle e-mail. The focus here is only on the Web-hosting aspect because this book is about Web sites.

Dedicated servers used to cost a small fortune, but a combination of generally lower computer prices and competitive pressures has dropped the expense of leasing one. At a rock-bottom price of around $50–$100 per month, dedicated servers are still maybe a bit pricey for a private individual, but for any serious commercial operation, they're a great bargain. After all, that's only $600–$1,200 a year, although hiring a single network administrator to work at your company can easily set you back 100 times that or even more.

Why compare those two costs? Aren't they apples and oranges? No, not at all. When you lease a dedicated server, the people you're leasing it from take care of keeping it up and running, which is what a network administrator does. Like virtual servers, dedicated servers are located at the facility of a Web space provider, such as Verio (www.verio.com — see Figure 5-1), and you don't have to worry about regularly backing up your data, restoring after a crash, upgrading things like Linux kernels, or any of the million things that keep technical staffs hopping.

Figure 5-1:
Verio offers
a variety of
specialized
services.

Finding your match

You can always run through the standard search engines and site guides
looking for information on Web hosts. Some search engines, such as
HostIndex (www.hostindex.com), however, are specifically designed to
help you track down the right host for you (see Figure 5-2). The Web sites in
Table 5-1 will help you do some comparison shopping.

Table 5-1	Web-Hosting Indexes
Web-Site Name	**Web Address**
budgetweb.com	http://blog.budgetweb.com/
CNET Reviews	http://reviews.cnet.com/web-hosting/
Findahost.com	www.findahost.com
HostReview.com	www.hostreview.com
WebHostingTalk.com	www.webhostingtalk.com

Figure 5-2:
HostIndex
is a search
engine
dedicated to
helping you
find the right
host for your
Web site.

Keeping It Cheap: Free Web-Site Providers

More than 23 zillion Web-space providers have an unbeatable price, which
you probably guessed already from the title of this section. If you set up a
personal or limited-interest site (such as a condo association's newsletter),
free Web-space providers may be the way to go. You can get lots more space
than your local ISP provides. It's not unusual to get 50 or more megabytes
(MB) of Web storage space without having to pay a dime for it.

If you plan on running any sort of professional site, though, the free Web
space providers aren't really the ticket for you. You need your own domain
name — .com, .org, or whatever — in order to be taken seriously. (See the
section "Getting Your Own Domain Name," later in this chapter.) Also, free
Web hosts make their money by slapping ads onto your site, and you can't
usually put up your own ads in competition with them.

Having to post a free Web host's ad on your site means you may not be able to use any add-ins such as opinion polls and chat rooms that feature their own banner ads.

Table 5-2 lists some free Web hosts.

Table 5-2	Free Web Hosts
Web-Site Name	*Web Address*
50Megs.com	www.50megs.com
Angelfire	www.angelfire.lycos.com
Bravenet	www.bravenet.com
Crosswinds	www.crosswinds.net
TopCities	www.topcities.com
Tripod	www.tripod.lycos.com

Getting Your Own Domain Name

Domain names, such as dummies.com, are the addresses of sites on the World Wide Web. Picking and registering your own domain name are two of the most critical phases in your site planning; I show you how to do both in this section. When you tell your Web browser to go to www.dummies.com, it's obvious where you're going to end up — at the *For Dummies* Web site. Your computer doesn't know that, though. It can't actually go to a named site; instead, it asks a *domain name server* (DNS) to translate that name into a more computer-friendly set of numbers known as an *IP address*. It's like getting into a cab and telling the driver to go to the Acme Building. He asks you where it is, and you tell him it's at 1123 Main Street.

Domain extensions — the final letters at the end of an Internet address — are known as the *top-level domain,* or TLD. They're called "top-level" because you read Internet addresses from right to left, and the part after the last dot is the highest step in a hierarchy that eventually leads down from the Internet as a whole, step by dotted step, to the particular computer you're going to. Here are the current domain extensions:

- ✔ .aero   Air transportation companies
- ✔ .asia   Pacific Rim companies
- ✔ .biz   Business firms

- ✔ .cat   Catalan language sites
- ✔ .com   Commercial operations
- ✔ .coop   Cooperatives
- ✔ .edu   Educational institutions
- ✔ .gov   U.S. government and agencies
- ✔ .info   All uses
- ✔ .int   Internationally recognized organizations
- ✔ .jobs   Human resources
- ✔ .mil   U.S. military
- ✔ .mobi   Mobile services
- ✔ .museum   Museums
- ✔ .name   Private individuals' sites
- ✔ .net   Internet service providers (ISPs)
- ✔ .org   Nonprofit organizations
- ✔ .pro   Professions
- ✔ .tel   For contact data
- ✔ .travel   For the travel industry

One problem with all these newer domains is that the general public identifies old standards with reliability, and some folks may tend to see the lesser-known alternatives as misprints or typographical errors. ("Dot what? Don't you mean dot com?") The term *dotcom* has, in fact, come into colloquial usage as meaning an Internet-based company.

The funny thing about all these TLDs is that there's no requirement (in many cases) for people to use any of them in the manner in which they were intended. Plenty of nonprofit organizations have .com addresses, and quite a few .nets have nothing at all to do with ISPs. Go figure. Some of the new TLDs, such as .museum, have stringent requirements; if you're not a museum, you can't get a .museum address.

The domain extensions that I mention in the preceding bulleted lists are called *generic TLDs,* but another kind of TLD exists as well — the *country-level TLD.* These TLDs specify the country in which the Web site is based. That's not necessarily where the Web server that holds the site is located, thanks to the global nature of the Internet. Registering the same name in many countries can be useful if you're an international organization with multiple languages to support. That way, you can have a Spanish-language page at mysite.es, a Japanese-language page at mysite.jp, and so on.

If you're into alphabet soup, you can toss around such terms as *gTLD* and *CLTLD* for the generic and country-level extensions, respectively, or even *iTLD* for international ones. Why there's a small *g* and *i* but an uppercase *CL* before the TLD parts is one of the Internet's great mysteries.

Picking a name

In the early days, it was easy to create a domain name because there weren't many of them in use yet. These days, if you want to pick a three- or four-letter abbreviation or a single word for your domain name, you're very likely to be out of luck. Everything short is already taken. The solution? Forget the acronyms and short names. Use phrases instead. The basic idea is to go for anything long enough that it's unlikely to have been used yet, but short enough to remember.

To find out whether a name is available, you either just enter a name at a commercial domain-name registrar (such as GoDaddy) that offers availability checks or use a WhoIs utility. One of the most familiar ones on the Web is the Network Solutions page at

```
www.networksolutions.com/whois/index.jsp
```

You might also try the nice set of tools at `www.whois.net` (see Figure 5-3) or use a stand-alone tool like WhoIs ULTRA, which you can get your hands on at

```
www.analogx.com/contents/download/network/whois.htm
```

Take your time and poke around the AnalogX site. You can get some other wonderful utilities there, too.

What do you do if you come up with a great domain name, but it's already taken — and you've just gotta have it? Well, it depends. If you're a company that already has a trademark, the domain name may well already "belong" to you as a matter of course, even if you haven't registered it yet. Well, at any rate, it probably can't be used *legally* by anyone else. If you've been trademarked and doing business as, say, Joe's Acme Fabuloso Garbanzo Beans and Unicyle Maintenance Company, and that name's your registered trademark, anyone else running a site named `www.JoesAcmeFabulosoGarbanzoBeansAndUnicycleMaintenanceCompany.com` is probably easy game for your lawyers.

Figure 5-3:
WhoIs.net
helps you
check for
domain-
name
availability.

You can often buy a domain name from the person or organization that's currently using it. It can't hurt to ask, anyway. Just don't ask Apple for www. apple.com or you'll hear all of the Bay Area laughing at you.

Another factor you need to consider when picking a domain name — besides the likelihood that some organization is actually using the name and has already registered it — is that some companies exist to do nothing but think up good names and register them. These companies, sometimes called "domain squatters," seem to have no intention of ever running real Web sites that use those names, but only — well, it's hard to think of it as anything but holding the names hostage. The only purpose they have is to own the name and sell it to you. And if you think you'll get it away from them for pocket change, think again. It'll cost hundreds of dollars at least — and the upper end? Limitless for a good name.

Finding a registrar

After you pick a name, you need to register it so nobody else can use it. This task is usually handled for you by your Web space provider — who's used to the job, probably has a bulk account with a major registrar, and fills out zillions of these applications every year.

The best-known registrar of domain names in America is Network Solutions (www.networksolutions.com). It registers your domain name for $35 a year if you sign up for one year or for as little as $9.99 a year for a hundred-year commitment (although that offer might appeal only to the most extremely optimistic, and you can find better deals with a much shorter commitment).

It used to be that you had to pay for the first two years at once, but in early 2000 this changed so you can pay for only one year if you prefer. Many sites that offer assistance in registering your domain name still say you have to cough up two years' money.

For a long time, Network Solutions was the only registrar on the block, but this is no longer the case. Today many other registrars compete with it. Prices vary quite a bit, so it's a good idea to shop around. The popular GoDaddy.com, for instance, has prices in the pocket-change range (like $1.99).

The organization that accredits domain name registrars is the Internet Corporation for Assigned Names and Numbers (ICANN). It maintains lists of the outfits that are authorized to register your domain name. To register a domain name by using one of the generic TLDs, go to

```
www.icann.org/registrars/accredited-list.html
```

and pick one of the registrars in your region.

To register one of the country-level TLDs, go to www.iana.org/cctld/cctld-whois.htm and click the name of the country; you find the URL of the country-level registrar at the bottom of the resulting page.

If you decide you don't like your current registrar, you can change. Any of the others will happily take your business away from its competitors.

Online Sources for Web Hosting and Domain Registration

Table 5-3 lists some places on the World Wide Web where you can find more information on the topics covered in this chapter.

Table 5-3	Online Resources for Web Hosting and Domain Registration
Web Site Name	*Web Address*
Better-Whois.com	`www.betterwhois.com`
checkdomain.com	`www.checkdomain.com`
Freedomlist	`www.freedomlist.com`
FreeWebspace.net	`www.freewebspace.net`
IANA (Internet Assigned Numbers Authority)	`www.iana.org/domain-names.htm`
ICANN	`www.icann.org`
Netcraft	`www.netcraft.com`
ServerWatch	`www.serverwatch.com/stypes/index.php/d2Vi`

Part II
Building Better Web Pages

The 5th Wave
By Rich Tennant

"Well, it's not quite done. I've animated the gurgling spit sink and the rotating Novocaine syringe, but I still have to add the high-speed whining drill audio track."

In this part . . .

1 go beyond the planning stage and get into the nitty-gritty of making your Web site work. Chapter 6 introduces the powerful tool of Cascading Style Sheets (CSS). Chapter 7 tells you where to snag some cool graphics and what to do with them once you've got 'em. Chapter 8 shows you how to get input from the folks who come to your site through forms.

Chapter 6

Using Cascading Style Sheets

*H*TML was designed to specify the appearance of a Web page, but the initial implementation left a lot to be desired. In the name of standardization (admittedly, a laudable goal at the time), a great deal of creative control was left behind. An <H1> (major heading) element, for example, would always look the same, no matter what the designer wanted to show with it. It would always be the same size, the same color, the same font, and so forth.

With the advent of Cascading Style Sheets (CSS), however, all that changed. Suddenly Webmasters could make anything on a Web page behave any way they wanted it to. This led, naturally, to a greater degree of creative control — and more than a little bit of confusion.

In this chapter, I cover the basics of CSS and show you how you can use it to make your own Web pages dance to the tune of your dreams. There is *so* much you can do with CSS that's beyond the scope of this book, I highly recommend that (after you read this chapter, of course) you rush out to the bookstore and get a copy of *CSS Web Design For Dummies* by Richard Mansfield (Wiley Publishing).

That said, let's take a look at CSS and the kinds of things you can accomplish with it.

Merging CSS and HTML

There are three ways to add CSS to your Web pages — inline styles, a style declaration, or a separate .css file:

✔ **Inline styles:** With this method, the effect is totally localized. That is to say, the style you create with this method applies only to the element that contains it — and to nothing else on the Web page (or on any other Web pages in your site). An inline style is the simplest kind of CSS, but lacks flexibility. It uses the style attribute to add CSS. An inline style that sets the color *only* for the H1 element *in which it is declared* looks like this:

```
<H1 style="color: blue">This is a major heading in
   blue.</H1>
```

✔ **Style declaration:** This permits you to use the full range of CSS, applying it throughout a single Web page, but it's of limited utility when dealing with a large number of pages on a significant Web site because its effect is limited to the page on which it is declared, which means you have to make a separate declaration on each Web page in your site. Such a declaration must occur within the HEAD element of the HTML document. A style declaration takes a form that looks like this:

```
<HEAD>
<STYLE>
H1
{color:blue}
</STYLE>
</HEAD>
```

After such a declaration, the text in all H1 elements on this Web page will be blue in color.

✔ **Separate .css file:** This file is linked to the .html files on your Web site. With this approach, all the creative elements (color, font size, and the like) are specified in a different file (.css) from the ones that define the content of the Web pages on your site (.html). This has a tremendous advantage over either of the other two approaches: One .css file can control the appearance of multiple Web pages. Say, for example, that you have a Web site with 87 pages. You can readily imagine the amount of effort involved if you have to go into each and every one of those Web pages and manually alter all the CSS properties you'd entered into each of them. Now imagine that there's just one .css file that you have to change to effect a new style on every single Web page in your site. You get the picture, right?

A .css file isn't anything fancy. It's just a plain text file, like a regular .html file. You can create one in anything from Windows Notepad to the fanciest Web page editor. Just make sure you give it an extension of .css (if your program doesn't already do that for you), and you'll be fine.

All you have to do is put a link to the .css file in each of your Web pages; after that, any change in the linked file is reflected automatically in all your Web pages.

Here's how it's done:

1. **Create the** .css **file with the variables relating to font size and color or whatever other features you want to specify.**

2. **Create the** .html **files that define the content of your site.**

3. **In the** HEAD **element of each Web page on your site, add the following lines of code:**

```
<HEAD>
<LINK rel=stylesheet href="file.css" type="text/css">
</HEAD>
```

Of course, you replace the *file* part with the name of your actual .css file.

4. **Upload both the** .css **and** .html **files to your Web server.**

There. You're done.

After that, if you want to change the appearance of every page on your site, just alter the .css file and upload the new version. Yep, simple as that. No kidding.

You can add several different .css files to one .html file by simply listing them all. Say you have three different style files that apply to your site. The following code would add them all:

```
<HEAD>
<LINK rel=stylesheet href="file1.css" type="text/css">
<LINK rel=stylesheet href="file2.css" type="text/css">
<LINK rel=stylesheet href="file3.css" type="text/css">
</HEAD>
```

Perhaps the hardest thing to keep in mind when dealing with a separate .css file is also the simplest: You don't use the <STYLE> tag. In fact, a .css file doesn't use any HTML tags at all. Ever. Other than that, the syntax is exactly the same. Take a look at how the code changes between the two:

✔ **Declared style in an** `.html` **file:**

```
<HEAD>
<STYLE>
H1
{color:blue}
</STYLE>
</HEAD>
```

✔ **Declared style in a separate** `.css` **file:**

```
H1 {
color:blue
}
```

There's actually a fourth level of CSS, but Webmasters have no control over it. A visitor to your site can specify in his Web browser that his own personal style sheet be used instead of any that is stipulated on the site.

Selectors, Classes, and IDs

Cascading Style Sheets — hmm — the *style sheets* part of that seems pretty obvious. Well, with a little struggle, maybe. I honestly cannot tell you why the inventors decided on *sheets* instead of *files* or some other more common term — that's just one of life's little mysteries. But the *style* part, at least, should be obvious: It's a way of establishing the style (appearance) of your Web pages, giving you much more control than standard HTML does. The *cascading* part is, after a moment's reflection on the way CSS works, also obvious: The style formatting flows from the top down, just the same as a waterfall or cascade does. (Perhaps its originators had a *sheet of water* in mind. . . .)

The preceding section describes three methods of adding CSS to your Web pages. The top level in this case is a separate `.css` file, the next level down the cascade is a general style declaration, and at the bottom of the cascade you find your inline styles. Each of these is interpreted in that order.

Whether or not you realize it, you already have a way of using *selectors* in CSS. A *selector* is simply the name of the element or elements that you're altering. The `H1` element that was used in the preceding examples, for instance, is a selector, because it selects which parts of your Web page are affected by your choices.

Using classes

What if you don't want to change all instances of an element, but just want to change some instances of them? That's where classes and IDs come in. You create a class in either a style declaration in the HEAD element of a Web page or in a separate .css file. The syntax is, by now, familiar:

```
<HEAD>
<STYLE>
.class1 {color:blue}
.class2 {font-family:Arial, Helvetica, sans-serif}
</STYLE>
</HEAD>
```

If this is done in a separate .css file, you have to leave out the HTML parts (HEAD and STYLE). Thus the version of the preceding code in a separate .css file would simply look like this:

```
.class1 {color:blue}
.class2 {font-family:Arial, Helvetica, sans-serif}
```

Pay particular attention to the curly brackets — { } — when you're choosing styles. In either declared styles or a .css file, the selector comes first, followed by the opening curly bracket, then the name of the property whose characteristics you want to specify. Next comes a colon to separate the property from its value (in the preceding example, the property of .class1 is color and the value is blue). Finally, you close the declaration with the last curly bracket. Failure to include either bracket (or the colon) will confuse your visitors' Web browsers to the point where they probably won't show what you intended.

The two lines of code just given declare that any element that is assigned class1 will be blue, and any element assigned class2 will be in the Arial font. (The other terms in that font family are the most likely similar fonts in descending order. Any modern operating system, whether Windows, Unix, Apple, or whatever, will recognize at least one of them — and use it to display something close to what the Web site designer intended.)

The .class definition is CSS. You recall that CSS and HTML aren't the same thing, of course, and HTML has a slightly different way of actually assigning the declared classes. To use this technique in HTML, about all you have to do is to drop the dot at the beginning:

```
<H1 class="class1">This text will be blue.</H1>
<H2 class="class2">This text will be in the Arial
    font.<H2>
```

Using IDs

The id method is pretty similar to the class method, but with extreme limitations: Unlike a class definition that can be applied to several elements on a single page, the id method can only be used for a single element per page. No two elements on one page can have the same id.

So — what good is an id? Say you have some element that is common to several Web pages but shows up in only one context in each page. (Headers and footers are good examples of this sort of situation.) In such a case, you might want to assign an id rather than a class, because there is no class, per se, involved (that is, there is no situation in which you'd want to alter multiple elements on the same page). Just in case you meet up with a situation like this one, you can handle it if you follow these steps:

1. **In a** `.css` **file (external style sheet), specify the** **id's** **name with a number sign (also called a** *hash mark***), like this:**

   ```
   #makethisred {color:red}
   ```

   The number sign and the following text specify the name of the id involved (in this case, `makethisred`, which should be self-explanatory, like all good id names), whereas the attributes specified between the curly brackets set the appearance of the item the id is assigned to.

2. **Next, on each Web page where the item appears (only once, remember!), add the** **id** **name as an attribute in the appropriate place so the specified values will be applied to it, as in the following example:**

   ```
   <P id="makethisred">This text will be colored red.</P>
   ```

   You use the number sign (#) only in the *definition* of the id in the `.css` file, not in the *application* of it in the separate HTML file.

Redefining Elements

If you think you're stuck with the official definitions of various elements in HTML, the good news is that you're wrong. With CSS, you can redefine *any* element to have the properties you desire. Don't care for the Arial or Times New Roman fonts? No problem. You can substitute anything else for them you like.

Take the H1 (major heading) element, for example: Without CSS, it's always going to have a size of 24 points, a black color, and a bold attribute. In plain HTML, the H1 element is also in Times New Roman font, even though many non-European publishers commonly use Arial for headings and Times New

Roman for text. You'll probably want to make such an obvious change, and CSS lets you do just exactly that. Here's how you redefine it:

```
<HEAD>
<STYLE>
H1 {font-family:Arial, Helvetica, sans-serif}
</STYLE>
</HEAD>
```

Henceforth, every H1 element will have that value.

You can, of course, get even fancier if you wish, redefining things to suit yourself by using various attributes. If you want your H1 elements to use gray, italicized lettering as well as the Arial font, just add those attributes to the definition:

```
<HEAD>
<STYLE>
H1 {font-family:Arial, Helvetica, sans-serif;
    color:gray;font-style:italic}
</STYLE>
</HEAD>
```

Whenever you're adding multiple attributes, be sure to separate them all with semicolons, as in the preceding example.

The following code shows the effect of altering just the H1 element in this manner while leaving the H2 element alone:

```
<HTML>
<HEAD>
<STYLE>
H1 {font-family:Arial, Helvetica, sans-serif;
    color:gray;font-style:italic}
</STYLE>
</HEAD>
<BODY>
<H1>This is an H1 heading in Arial, colored gray, and
    italicized.</H1>
<H2>This is an H2 heading, unaltered from the
    standard.</H2>
</BODY>
<HTML>
```

Figure 6-1 shows how this works.

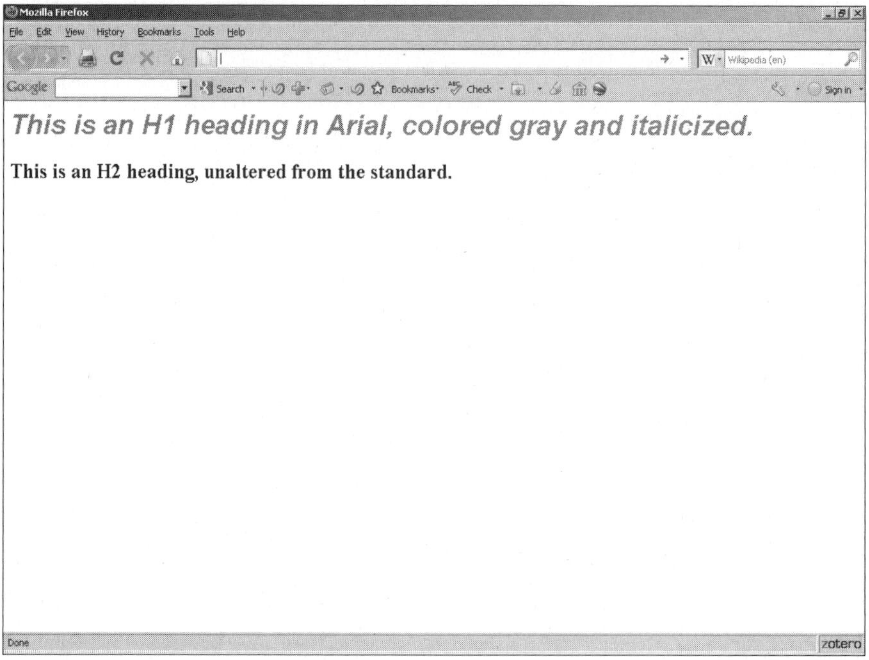

This is an H1 heading in Arial, colored gray and italicized.

This is an H2 heading, unaltered from the standard.

Figure 6-1:
An altered
H1 element
with an
unaltered
H2 element.

Contextual Selectors

A *contextual selector,* as you might guess from the apt description, is a selector that works only within a certain context. The context that's referred to is the parent element of another element. Normally, when one element is contained within another — as when a heading contains some kind of emphasis on a particular word (such as bolding it) — the contained element inherits the properties of its parent element.

Okay, that's a long-winded way of saying that if you set your H1 elements to be blue and you add <B></B> tags around one word in one H1 element, that bolded word will also be blue. But what if you want all the B elements that appear within an H1 element to turn green? You can do that, no problem. And, because you're using contextual selection, no B elements that appear outside an H1 element (that is, outside the context) will be affected. Here's how the code for such a style declaration actually looks:

```
<HEAD>
<STYLE>
H1
{color:blue}
H1 B
{color:green}
</STYLE>
</HEAD>
```

Going Beyond the Basics

You're not even remotely limited to just altering the style of common textual elements, of course. With CSS, you can play with the settings of anything and everything on your Web pages. The following examples show just a few of the possibilities that are at your disposal via various CSS attributes.

CSS colors

As previously shown, you can set the background color of any element via the CSS background-color attribute. In the preceding examples, the value of the color was set via the simplest method of specifying a textual color such as "red" or "black."

There were 16 common text values for colors defined in HTML 4.01: black, green, silver, lime, gray, olive, white, yellow, maroon, navy, red, blue, purple, teal, fuchsia, and aqua.

Color names can be used in any color situation, not merely as background colors. As an example, you can set a font to be colored silver or a border to be lime.

In addition to these official basic colors, however, several other color names are commonly recognized by the major Web browsers, and you can also utilize hexadecimal (base 16) or decimal (base 10 in shades of Red, Green, and Blue) numbers as color values to set a much wider variety of shades. You can

check out the color set known officially as "X11," complete with examples, at
www.w3.org/TR/css3-iccprof#x11-color.

You should remember to put the number sign (#) in front of hexadecimal numbers; that's what tells a Web browser that it's dealing with a hex value. If you forget to do that, some browsers will forgive you, but others won't.

Borders

Chapter 3 discusses the use of borders when you're using frames — but thanks to the versatility of CSS, you can also use borders with *any* element on your Web pages.

To set the kind of border you want to surround a particular element, use the border attribute. You have several options here: none, dotted, dashed, solid, double, groove, ridge, inset, or outset.

Obviously, the none value is pretty much useless, as very few elements have a border by default. Figure 6-2 shows the other options as specified in the following code example:

```
<HTML>
<HEAD>
<STYLE>
.class1 {border:dotted}
.class2 {border:dashed}
.class3 {border:solid}
.class4 {border:double}
.class5 {border:groove}
.class6 {border:ridge}
.class7 {border:inset}
.class8 {border:outset}
</STYLE>
</HEAD>
<BODY>
<H1 class="class1">This has a dotted border.</P>
<H1 class="class2">This has a dashed border.</H1>
<H1 class="class3">This has a solid border.</H1>
<H1 class="class4">This has a double border.</H1>
<H1 class="class5">This has a grooved border.</H1>
<H1 class="class6">This has a ridged border.</H1>
<H1 class="class7">This has an inset border.</H1>
<H1 class="class8">This has an outset border.</H1>
</BODY>
</HTML>
```

CSS and WYSIWYG

When you're using a sophisticated Web-development environment (such as CoffeeCup or Dreamweaver), you can ease your workload a great deal by simply letting the program take care of most of the drudgery for you. Every major WYSIWYG program has some sort of CSS feature that allows even a novice Webmaster to take control like an old pro (see Chapter 10 for using CSS to create button-based menus in CoffeeCup).

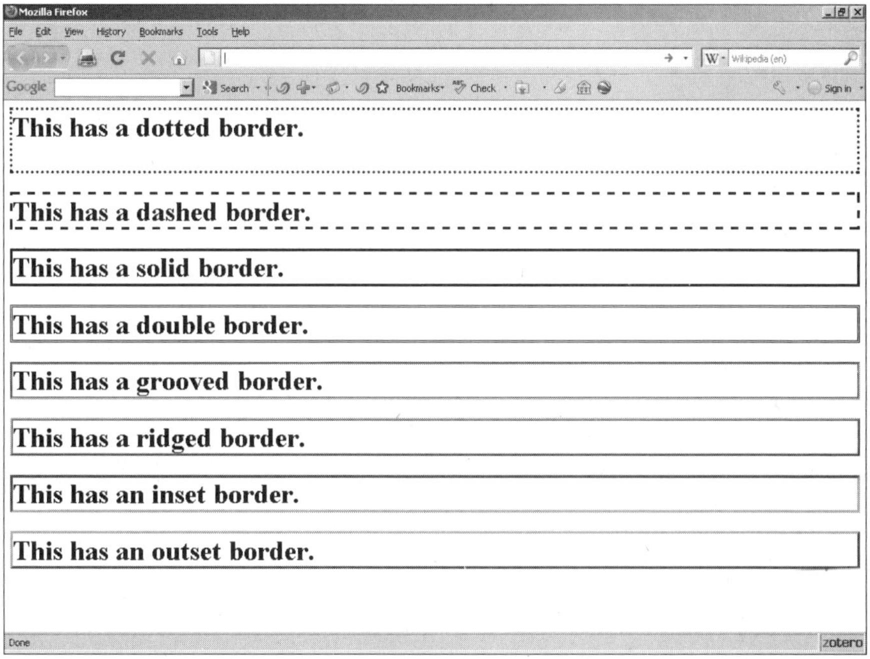

Figure 6-2: Various border designs in CSS.

To add styles to your Web page using CoffeeCup, follow these steps:

1. **Starting from a new or existing Web page loaded in CoffeeCup, click the Style Sheet Items icon on the toolbar and select Style Sheet Wizard as shown in Figure 6-3.**

   Doing so brings up the dialog box shown in Figure 6-4.

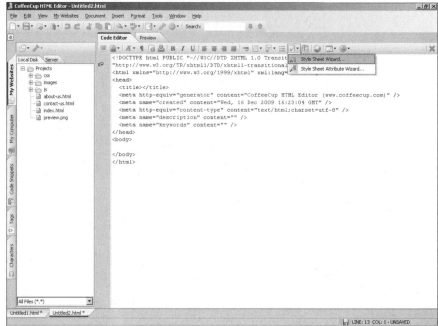

Figure 6-3:
Creating
styles.

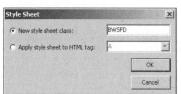

Figure 6-4:
Naming a
style.

2. **Enter the name of the style in the text box, then click the OK button.**

   You're now looking at the Style Sheet Wizard, shown in Figure 6-5.

3. **Select the font attributes you want to apply to this style, if any, by clicking the downward-pointing arrows on the right side.**

4. **Next, click the Color and Background tab.**

   This opens the related options as shown in Figure 6-6.

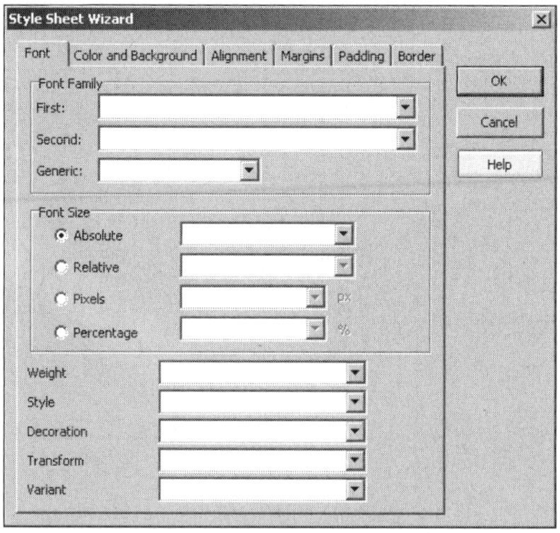

Figure 6-5:
The Style
Sheet
Wizard.

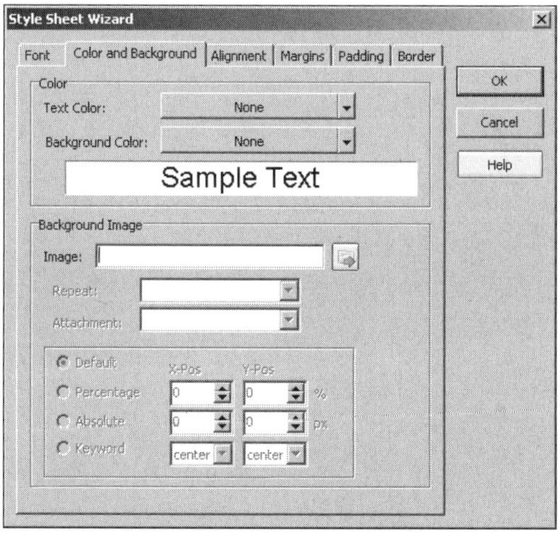

Figure 6-6:
Setting
color and
background
options.

5. **Click the downward-pointing arrows to the right to select text or back-ground colors from a color chart (see Figure 6-7).**

   If you don't see what you want, click the More Colors button to open a color wheel. Click on the colors in that wheel to choose one.

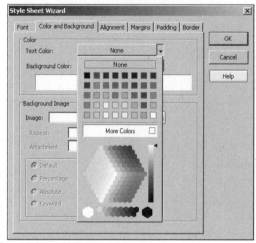

Figure 6-7:
Choosing a
color.

6. **To add a background image to the style, click the Browse button, navigate to the desired graphics file, and select it.**

   If you want to select characteristics of the background image, go ahead. You can decide whether it repeats or shows only one copy, whether it scrolls or remains fixed in position, and where it shows up on-screen (this works just like positioning layers — see the later section on positioning with layers).

7. **Click the Alignment tab to access the choices shown in Figure 6-8.**

   You can set the Indentation as a length in pixels or as a percentage. Whichever you select, you can specify the value by selecting from the scrolling values at the right.

   With Line Height, you have those two options — as well as one called Multiplier, which lets you specify a whole-number value (such as twice the usual height, for example).

   For Alignment, you can set either the vertical or horizontal value. For the vertical value, the Keyword option specifies the HTML attributes such as middle or top; you may also set the vertical alignment as a percentage. Horizontal alignment options are simply center, justify, left, or right.

   Word and letter spacing are simple pixel values.

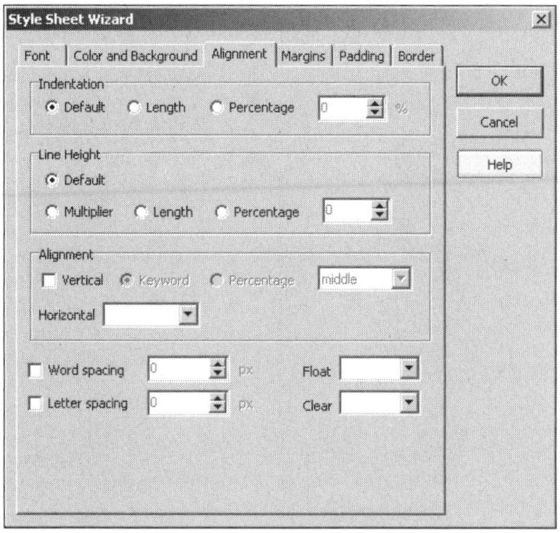

Figure 6-8:
Setting
alignment.

8. Click the Margins tab (see Figure 6-9).

The Left and Right Margins have three options, as does Width: Auto (or the default, the same as setting nothing), Absolute (in pixels), and Percentage. Top and Bottom Margins and Height have Absolute and Percentage values.

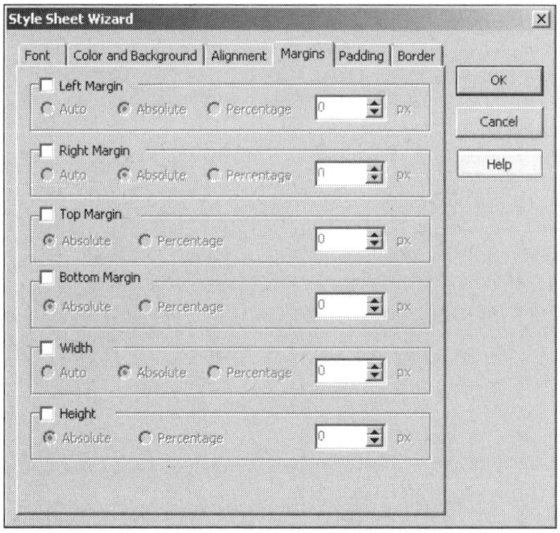

Figure 6-9:
Choosing
margin
values.

9. **Click the Padding tab (shown in Figure 6-10).**

   Recall that all CSS values are applied to a rectangular area. Just as with table cells, you can set the contents so there's some space (padding) between them and the edges. The only options are absolute (a certain number of pixels) or percentage.

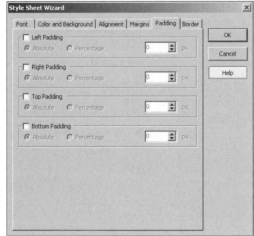

Figure 6-10:
Setting the padding values.

10. **Click the Border tab (see Figure 6-11).**

    The style's borders (see the section on borders earlier in this chapter) can be set via these options. All four have the same choices: Fixed, Absolute, or Percentage. The options on the right will change, depending upon your choice. For Fixed, you get a drop-down list allowing you to choose values of none, thin, medium, or thick for the lines of the border. The other two work just like similar options already discussed.

    Colors are chosen the same way as text colors (see Step 5).

11. **Click the OK button to finish the style.**

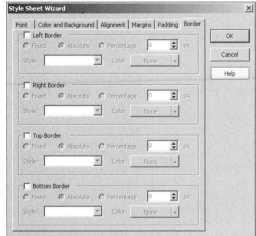

Figure 6-11:
Specifying
border
settings.

Layers

Layers? Okay, not layers, DIVs. This is an old argument going way back to the old browser wars between Microsoft's Internet Explorer and Netscape Navigator (the program that was the ancestor of both IE and today's Firefox browser). Microsoft, having much more money and clout, clearly won that war; few people today even remember what Netscape was, but the older, more aptly descriptive terminology has stuck, despite the fact that the official name for a layer today is a DIV (division of a Web page).

The DIV goes in the BODY element of your Web page. A DIV is defined as a rectangle with a specified width, height, and upper-left corner position. These three factors are all that a Web browser needs to know to create the layer: Start at this location, and then extend a rectangle downward and to the right by this many pixels. That rectangle acts as a kind of miniature Web page within the larger Web page; it can contain anything that a normal Web page can.

The concept of layers actually goes back further than that, to the days when an overhead projector was the hottest high-tech item on the market. If you're old enough (or recently attended a low-tech school), you probably have memories of your teachers placing one transparency on top of another on an overhead projector, which resulted in the information on the second transparency showing up on the screen on top of the information on the first one. The first transparency was the lower layer; the second was the higher layer; and so forth.

Web pages can be thought of in the same way — as one layer of information superimposed upon another, lower layer. A third, higher layer can then be placed on it, and so forth, ad infinitum.

Many Web site designers take advantage of this ability to provide distinct types of information on top of one another. This may be a series of maps showing (for example) Europe before, during, and after the Napoleonic Wars, with a user interface that allows Web-site visitors to view them in whatever sequence they desire. This is called an *overlay* in cartographic terminology, which you'll often find in sophisticated mapping programs such as Google Earth. (Shameless plug time: Be sure to see this author's *Google Earth For Dummies* [Wiley Publishing] if it's not already a part of your collection.)

Absolute positioning

Absolute positioning is placing a DIV element based on the upper-left corner of the Web page itself, rather than basing the position on anything contained within the Web page. Thus, a DIV that is absolutely positioned at, say, 50 pixels in and down from the upper-left corner will be only half as far from the left and top margins as one that's absolutely positioned 100 pixels in and down.

To set a DIV to an absolute position, you simply need to specify that this is what you want — and set how far from the left and top of the Web page you want the upper-left corner of your DIV to be. For example, for a rectangle that's 100 pixels by 100 pixels in size, use the following code to set its absolute position to 50 pixels in and 50 pixels down:

```
<BODY>
<DIV
style="position:absolute;top:50;left:50;width:100;
    height:100">
</DIV>
</BODY>
```

To specify this — as well as one that is 100 pixels in and down, as in the example mentioned in the first paragraph — you'd change the code to read as follows:

```
<BODY>
<DIV
style="position:absolute;top:50;left:50;width:100;
    height:100";background-color:gray>
</DIV>
<DIV
style="position:absolute;top:100;left:100;width:100;
    height:100";background-color:black>
</DIV>
</BODY>
```

Note that both DIVs in this style declaration go within the BODY element. Also, for the purpose of better showing them in this example, each DIV has a different background color assigned to it — specified by (as you may have guessed) the background-color attribute.

Figure 6-12 shows the two DIVs given absolute positions.

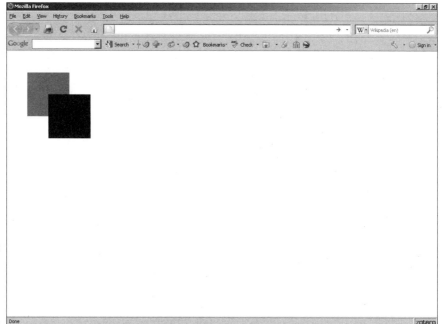

Figure 6-12:
Setting an absolute position.

Relative positioning

Relative positioning is simple to implement: You simply use the word relative instead of the word absolute in your HTML code. Otherwise it works the same as absolute positioning does except for one critical factor — its origin point. It's based not on the upper-left corner of the Web page, but on the upper-left corner of *the containing element.* Doubtless you recall that everything on a Web page is contained within something else — the BODY element is contained within the HTML element, and so forth — thus, with relative positioning, you have to pay careful attention to this container relationship unless you really, *really* like dealing with unpredictable results on your Web pages.

If, for example, one DIV is contained within another one, then you have to calculate the second one's positioning relative to its parent DIV element's position, not to the Web page as a whole. Say the contained DIV is set to a relative position of 200 pixels in and 200 pixels down. If the parent DIV is set to 100,100, then the position of the child DIV is going to be 300,300 (the position of the upper-left corner of the parent DIV plus the position of the child DIV).

To modify the earlier example to do that, you'd change the code to read something like this:

```
<BODY>
<DIV
style="position:absolute;top:200;left:200;width:100;
    height:100;background-color:gray">
<DIV
style="position:relative;top:100;left:100;width:100;
    height:100;background-color:black">
</DIV>
</DIV>
</BODY>
```

Notice that the second <DIV> tag begins before the first layer is closed with its </DIV> tag. Thus, the second one is enclosed within the first one. Because the second one's relative positioning values are the same as the size of the first DIV, the upper-left corner of the second DIV is located exactly where the first one's lower-right corner falls — instead of in the middle of it, as in the preceding example (see Figure 6-13).

Online Sources for CSS

Table 6-1 lists some places on the World Wide Web where you can find more resources like the ones covered in this chapter.

Table 6-1	Online Resources for CSS
Web-Site Name	*Web Address*
CSS Beauty	www.cssbeauty.com
CSS Standard	www.w3.org/TR/CSS2
CSS Tutorial	www.w3schools.com/css
CSSplay	www.cssplay.co.uk
Dynamic Drive CSS Library	www.dynamicdrive.com/style
Guide to Cascading Style Sheets	http://htmlhelp.com/reference/css

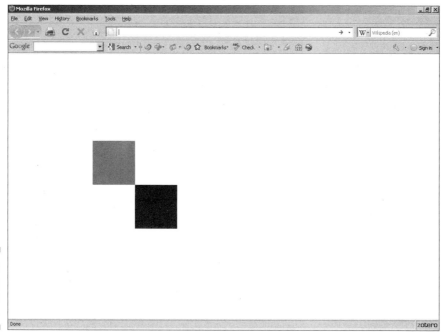

Figure 6-13:
Using
relative
positioning.

Chapter 7

Adding Images

In This Chapter

▶ Getting free graphics

▶ Optimizing graphics files

▶ Creating free logos

▶ Editing images

▶ Designing with images

*Y*ou can have a perfectly functional Web site without images. But if you compare your site with one that's just as functional but also uses graphics, yours will probably lose out in terms of attracting visitors. Most people will go to the other site and leave yours gathering electronic dust.

In this chapter, I take you on a whirlwind tour of places where you can download images by the bushel, I suggest methods for modifying images in fabulous ways, and I share lots of other tips to improve your site's appearance.

Getting Graphics — for Free!

Most of us aren't artists, and even if I know an artist or three, most of them spend their time mucking about with paintbrushes and canvases. Many aren't really comfortable with electronic media. So how do average people who want nice graphics for their Web sites get them? The good news is that excellent graphics are all over the place. Graphics are an integral part of the World Wide Web, and the quality of those graphics has improved tremendously from the early days of the Internet.

Heeding copyrights and credits

Every Web browser is a funnel for graphics. Any image that you can see in it, you can download and put on your site — technically speaking, anyway.

But you need to consider a few factors before you use graphics. Yes, you can grab every image file you find. But you can't necessarily use them all without consequences.

When an artist creates an image, that artist owns the *copyright* to that image. Just as the word says, that gives the artist — and the artist alone — the *right* to make *copies*, electronic or otherwise. The artist can give other people permission to make copies of the image — or even sell the copyright to someone — but unless he or she does so, the artist retains total control over the image.

Never take legal advice from anyone who spells copy*right* as copy*write.*

One of the few ways in which someone can lose a copyright is by stating that he's placing a work in the *public domain,* which means that he's surrendering his copyright, and others can do anything that they want with the work. Many people don't understand what public domain means, though — and you sometimes run across a statement on a Web site that says something incredible like, "I retain the copyright to all these images, but I'm placing them in the public domain, so feel free to use them." If you find one of these contradictory disclaimers and you really want to use the images, your best course is to contact the artist for clarification.

Typically, you find five different situations with fine print on an artist's Web site, as the following list describes:

- ✔ The artist states that you can't use the images. Just walk away — you can find plenty of others out there.

- ✔ The artist states that you can use the images without any conditions. Go ahead and download to your heart's content.

- ✔ The artist states that you can use the images if you do certain things, such as include a link back to the page they're on or include a copyright notice under the image. Do what the artist asks and use the images.

- ✔ The artist states that you can use the images freely if you run a noncommercial site but that commercial sites must pay. If you're commercial and the work is good, pay up — it's not going to break the bank. After all, you're not buying a Renoir original here.

- ✔ The artist provides no information at all about usage. Either walk away or e-mail the artist to find out the policy.

Creating your own images

The easiest way to avoid copyright problems is to make your own images. That way you own the copyright — unless you're working under contract for someone such as a Web design firm, in which case that company probably owns the copyright. It's impossible for me to cover all you need to know about copyright in the limited space available here, but the subject is well covered in *Creating Web Graphics For Dummies,* by Bud Smith and Peter Frazier (Wiley Publishing).

Of course, the digital camera revolution also gives you an unprecedented opportunity to create your own Web-ready graphics (check out *Digital Photography For Dummies,* 5th Edition, by Julie Adair King), and programs like Photoshop and Fireworks make it relatively easy for even those of us who aren't very graphically talented to come up with professional-level graphics. Table 7-1 shows the URLs for several popular graphics programs.

Table 7-1	Online Resources for Graphics Programs
Program	*Web Address*
Adobe Fireworks	www.adobe.com/products/fireworks
Adobe Photoshop	www.adobe.com/products/photoshop
Corel Painter	www.corel.com/painter
Corel Paint Shop Pro	www.corel.com/paintshoppro
CorelDRAW	www.corel.com/coreldraw

Differentiating among graphics file formats

Sometimes it seems there are about as many different graphics file formats as there are people in Manhattan on a Monday afternoon. Every company from Adobe to Kodak has its own way of showing electronic images. When it comes to the Web, though, you really need to consider only three formats — the three that work in all major (and most minor) Web browsers:

- **GIF:** The venerable old *GIF* (Graphics Interchange Format) file format still sees a lot of use on the Web. Because GIF limits you to 256 colors, it's best to use for images that don't have lots of colors or much in the way of subtle shifts between colors. GIF also has a unique capability — it can contain several images in a single file. These images appear sequentially as you view the GIF file, resulting in a cheap and easy form of animation.

- **JPEG:** The relatively newer *JPEG* (Joint Photographic Experts Group) format, also commonly known as *JPG* because people still have the habit of using DOS 8.3-type filenames, has radically different capabilities. JPEG is a true color format, so you don't need to worry about any color limitations. It also stores image information in a different way, resulting in a highly compressed file that's usually much smaller than a GIF file of the same image.

✔ **PNG:** The latest puppy in the window is the *PNG* (Portable Network Graphics) format. (You pronounce it *ping.*) PNG does everything that the GIF format does, except create animated images, and does quite a few things much better — such as providing better transparency capabilities. (A more sophisticated format known as *MNG* — Multiple-image Network Graphics — that's currently in the works includes the capability to create animated images.)

Putting Your Graphics on a Diet with GIFWorks

Fat files are embarrassing. They slow down a page like nothing else, turning a fabulous site into a sluggish turkey. A really good graphics program can trim your overweight files, but such a program will also set you back a pretty penny, and you'll have to work with it for a while if you want to get the most out of it. Instead of putting all that money and effort into solving the file-size problem, try some of the following Web sites that do the job for you — for free.

GIFWorks is absolutely one of the best tools you'll find on the Web. Period. You get the idea I like it? A lot? There's a good reason: This is one truly full-featured program, and it's something you may not be familiar with yet — but I think it's the wave of the future on the Web. This program isn't one you download and use on your computer. It stays put, and you use it right on the GIFWorks site.

With GIFWorks, you can do everything to GIF files (but only GIF files), from reducing colors to adding special effects. So what does it cost? Nothing, nada, zip. And to top it all off, the same folks have a site that lets you get your hands on zillions of high-quality images (the Animation Factory, at www.animfactory.com). I'm not exaggerating when I say *quality,* either. This is some of the best stuff I've seen.

Unlike GIFWorks, you have to pay for The Animation Factory, but their rates are within just about any budget — anywhere from $59.95 for a year's download privileges to the highest rate of $199.95 for a year of the top pro-level service. You don't have to pay any further fees for using the images. The Animation Factory is well worth the price, even if you don't run a commercial Web site — and GIFWorks shows the same attention to quality but costs nothing at all.

Here's how to upload your image to GIFWorks:

1. **Go to** www.gifworks.com/image_editor.html.

2. **Choose File↪Open Image from the GIFWorks menu options, as shown in Figure 7-1.**

   Come back to this page later and check out the File↪New 3D Text option. It's a great way to create animated text banners.

3. **On the next page, open a file from the Web by entering its URL and clicking the Fetch Image button. Or upload a file from your local drive by clicking the Browse button, selecting the file, and then clicking the Upload Image button.**

   GIFWorks operates on a *copy* of the image you specify. It doesn't change the original file in any way.

   After the image is uploaded to GIFWorks, it appears in the program, as shown in Figure 7-2.

   I'm using a dog from the collection at www.bestanimations.com for this example. The dog is animated, which is one of the great strengths of GIFWorks. Many programs can modify and optimize individual GIF images, but an animated GIF is composed of many different images — eight of them, in this case — and GIFWorks can modify all of them simultaneously, thus altering the animated image.

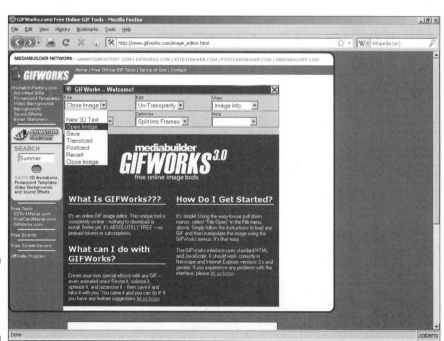

Figure 7-1: Opening a file in GIFWorks.

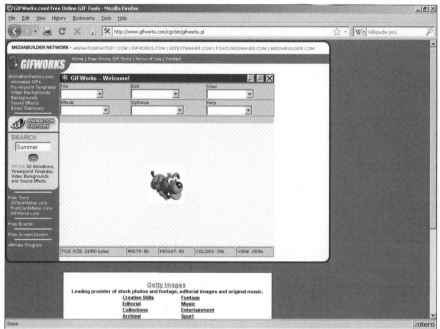

Figure 7-2:
An animated
image in
GIFWorks.

Before you begin to work with the image, click the Help menu and take a look at the FAQ.

After your image is at GIFWorks, what you do with the image depends on your situation. Here are some options you can choose from:

- ✔ **To reduce the file size quickly:** Choose Optimize⇨Reduce Colors from the menu bar. You get a whole page full of different versions of the original image, each with fewer colors than the preceding ones. You also get information about the file size, number of remaining colors, and percentage reduction. Scroll down the page, look at each image, and download the one that represents the best compromise between image quality and file size.

- ✔ **To make a color transparent:** Choose Edit⇨Transparify from the menu options. In the pop-up window that appears, click the color you want to see through. To make a transparent GIF totally opaque, do the same thing, but start by choosing Edit⇨Un-Transparify.

- ✔ **To view information on file size, width, height, and so on:** Choose View⇨Image Info.

Okay, that's all the practical stuff that most Webmasters need. Now for the fun part. After you're done being responsible, head for the Effects menu and start playing. You can do so many things to your images that you may have a hard time choosing among them. Unless you're dead set on just trying anything that comes to hand, choose Help➪Effects Gallery to look at some examples. Figure 7-3 shows what applying some of the effects did to the image shown in Figure 7-2. Enjoy.

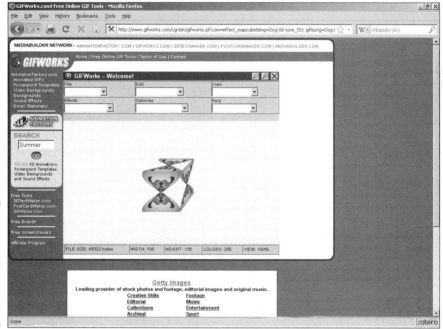

Figure 7-3: Special effects can radically alter the look of an image.

Creating a Logo with CoolText.com

If you want a free logo fast and you don't mind doing it yourself, try CoolText. com at — you guessed it — www.cooltext.com. This Web site generates graphics, according to the options that you choose, while you wait. The process is simple and fun, and there's no limit to the number of logos you can experiment with.

Not only are its logos cool, but so are the site's legal requirements: none, zip, nada. There's no copyright issue to deal with, no ads stuck in the middle of things, and no fine print of any kind. As an act of gratitude for such a great service, you may want to add a link back to this site from yours, but even that's not required.

Although CoolText.com doesn't hold a copyright on the logos you create, you probably do. I'm not a lawyer (and I don't even play one on TV), but it seems to me that the decisions you make during the course of designing the logos qualify them as artistic creations. Don't take my word for it, though. If this point is important for your situation, check with an attorney who really knows copyright law — or e-mail the U.S. Copyright Office at `copyinfo@loc.gov`.

To make a custom logo at CoolText.com, follow these steps:

1. **Go to** `www.cooltext.com`.

2. **Scroll down and click any logo style under Choose a Logo Style, as shown in Figure 7-4.**

   This takes you to the logo design page, shown in Figure 7-5.

Figure 7-4: CoolText.com's logo page, showing the styles you can use to create your own custom logo — for free!

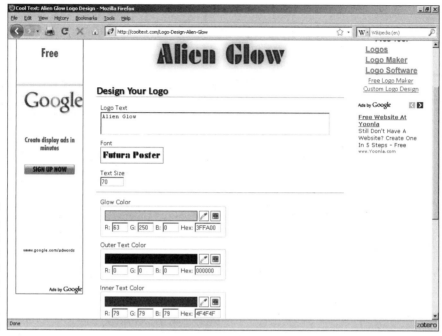

Figure 7-5:
The logo design page, where you choose options for your logo.

Different logo styles offer different options. Depending on the style that you choose, these options may set colors, determine whether text is engraved or raised, and so forth. In this example, I'm using the Alien Glow design.

3. Type the text for your logo in the Logo Text text box.

You usually type your site or company name here, although you can type anything that you want. If you need more than one line, you can put a new line symbol (\n) in the text, as in the following example:

```
First Line\nSecond Line
```

4. Click the font name (in this example, Futura Poster), and then select a font category from the list that's presented. Finally, select the name of a particular font.

You're returned automatically to the design page.

5. Enter a font size in the Text Size text box.

6. Click the Predefined Color picker (to the right of the color bar) for the Glow Color category and then select a glow color from the resulting color picker Web page. (See Figure 7-6.)

This Web page gives you a long list of named colors, with examples of each color. Just decide which color you like and click it to return to CoolText.com with that color selected. You can specify a glow color either by entering numerical values in the R, G, and B text boxes to indicate the RGB (red, green, and blue) components, or by entering its hexadecimal value to the right.

7. **Repeat Step 6 for the other three color settings (Outer Text Color, Inner Text Color, and Background Color).**

8. **Click the current background image in the Background Image category (if one hasn't been chosen, click None), and then click one of the textures on the resulting Web page. (See Figure 7-7.)**

   You're returned to CoolText.com with that texture selected.

   If you need more textures, click the links at the top of the textures page to view more pages.

9. **If you want to specify a file format, click the Edit button for the File Format category and then select one of the file formats in the resulting list.**

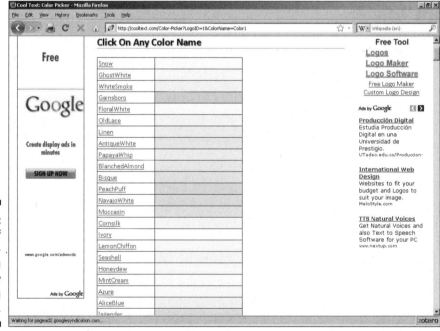

Figure 7-6:
The list of named colors lets you choose by just clicking one.

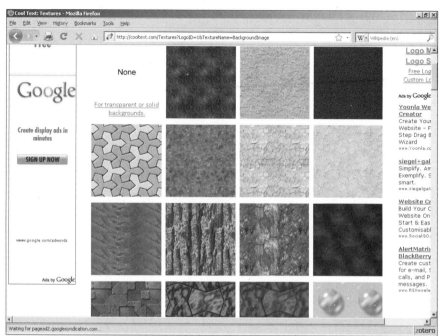

Figure 7-7:
Choosing a
texture for
your logo.

10. **After you set all the options for your logo, click the Render Logo button.**

Now, all you have to do is sit back and wait until your logo shows up. If you like it, download it right away because it exists on CoolText.com's server for only about an hour. If you don't like it, back up and monkey with the settings until you get what you want.

While you're at CoolText.com, check out the button generator, too. You access it by clicking the Buttons link at the top of the page.

Editing Images

There are plenty of times when you'll need to tweak an image to get it "just so" for your site. All graphics programs give you some options for doing this sort of thing, and they all work pretty much the same way. In this section, I show you how to use a handy little graphics editor called IrfanView (`www.irfanview.com`) to spiff up your Web graphics quickly and easily.

Resizing

Although you can make an image appear smaller on a Web page than it really is (see the "Sizing images in HTML" section, later in this chapter), it's usually best to set the size deliberately before the image ends up on your site.

This is a simple process, although there are a couple of caveats. When you resize an image, your graphics program has to change the *pixels* — the color dots that make up the image. Obviously, a larger image will take more pixels and a smaller one will take fewer. This means either adding pixels *(interpolation)* or subtracting pixels *(resampling)*.

Although graphics interpolation has come a long way, any image-resizing process still has to make some compromises. Shrinking an image usually doesn't damage the capability to view the picture, but it always has to mean some loss of detail. Enlarging an image can add areas of blockiness due to the additional pixels needed to fill the new space.

The best resizing is a minor resizing.

Open the image you want to resize in IrfanView, and then follow these steps:

1. **Choose Image⇨Resize/Resample from the menu.**

   In the Resize/Resample Image dialog box, shown in Figure 7-8, there are three methods of setting the new image size:

   - *To specify a particular physical size,* in the Set New Size panel, select pixels, centimeters, or inches, and then enter the new width and height in the Width and Height text boxes.

     If the Preserve Aspect Ratio check box is selected, you have to enter only one of the values; the other will be automatically entered.

   - *To use a percentage,* select the Set New Size as Percentage of Original radio button, and then enter the appropriate numbers in the Width and Height text boxes.

   - *To use common sizes,* click the appropriate button or select a radio button in the Some Standard Dimensions panel.

2. **Click the OK button.**

3. **Save the image.**

   If you don't save the image after you make your changes, you'll lose it.

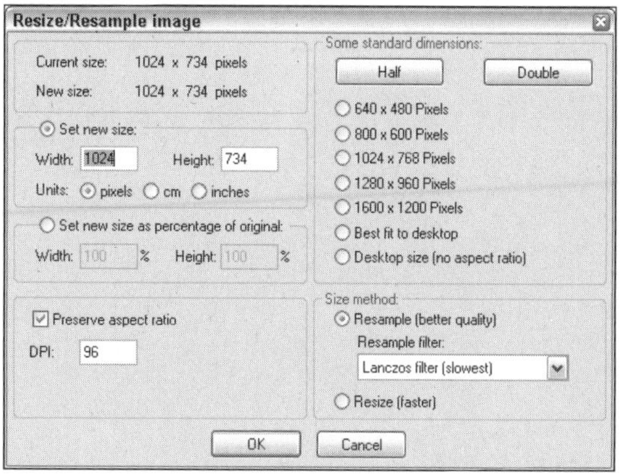

Figure 7-8:
Setting the
new image
size.

Cropping

What if you want part of a picture but not all of it? Get out the scissors — it's croppin' time. You can cut out any rectangular section you want — you'll probably do this a lot, so you'll be happy to hear how easy it is.

Open the image you want to crop in IrfanView, and then follow these steps:

1. **Place your mouse pointer at one corner of the area you want to crop and then click.**

2. **While holding down the left mouse button, drag the mouse pointer to the opposite corner of your area.**

   As you do so, a guide box shows you the currently selected area. (See Figure 7-9.)

3. **When you have the area you want selected, release the mouse button.**

4. **Choose Edit⇨Crop Selection from the menu.**

   Alternatively, you can press Ctrl+Y.

Rotating and flipping

Just like a picture hanging on a wall, an image on your Web site can sometimes look better if it's repositioned. A slight turn to the right, perhaps, or maybe even a complete inversion for a shocking effect. Graphically, I'm talking about rotation and flips.

Figure 7-9:
Cropping an
image.

Photo courtesy of NASA.

There are two kinds of rotation in IrfanView. Simple rotation is always by 90 degrees. Four of these rotations in a row return the image to its original state. Custom rotation allows you to specify an exact number of your choice instead.

To do a simple rotation, just choose Image from the menu, and then click Rotate Right or Rotate Left.

For a custom rotation, do this instead:

1. **Choose Image⇨Custom/Fine Rotation from the menu.**

   The Rotate by Angle dialog box appears.

2. **In the dialog box shown in Figure 7-10, enter the degree (up to two decimal points) of rotation. Use a minus sign (–) for leftward rotation.**

3. **The dialog box displays the original image on the left and the altered one on the right. If you aren't satisfied with the results of your rotation, repeat Step 2 until the altered image suits your needs.**

4. **Click the OK button.**

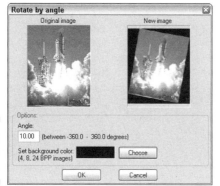

Figure 7-10:
Doing a fine
rotation.

Photo courtesy of NASA.

Flipping an image is done in pretty much the same way as a simple rotation — choose Image⇨Vertical Flip or Image⇨Horizontal Flip from the menu — but it isn't the same thing as rotating an image 180 degrees. Remember that a *flip* is a mirror image instead of a turned one.

Adjusting color

Color adjustments include a range of possibilities. The most basic are color reduction (for example, making a 256-color image into a 16-color one) and grayscale conversion. The more complex include setting the proportions of red, green, and blue and monkeying with the contrast and brightness.

Gamma correction is a highfalutin term for fixing an image that's too light or dark. You'll often find this situation when viewing an image on a PC that was done on a Mac.

To do a simple color reduction with IrfanView, follow these steps:

1. **Choose Image⇨Decrease Color Depth from the menu.**

   The Decrease Color Depth dialog box appears.

2. **In the dialog box shown in Figure 7-11, select one of the radio buttons to select a standard color depth.**

   If you select the Custom radio button, be sure to enter another number of colors into the Custom text box.

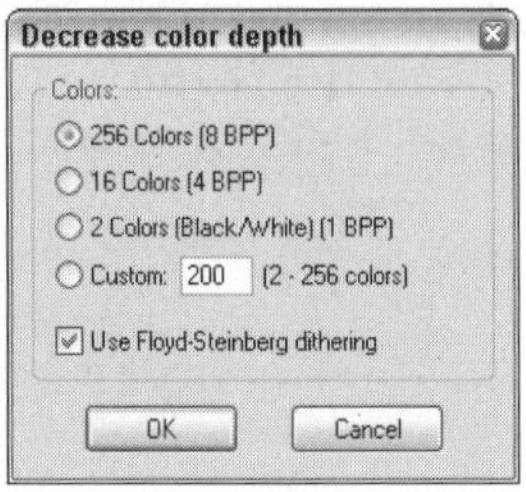

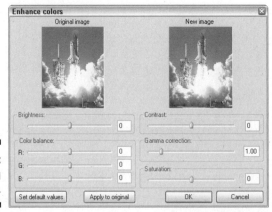

Figure 7-11:
Reducing
colors is
easy.

3. **Click the OK button.**

Grayscale conversion is even easier. Just choose Image⇨Convert to Grayscale from the menu.

Although the most complex color adjustments are a bit more involved, IrfanView wraps them in an easy-to-use package with lots of options. Load up an image and give it a go:

1. **Choose Image⇨Enhance Colors from the menu.**

2. **In the Enhance Colors dialog box (see Figure 7-12), drag the sliders or type values into the text boxes.**

   As you do so, the reference image on the right shows the changes you're making; the original image isn't affected by your experimentation, so feel free to play around with all the settings. You can, at any time, click the Set Default Values button to put everything back to normal.

3. **If the reference image isn't large enough for you, click the Apply to Original button.**

Figure 7-12:
Enhancing
colors.

Photo courtesy of NASA.

This adds all your changes to your full-size original image. Note, however, that you still haven't actually altered it; all you have to do is click the Cancel button to return to normal.

4. **When you're finished, click the OK button to keep your changes or the Cancel button to abort them.**

Using special effects filters

There's a lot you can do with most of today's graphics programs, but there's always something more that's possible. That's where *filters* come in. A filter is a special-effects wizard that alters your images automatically in various ways. You might, for example, apply a filter to a photograph to make the photo look like an oil painting or pencil sketch.

IrfanView has its own set of ready-to-use filters. It can also use your Photoshop-compatible filters. The best way to gain a quick understanding of what filters can do is to check out the Effects Browser:

1. **Choose Image⇨Effects from the menu.**

2. **Choose the Effects Browser option from the resulting submenu.**

3. **In the Image Effects dialog box shown in Figure 7-13, select the names of the various built-in effects filters.**

   As you do so, the twin images show you how the original compares to the filtered version.

4. **Enter any requested values required by the filter.**

5. **When you're done, click the OK button to keep your changes, or click the Cancel button to abort them.**

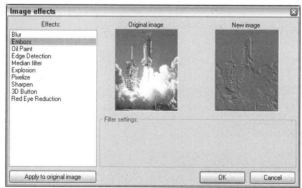

Figure 7-13:
Previewing
effects.

Photo courtesy of NASA.

Basic Design with Images

Getting or creating images is one thing. Knowing the right images to get (or to make) is another, and knowing what to do with them is perhaps most important of all. Misusing graphics — using either too many or too few — can make an otherwise outstanding Web site into an unpleasant mess. This section explores the proper use of images in Web page design.

Placing images for maximum effectiveness

It's easy to overdo any element on a Web page. It's not uncommon to run across sites that are all, or almost all, text — which is fine for some technical material, but pretty dicey if you're trying to appeal to the general public. At the opposite extreme, you'll find pages that are (in effect) nothing but one image after another, with perhaps a small bit of text that often leaves you more confused than when you started.

Balancing visual elements with text is key to good Web site design. The CNN. com front page illustrates this point well. It's functional, eye catching, and well balanced. Figure 7-14 shows the top portion of the Web page. Note that it's strongly graphical. Even the text and links are all tied in to their attendant graphical background, their colors nicely suiting the overall look of the page.

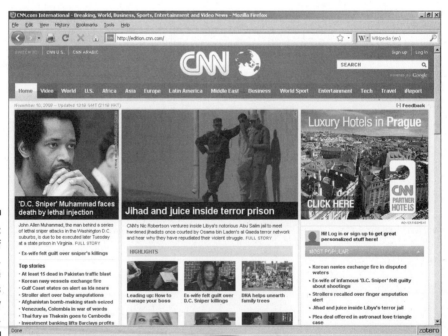

Figure 7-14: The top of the CNN. com home page is strongly graphical.

The major image at the top — a photo and its surrounding frame — is the largest single graphical element on the page, reflecting its importance as showing the latest top story. Farther down (see Figure 7-15), there are smaller photos illustrating other stories; the whole is well balanced by the set of text links leading to various news reports.

This site has a particularly interesting feature: Except for the news story's text links, virtually all the text is either embedded in or otherwise associated with a graphic. And very little of the graphic material is in the form of photos, drawings, or other commonly used image types. You do find heavy use of graphical dividers to help structure the visual appeal of the page — but they're small and don't overpower the other elements nearby.

Your own artistic judgment must be the ultimate guide, but these guidelines will help you to create better-designed Web pages:

✔ Keep most images relatively small. How small depends upon two factors: the number of images you have on the page and simple visibility.

✔ Use your largest picture or artwork as the lead-in to the rest of your material. If it's not the most important image, it probably shouldn't be the biggest one, either.

✔ Use small divider images to separate subject areas.

✔ Don't allow advertising images to overwhelm the basic material of the Web page.

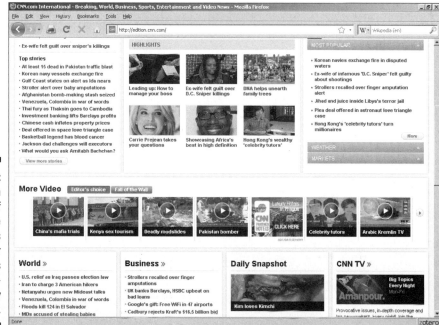

Figure 7-15: The main portion of the page contains smaller graphics and is broken up by text.

Sizing images in HTML

Besides file size, you need to consider the physical size of images. Each image, when displayed in a Web browser, takes up a certain amount of real estate on your visitors' screens. Very often, a particular image you want to use just doesn't happen to be the size you want it to be.

You can fire up your favorite graphics program, load the image, resize and resample it, and then resave it. Or you can just let your visitor's Web browser do all the work for you. The ability to alter the size of an image on a Web page is built in to HTML. Although it isn't required, it's good form to specify the width and height of an image, as demonstrated here:

```
<IMG width="100" height="30">
```

Normally you would use the actual size of the image, of course. But you can use any values. To make the image take up more space on a Web page, just enter larger numbers. To make it smaller — you guessed it — enter smaller values instead.

You have to be careful to resize the image proportionally, unless you're looking for some weird effect. If you want to quadruple the area of the example image — from 3,000 pixels to 12,000 pixels, for example — you set the width to 200 and the height to 60.

See Chapter 2 for details on how to place images.

Online Sources for Quality Graphics

Table 7-2 lists some places on the World Wide Web where you can find lots of high-quality graphics for your site.

Table 7-2	Online Resources for Quality Graphics
Web Site Name	**Web Address**
CoolNotions.com	www.coolnotions.com
All Free Original Clip Art	www.free-graphics.com
Goddess Art of Jonathon Earl Bowser	www.jonathonart.com
Graphics-4free.com	www.graphics-4free.com
Grazia A. Cipresso	www.gcipresso.com
Lindy's Graphics	www.theiowa.net/lindy

I don't list any image repositories in this table. An *image repository* is a Web site that simply provides about a zillion images for download without any regard for where they came from or what kind of legal troubles they may cause for you. They typically involve all sorts of copyright and trademark violations — and the fact that such a repository provides the Donald Duck images that you put on your site doesn't keep Disney's lawyers off your back. Stick with sites like the ones in this table, and you'll keep out of trouble.

Chapter 8

Adding Forms

● ●

In This Chapter

▶ Adding the FORM tag

▶ Setting up interaction

▶ Getting text info

▶ Offering visitor choices

▶ Checking for CGI access

▶ Implementing CGI scripts

▶ Using form makers

● ●

A Web *form* consists of a series of elements that, together, enable you to gather information from your visitors. A Web form's two most common uses are for getting user data when a visitor signs up for "membership" and getting purchaser info when making a sale.

The first step in your form design process is, of course, to figure out what information you need from your visitors. Next you need to determine which form elements are best suited for getting that info. After you've done that, you type the HTML and (finally) arrange to submit the form's data for processing.

You doubtless recall from Chapter 2 that all HTML tags are enclosed within other tags, and forms are no exception. The <FORM> tag goes within the BODY element, so your basic form setup will look like this:

```
<HTML>

<HEAD>
</HEAD>

<BODY>

<FORM>
</FORM>

</BODY>

</HTML>
```

If you fail to follow this pattern properly, in which each element is properly nested, the form may not work. Web browsers are very forgiving, however, so you might still get away with it.

Getting Input

The most important part of a Web form, next to the <FORM> tag itself, is the <INPUT> tag. The various permutations of the INPUT element allow you to get input in a wide variety of formats, ranging from simple text to a series of Yes and No options.

The INPUT element includes several types such as check boxes, password fields, and even an option for a user to upload a file. I'll go over the most useful of these in the following sections, but here's the basic way to handle specifying the particulars:

```
<FORM>
<INPUT type="text">
<INPUT type="checkbox">
<INPUT type="submit">
</FORM>
```

Note that there is no closing tag for the INPUT element.

As shown in Figure 8-1, this simple code example results in the elements all lying side by side. To put them all on separate lines for layout purposes, you'd need to add a line break between each pair, like this:

```
<FORM>
<INPUT type="text">
<BR>
<INPUT type="checkbox">
<BR>
<INPUT type="submit">
</FORM>
```

The version with line breaks results in the layout shown in Figure 8-2.

For a really neat form layout, try putting its elements into a table (see Chapter 3).

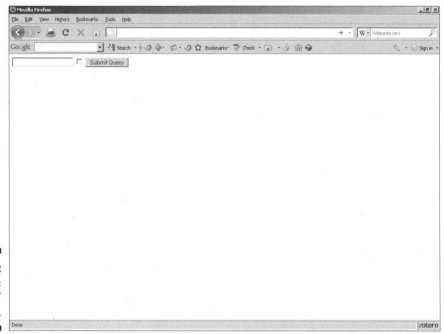

Figure 8-1:
Some basic
INPUT
types.

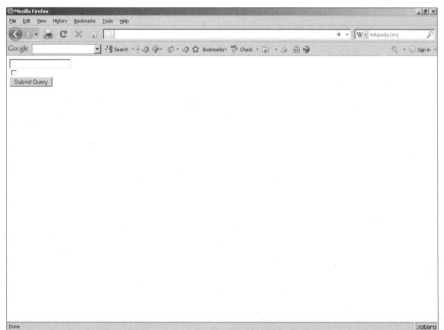

Figure 8-2:
Separating
lines.

Of course, a typical form uses several of the same INPUT types over and over again. You'll need to give each element a particular name in order to distinguish it from similar elements. Otherwise it would be impossible to tell the difference between (for example) the three text boxes asking for a visitor's first name, middle initial, and last name.

You do this via the name attribute, as you might expect. The example just mentioned would be coded like this:

```
<FORM>
<INPUT type="text" name="firstname">
<INPUT type="text" name="middleinitial">
<INPUT type="text" name="lastname">
</FORM>
```

Typing in text boxes

Text boxes are simple, one-line rectangles that typically contain information such as names and addresses, and you've got a bunch of options you can specify when it comes to using them.

The most obvious of these is setting the length of the text box. This capability enables you to create a more pleasing layout and (incidentally) save space. To expand on the example in the preceding section, you might set the length of the user name text boxes like this:

```
<FORM>
First Name: <INPUT type="text" name="firstname" size="15">
Middle Initial: <INPUT type="text" name="middleinitial"
          size="1">
Last Name: <INPUT type="text" name="lastname" size="20">
</FORM>
```

Figure 8-3 shows the results (note that, despite the size limit on the middle initial, both Firefox and Internet Explorer expand it to three characters).

The size attribute specifies the number of typed characters, not the number of pixels, and the width of characters depends on the font being used.

Of course, when it comes to setting the length, you have to just take your best shot at what will work best. Some last names are five letters long whereas others may be more than 20. Fortunately, the size of the text box doesn't actually limit the size of the data entered into it. If someone types a 100-character entry into a size 20 text box, all 100 characters will still be entered, and the text will simply scroll as it's typed.

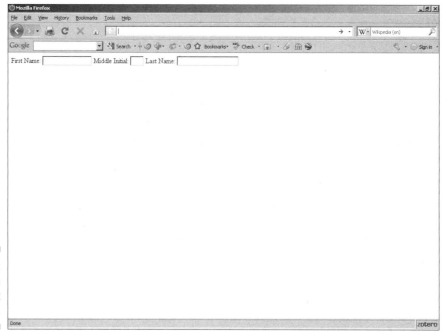

Figure 8-3:
Limiting the
size of text
boxes.

But what if the program you're using to process the data has a limit on the size of the data it will accept? This is a pretty common situation, and you'll be happy to know that there's a simple way to handle this problem: You use the maxlength attribute. The following code shows how to adapt our example to accept no more than a particular number of characters:

```
<FORM>
<INPUT type="text" name="firstname" size="15"
        maxlength="50">
<INPUT type="text" name="middleinitial" size="1"
        maxlength="1">
<INPUT type="text" name="lastname" size="20"
        maxlength="50">
</FORM>
```

In this case, the first and last names are limited to 50 characters in length; the middle initial, of course, is set to a single character.

If you're using a form that requires a user to enter a password, it's customary to use, in the place of a regular text box, a specialized password text box that — you guessed it — you enter by typing this line:

```
<INPUT type="password">
```

With password text boxes, when a user enters his or her password, a series of asterisks is shown instead of the typed letters, thus protecting the user's security if someone else is peeking at the screen. That's the only difference; You use the same options as with regular text boxes.

The following code sets up the example shown in Figure 8-4:

```
<FORM>
User Name: <INPUT type="text" name="username" size="25"
          maxlength="50">
<BR>
<BR>
Password: <INPUT type="password" name="middleinitial"
          size="25" maxlength="50">
</FORM>
```

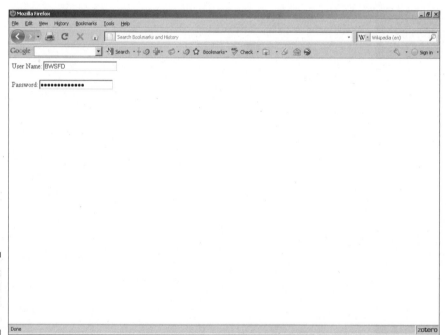

Figure 8-4:
Regular and
password
text boxes.

Using text areas

There are lots of cases when you'll want to get some textual data that just doesn't fit comfortably in a one-line box. Say, for example, that you have an order form where you ask buyers if they have any special instructions. The answers you get to such a question may run to several paragraphs rather than just a few words.

That's where *text areas* come in handy: You can use them to set up a box as wide and as tall as you want.

The most important way text areas differ from text boxes is that they are *not* (as you might normally expect) yet another type of the INPUT element. Instead, you use the TEXTAREA element.

This code example shows the difference between the two:

```
<FORM>
User Name: <INPUT type="text" name="username" size="25"
          maxlength="50">
<BR>
<BR>
Special Instructions:
<BR>
<TEXTAREA name="specinst" cols="100" rows="20">
</TEXTAREA>
</FORM>
```

This specifies a text area with a width of 100 columns and a height of 20 rows, as shown in Figure 8-5.

You have to use the </TEXTAREA> end tag!

Choosing radio buttons or check boxes

When it comes to basic choices, you'll want to use check boxes or radio buttons. The round radio buttons (also called *option buttons*) are used for mutually exclusive choices; the square check boxes are used in situations where several simultaneous choices might be made.

For example, if you have a Yes or No situation, you'd use radio buttons, as in the following example (see Figure 8-6):

```
<FORM>
Yes <INPUT type="radio" name="yesorno" value="yes">
No <INPUT type="radio" name="yesorno" value="no">
</FORM>
```

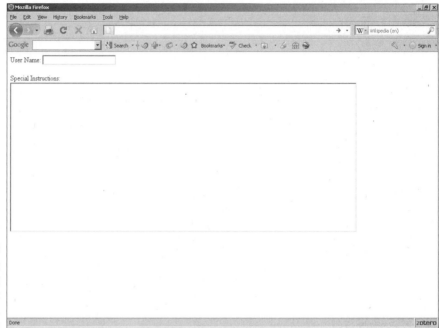

Figure 8-5:
Text box
and text
area.

The name attribute for radio buttons works differently from other INPUT types. A set of radio buttons has the same name for everything in it; it is the value attribute that specifies the difference between them. That's because there can be only one answer — if you choose Yes, then there's no possibility of selecting No, and vice versa.

You would choose check boxes if (say) you're asking whether a user wants to subscribe to various magazines. In that case, the visitor may want to order several (both *Time* and *Newsweek,* for example). Here's how it's done:

```
<FORM>
Time <INPUT type="checkbox" name="time" value="subscribe">
<BR>
<BR>
Newsweek <INPUT type="checkbox" name="newsweek"
         value="subscribe">

</FORM>
```

Figure 8-7 shows how this looks on a Web browser.

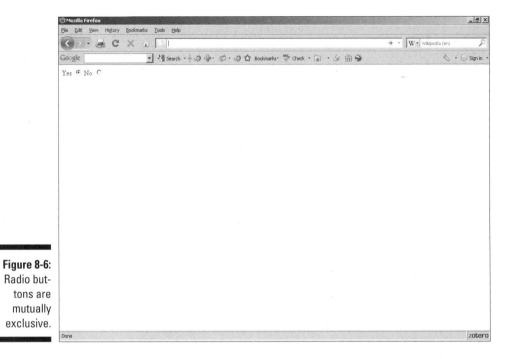

Figure 8-6:
Radio buttons are mutually exclusive.

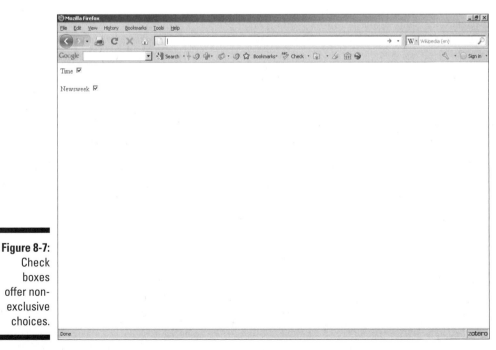

Figure 8-7:
Check boxes offer non-exclusive choices.

Setting up SELECT and OPTION

What if you have, instead of just a few choices, a whole long list of possible choices, such as which country a visitor is from? Setting up a form with dozens of radio buttons would leave your Web page so cluttered and confusing that nobody would want to fill out the form.

Setting up a single SELECT element that has several OPTION elements nested within it, however, lets you add as many choices as you want — in a very small space — by using drop-down menus or list boxes.

Here's a code example that lets visitors choose which continent they're from:

```
<FORM>
<SELECT name="continent">
<OPTION>North America</OPTION>
<OPTION>South America</OPTION>
<OPTION>Europe </OPTION>
<OPTION>Asia </OPTION>
<OPTION>Africa </OPTION>
<OPTION>Australia</OPTION>
<OPTION>Antarctica</OPTION>
</SELECT>
</FORM>
```

The SELECT element is not a type of INPUT element, but a separate one, and both it and the nested OPTION element require closing tags.

Figure 8-8 shows how this works. (I've added a second copy in the image, not reflected in the preceding example, that shows both the original result — a one-line box with a clickable arrow — and what happens when a user clicks that arrow: The expanded, complete list of options appears.)

If you don't want just a single line as in the preceding example, you can use a list box instead of a drop-down menu. All you have to do is just add one attribute to the SELECT element, called size:

```
<FORM>
<SELECT name="continent" size="4">
<OPTION>North America</OPTION>
<OPTION>South America</OPTION>
<OPTION>Europe </OPTION>
<OPTION>Asia </OPTION>
<OPTION>Africa </OPTION>
<OPTION>Australia</OPTION>
<OPTION>Antarctica</OPTION>
</SELECT>
</FORM>
```

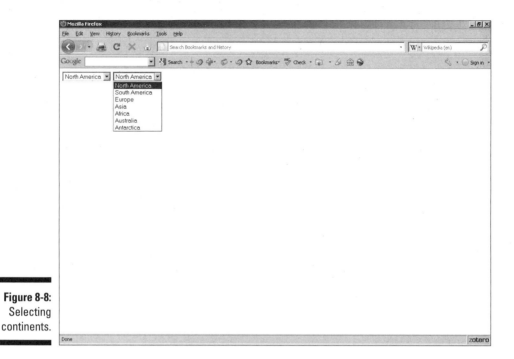

Figure 8-8:
Selecting
continents.

As you can see in Figure 8-9, four of the choices now show instead of just the first one. The other choices that aren't shown are accessed by scrolling.

Submitting the form

After a user is finished filling out the form, the next task is to submit the information so it can be processed. Usually you give the user the means to do this by adding a Submit button at the bottom of the form, like this:

```
<FORM>
Time <INPUT type="checkbox" name="time" value="subscribe">
<BR>
<BR>
Newsweek <INPUT type="checkbox" name="newsweek"
          value="subscribe">
<BR>
<BR>
<INPUT type="submit" value="Send me my magazines!">

</FORM>
```

Any value you enter for the Submit button will be displayed, as shown in Figure 8-10, and the size of the button will expand automatically to accommodate it.

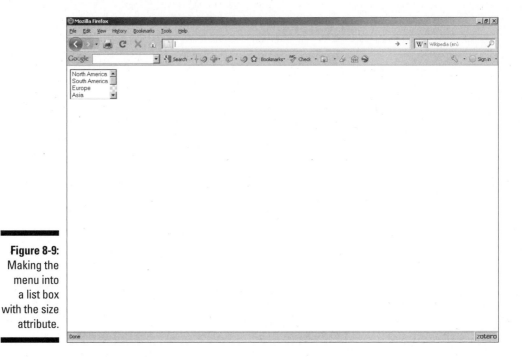

Figure 8-9:
Making the
menu into
a list box
with the size
attribute.

Figure 8-10:
Adding a
Submit
button.

Processing the Form

You've seen how a form is designed and how to submit its contents after a user fills it in, but what do you submit it to? HTML has no form-processing capabilities at all, so you need to send it to an external program for processing. You'd normally, of course, have that program in mind from the very beginning and design the form to mesh with it.

Although the various form-processing programs (such as shopping carts) are written in a variety of programming languages, you don't need to know anything about programming in order to use them. Instead, many of them are hooked up to your Web page by using the *Common Gateway Interface* (CGI). There's nothing mystical or particularly difficult about using the CGI, and I give you the basics in the section "Adding CGI Scripts," later in this chapter.

If you're going to use CGI with your Web pages, first you have to make sure that you have the capability to do so. This sounds obvious, of course, but you may or may not have CGI access for your Web site. *CGI access* means you can run programs on your Web server that use the Common Gateway Interface, a method of sending form data from a Web page to an external program for processing.

Okay, yeah, CGI *also* stands for Computer-Generated Imagery, referring to the special-effects technology that puts monsters, disasters, and other realistic animations in Hollywood blockbuster movies. The Common Gateway Interface may not be as spectacular, but it sure is handy for Web sites.

Nine times out of ten, these programs are kept in a subfolder called `cgi-bin`, so your first step is to look to see if you have such a subfolder on your server. If you do, odds are that you have CGI access, because that subfolder doesn't have any other purpose. If it's there, go ahead and try to use a CGI program. If you follow all the instructions carefully and the program still doesn't work, you may need to have a talk with your network administrator or ISP.

Why your ISP often won't help

When your Web site is hosted by the same ISP that you get your Internet access from, you'll probably find that it's not too supportive of your desire to run CGI scripts. There are a couple of reasons for this, which make good sense to your ISP but don't help you at all:

✔ Badly written programs using CGI can represent a security hazard, poking holes in the normal running of things. Because ISPs want everything to run smoothly and under their control instead of someone else's, ISPs tend to frown on this possibility.

✔ Most ISPs don't really care about your Web site. They're not bad people, but they're mostly in the business of providing Internet access to their customers, and anything else they have to deal with is just an annoyance that gets in the way of their main job.

If your ISP allows you to run CGI scripts, it may be a painful and expensive process on your end. I once had an ISP that wanted to approve the scripts in advance, put them on the server sometime over the next couple of days (it was apparently too much trouble to allow the paying users to access their own files and get the job done instantly), and charge me $25 a pop for doing so. From an ISP's point of view, that's reasonable. From my point of view, it was a definite no-go. For starters, I like to do things right away instead of taking days to get around to it. On top of that, you often have to monkey with a CGI script before you get it working just the way you want. Every time I wanted to make a change, it cost another $25 and set me back a couple more days.

Finding a CGI provider

Fortunately, many Web space providers do provide you with CGI access. If you live in a city or large town, you can easily shop around and find a new ISP that's on your side, CGI-wise. If not, thanks to the way the Internet works, you don't need to deal with your local ISP at all.

You can go with a virtual server or other commercial remote Web-space provider (see Chapter 5 for details), or you can easily find free Web-space providers by using the search engine at FreeWebspace.net. Go to the main page at www.freewebspace.net and click the Advanced Free Hosting Search link, or just go straight to www.freewebspace.net/search/power. shtml, as shown in Figure 8-11. In the search form, select the CGI check box under Features. Select any other options you desire, and click the Search button. My test search, using the default options and the CGI check box, came up with 15 free providers that grant CGI access.

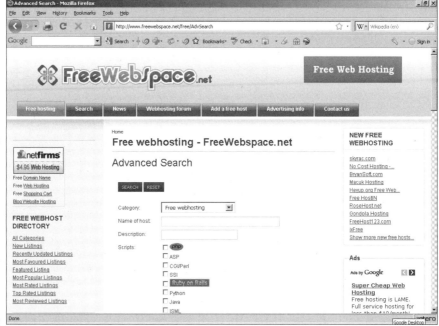

Figure 8-11: FreeWeb space.net's Advanced Search form can help you find a provider that gives you CGI access.

Using remotely hosted CGI scripts

The CGI scripts that you use don't have to reside on the same server that houses your Web pages. This is good, because CGI scripts are run by the Web server on which the script is located — and using them puts an added load on your server, if that's where you keep them. If you have lots of visitors, the data-processing demands on your server can be pretty strenuous. If you don't have your Web site on a dedicated server with plenty of power, things can get really slow.

When the script is on someone else's server, however, you don't have to worry about the server load. Happily, there are lots of remotely hosted CGI scripts, which means you can still add their capabilities to your own pages while avoiding the server-overload problem. Many of the add-ons in this book are remotely hosted.

Free CGI Resources provides free scripts that work via links to its server. (See Figure 8-12.) Check out some of them at www.fido7.com/free-cgi.

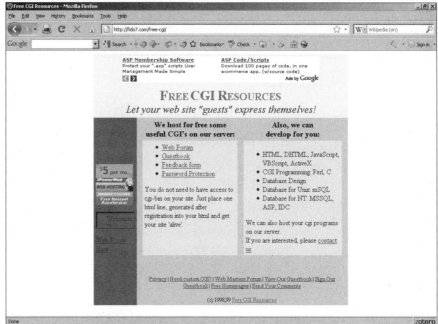

Figure 8-12:
Free CGI
Resources
provides
you with CGI
scripts that
work on its
server, not
yours.

Adding CGI Scripts

A CGI script works by taking input from your Web page and sending that input to an external program for processing. Usually it returns a new Web page that incorporates the results of that processing. The input is most often data from a form, but it can sometimes be just a link that a user clicks to activate the program.

Basic techniques

Before you do anything, you have to get the script. Whenever I describe a script in this book, I provide you with the URL of the site from which you can download the script. After you have the script, follow these basic steps to use it:

1. **Read the instructions for the script. Let me say that again: Read the instructions.**

   After you've worked with a few scripts, it's tempting to just plunge right ahead without looking. After all, most scripts plug in pretty much the same way, and often you can get away with skipping the instructions.

Of course, that's *also* the cause of about 900 percent of the problems people have with scripts. All it takes is to misunderstand or misinterpret one little setting, and then the whole script won't work.

The instructions are often in the standard ReadMe.txt file. Sometimes, the script doesn't have a ReadMe file, though, and the instructions are embedded in the text of the script itself in the form of comments. (*Comments* are notes the programmer adds to provide information; they're marked so they're differentiated from the program code and don't interfere with the running of the program.)

2. **Open the script file in a text editor and make any necessary changes so that it works with your particular setup. After you do this, save the modified script.**

   You may, for example, want to add a list of URLs for a link menu, an e-mail address to send a message to, or the location of your site's main Web page. You don't have to understand the programming in order to do this little chore. Just follow the instructions and replace the sample values in the script with your own values.

   If you use a word processor to make the changes, make sure that the script gets saved as plain text and that the original file extension doesn't get changed. You don't want a bunch of word-processor formatting codes embedded in the script, which you'll get if you save the original plain text as, for example, a Microsoft Word .doc file!

3. **Add the HTML code that the script's instructions say to add to your Web page.**

   As with the script, you probably need to change a few sample values to the actual values. The HTML code is usually nothing more than the location of the CGI program, entered as the action attribute of a form.

4. **Upload the script and the modified HTML file to your Web server.**

   The HTML file goes in the normal HTML folder, and the script goes into the cgi-bin folder.

Solving problems

The basic techniques described in the preceding section work in almost all cases, but in some situations, you may need to modify the script a bit more to get everything working just right.

For example, nearly every script you find assumes your cgi-bin directory is called cgi-bin. Yours may be simply named cgi, for example. If that's the case, you need to change the typical folder references in the script to match your folder name.

You may also find that the standard file extensions, such as `.pl` for Perl files, aren't allowed in your CGI setup. In that case, you have to change the file extension to whatever your server demands. A file named `search.pl`, for example, may need to be renamed `search.cgi`.

If you try to run the script and nothing happens, here are some troubleshooting options:

✔ **Go back over the instructions and see if you did anything wrong.** Nine times out of ten, it's something simple but so small and insignificant that it's easy to overlook. You may have left out a required comma between two values, or forgotten a quotation mark. Perhaps you misspelled the URL of a Web site. Very carefully go over everything you did, and you'll usually find the problem.

✔ **If the script is fine, make sure that you uploaded all the necessary files.** Some scripts have data files that you must upload along with them in order for them to work properly.

✔ **Check to see that your** `cgi-bin` **folder has the correct permissions settings.** If you're not familiar with permissions, ask your ISP to check them for you.

✔ **If all else fails, send an e-mail message to the program's author explaining the nature of the problem and ask for help.** Because most of these programs are free, don't expect too much in the way of technical support. Nobody can afford to both give away programs and spend all their time providing free technical support as well. The best approach is to be polite, perhaps tell the program's author how much you want to use the program (if you don't feel that way about it, you haven't come this far) — and be sure you give all the information you can about the settings you used.

Trying Out Form and Poll Makers

Hardly a day passes without someone announcing the results of some kind of poll: "Thirty-two percent of city residents prefer smog." "The *For Dummies* nerd's approval rating climbed by 4 percent in the past week." "Quantum physics confuses nine people out of five." For whatever reason, people are fascinated by other people's feelings about different subjects. And people love to toss in their two bits' worth whenever they see a survey form. Here are a few common uses for Web-site survey forms:

✔ **Feedback on product quality:** "How do you rate our new release?"

✔ **Opinions on social issues:** "Should we pay more attention to threatened species?"

> ✔ **Preferences between political candidates:** "Do you plan to vote Democrat, Republican, or Independent?"
>
> ✔ **Requests for new site features:** "Check the services you want us to add."

It's not just polls, though. The amount and variety of information gathered via forms on the Web are staggering. Visitor information, prospect inquiries, and product orders are only a few uses of forms. If the idea of using forms interests you, but you're not comfortable with the CGI — that's short for Common Gateway Interface — you may want to try out some of the form makers and processing services described in this section.

A tremendous amount of overlap exists between the folks who offer free forms and those who offer form-processing services. Many of the form makers also provide CGI services, although they usually limit them to servicing their own custom forms. A pure form-processing service, however, handles forms that you create on your own. This type of service gives you much more control and power over your Web site's content.

Response-O-Matic

Response-O-Matic — which you can find (predictably) at `www.response-o-matic.com` on the Web — is one of the best form-processing firms around, and it gives you tremendous flexibility. It handles any form you want to throw at it. Well, okay, it does have a few restrictions. But they're minimal and reasonable. You can't, for example, transmit more than 50K of data with one form submission. That's plenty, however, with scads and bunches to spare.

The questions that you add to the form are up to you, but they require a bit of HTML knowledge. (If you're totally at sea when it comes to HTML, try Freedback.com instead.)

To create a form by using Response-O-Matic's service, follow these steps:

1. **Go to `www.response-o-matic.com` and then click the Get Started button.**

2. **On the Sign Up page (see Figure 8-13), enter your name, e-mail address, and a password.**

3. **Click the Sign Up button.**

   You get an e-mail message asking you to confirm your account creation. Click the link in it.

4. **The resulting Form Builder page, shown in Figure 8-14, has a rudimentary form that asks for only a name and an e-mail address.**

   Don't fill in the information — it's just part of the form you're building for someone else to fill in.

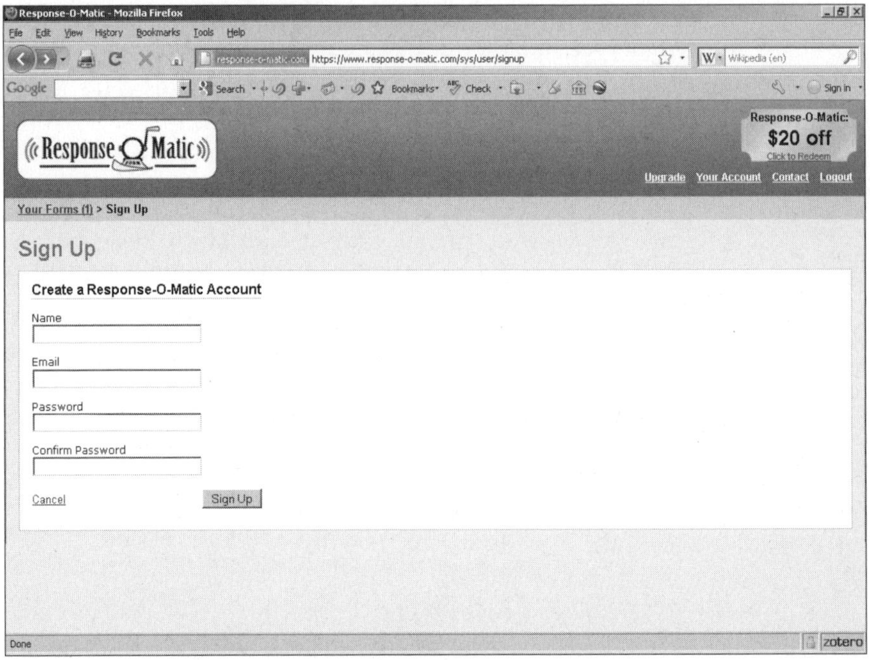

Figure 8-13:
Entering
your data.

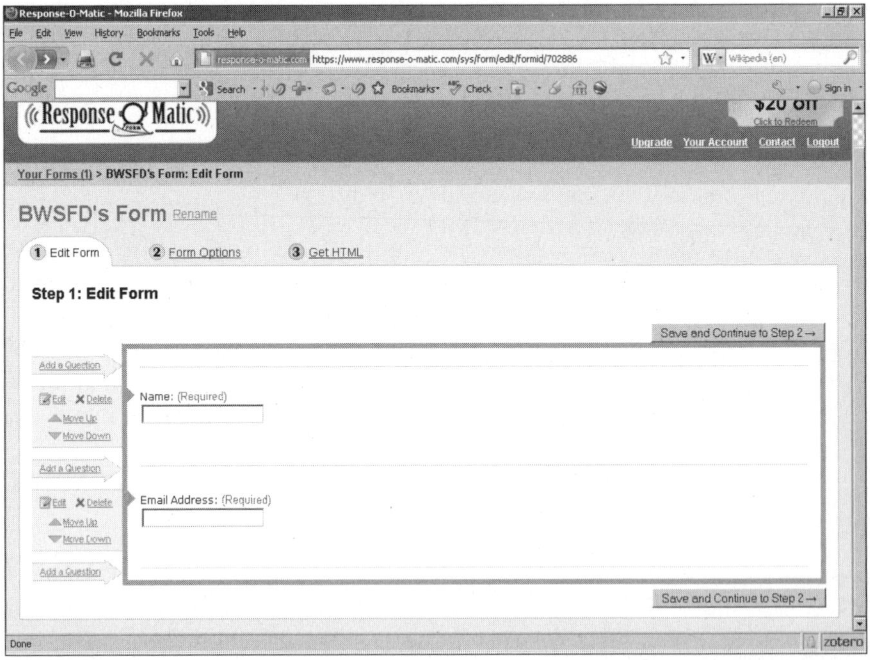

Figure 8-14:
Adding form
elements.

5. **If you don't want those two form elements, click the Delete link to the left of each of them.**

6. **To add other elements, click the Add a Question link.**

7. **In the Choose a Question Type box (see Figure 8-15), select the desired kind (check box, radio button, and so on).**

Figure 8-15:
Adding new
form ele-
ments.

Figure 8-16 shows the results of selecting the Short Answer option.

8. **Enter the question you want to ask. If an answer is absolutely neces-sary, select the Required check box.**

9. **Click the Save button. Figure 8-17 shows the result.**

10. **When you're satisfied with your form, click the Save and Continue to Step 2 button.**

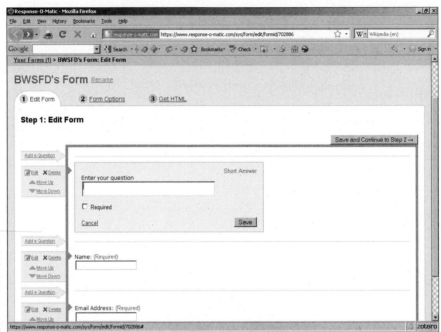

Figure 8-16:
Selecting
the Short
Answer
option.

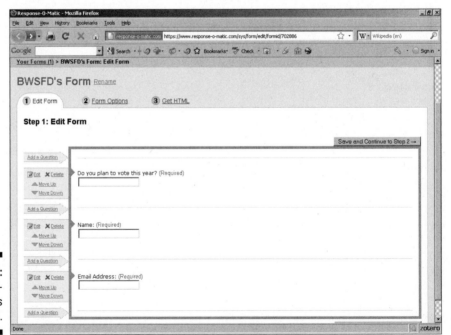

Figure 8-17:
The ques-
tion appears
on the form.

11. **On the Form Options page, shown in Figure 8-18, select whether to have your form users sent to your site or to the all-purpose Thank You page at Response-O-Matic.**

    If you choose the Thank You page, you then see a box in which you can enter your Web site's address, which will be displayed on the Thank You page. You can also select an option to show the form results on that page.

12. **Under Email, it is advisable to select the check box to have the form submissions e-mailed to you.**

    You'll get to enter a subject for the form e-mails you'll receive.

13. **Click the Save and Continue to Step 3 button.**

14. **On the resulting Get HTML page (see Figure 8-19), copy the code and then paste it into your own Web page.**

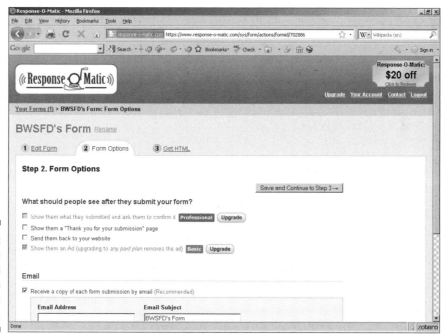

Figure 8-18:
The Form
Options
page gives
you more
choices.

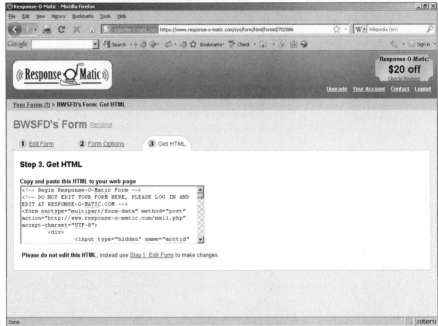

Figure 8-19:
The code is
available for
copying and
pasting.

FormSite.com

FormSite.com (www.formsite.com) is another form maker that, in addition to creating a variety of general forms, has a specific survey form service. Like Response-O-Matic (described earlier in the chapter), the service is free if you accept its accompanying advertising — or you can pop for a few bucks to get rid of the advertising banners and pick up some extra features, such as secure forms.

To create a form with FormSite.com, follow these steps:

1. **Go to** www.formsite.com.

2. **Click the Sign Up Free button.**

3. **Type a username and a password in the appropriate text boxes on the User Profile form, shown in Figure 8-20.**

   You can optionally provide your e-mail address.

Figure 8-20: FormSite. com's User Profile page, your start-ing point for creating your survey.

4. **Click the I Agree, Create Account button.**

5. **When the next page opens, click the New Form button (see Figure 8-21).**

6. **On the resultant New Form Web page, shown in Figure 8-22, type the name of your form in the — you guessed it — Name text box.**

7. **To use a predesigned template, select the option button next to the survey template that most closely resembles the one you want to create.**

8. **To start from scratch, select the From a Blank Form radio button; then click the Create button.**

9. **On the next page (shown in Figure 8-23), drag items from the left and drop them into the white box above the Preview button.**

   To access more options, click the categories (such as Formatting Items).

   Figure 8-24 shows the results of adding the Image form element. To add an image to the form, click the Upload button. Among the available options, alternate text (shown in a Web browser if the image is unavail-able) can be added, and you can make the image a clickable link by sup-plying a connecting URL.

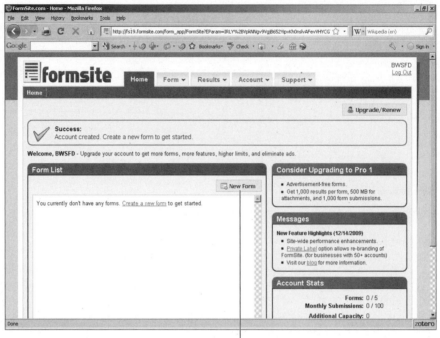

Figure 8-21:
Click the
New Form
button.

New Form button

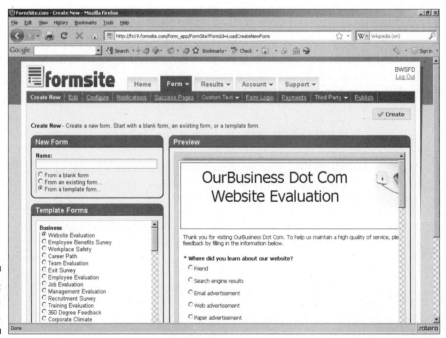

Figure 8-22:
Creating a
new form.

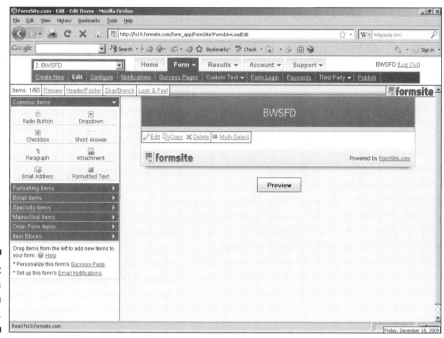

Figure 8-23: Selecting a new form element.

Figure 8-24: Setting the options for an element.

10. **When you're satisfied with your choices, click the Save button to add the element to your form.**

11. **When the form is completed, click the Publish link at the top of the page.**

12. **On the resulting Web page, select the HTML radio button under Form Link.**

    Depending on the requirements of your particular Web page, there are various other choices you can make other than HTML. You can, for example, scroll down and copy a JavaScript version.

13. **Copy the HTML code and paste it into your own Web page.**

Online Sources for CGI and Forms

Table 8-1 lists some places on the World Wide Web where you can find more information on the topics covered in this chapter.

Table 8-1	Online Resources for Scripts and Applets
Web Site Name	**Web Address**
CGI Resource Index	www.cgi-resources.com
CGI: Why Things Don't Work	www.raingod.com/raingod/resources/Programming/Perl/Notes/CGIDebugging.html
Freewarejava.com	www.freewarejava.com
Intro to CGI	www.mattkruse.com/info/cgi
Java Boutique	www.javaboutique.internet.com
JavaScript Kit	www.javascriptkit.com
Perl Primer	www.webdesigns1.com/perl
WDVL: The Perl You Need to Know	www.wdvl.com/Authoring/Languages/Perl/PerlfortheWeb

Part III

Adding Frills and Fancy Stuff

The 5th Wave   By Rich Tennant

In this part . . .

Here you discover a ton of ways to make your site work, look, and sound great. Chapter 9 painlessly introduces you to the wonderful world of JavaScript; Chapter 10 walks you through adding image-based buttons and image maps. Chapter 11 introduces you to the world of Web multimedia. Chapter 12 covers the hottest thing going in generated content: blogging.

Chapter 9

Exploring JavaScript and DHTML

*F*irst off, forget any fears you might have about "being a computer programmer!" The processes I talk about in this chapter are things that anyone could do; in fact, they're largely the same kinds of things you already do on a daily basis, but just don't realize are basically the same as what programmers think about all the time.

When you use that programming mindset to create Web pages, JavaScript gives you an advantage: It's not only specifically designed for use on Web pages, but because it's also one of the simplest programming languages around, you'll find it much easier to learn than some of the more complex languages (like C++). Combining JavaScript with HTML creates a further advantage that goes by the name DHTML (or Dynamic HTML). DHTML is "dynamic" because it allows you to add a high degree of interactivity — making your Web pages not just a static grouping of words and images, but a highly entertaining and useful experience for your visitors.

Principles of Programming

A computer program is nothing more than a list of steps for the machine to follow when trying to complete some task. You already do that sort of thing for yourself during the normal course of your life, whether you realize it or not. If you set out to accomplish something as common as taking your children to visit the community swimming pool, you have to consider a whole variety of options: You have to make sure that they have the right kind of clothing (one kind of variable), that they understand the rules of using the pool (a set of constants), and so on.

So, let's set aside all your preconceived notions about how difficult it is to "do" programming — and admit at the outset that you've already been programming all your life.

That said, there's a caveat (my editor promised me I could use at least one Latin word in this book). That means "beware" — you need to pay careful attention to getting your JavaScript just right. I mean, if you dress your kid wrong for the pool, your life doesn't crash the way a computer program will. The difficulty with programming is that the computer is inflexible and understands no shades of gray. It takes effort and experience to think with the ruthless logic of a computer. However, if you follow the instructions in this chapter, you'll be well on your way to mastering that skill.

Constants and variables

There are two kinds of values you'll be using in JavaScript (or in any other kind of computer programming): *constants* (values that never change) and *variables* (which change depending on the circumstances). The first kind is like the dates of Christmas Eve or New Year's Eve — these will always fall on the 24th and the 31st of December, no matter what else is going on. The latter, however, are like Easter — which might fall on a different day in a particular year depending on the circumstances.

The first thing you have to do with a variable is to define it; no variable can have any value unless, of course, that variable actually exists first. As you'd imagine, this is a fairly simple affair: To establish that a particular variable exists, you simply *declare* that this is so by adding a line like this to your JavaScript:

```
var thisvariableexists
```

If you want to assign a starting value to a variable at the same time that you declare it to exist, the process is just a tad different:

```
var thisvariableexists=1
```

This line of code both declares the existence of a variable called `thisvari-ableexists` and assigns to it a value of `1`.

You actually don't have to use the `var` part at all. Most Web browsers will understand what you mean if you just say `thisvariableexists=1`. Even so, it's good programming practice to specify exactly what you mean rather than just leaving things to chance (and maybe hoping that, years later, you'll remember exactly what you meant by some nonstandard usage).

You'll probably want to use lots of *comments* or notes of just exactly what you meant when you entered certain lines of code. To do so in a JavaScript situation, all you have to do is to use the figures // at the beginning of a line of code, as in the following example:

```
//This is a JavaScript comment.
```

Normally that's all you need to do — just the double slash lines with nothing more. However, if a comment requires more space than one line can provide, you'd use opening and ending tags to specify it, as in the following example:

```
/*This is an example of
JavaScript code that exceeds several lines.
*/
```

The opening and ending tags, of course, would be /* and */.

Even if a value will never vary (in which case it's not technically a true variable) — the date of New Year's Eve, for example — you can still assign that value with a `var` declaration.

Variables can have one of three value types, and those types influence the kinds of calculations that you can perform based upon them. The first type (that we've already dealt with) is the *numeric* kind. Numeric values, as their name implies, are nothing more than numbers: 31 for the end of December, 12 for that month, and so on.

Strings, however, are composed of textual values rather than numerical ones, and a string (of letters) can have any value that human languages may impute to it. Thus the string value `"December"` may have many more possible interpretations than merely that it is 12th in a series of 12. Depending upon the particular application involved in interpreting that string, it may mean anything from "the month in which Christmas and Hanukkah occur" to "the time when winter begins."

In addition to numerical or string values, you'll have to deal with *Boolean* values. This sounds like a fearsome thing, but all it really means is whether something is or isn't logically true. (By the way, *everything* in computing revolves around this concept; the simplest possible computer program is one that tells whether or not a light bulb is lit, and the most complex conceivable 3D graphics software is merely a descendant of this sort of statement.)

String values, unlike their numeric or Boolean equivalents, are always enclosed within quotation marks.

Doing the math

You'll often need to compare two values for various reasons. Some of these include:

- ✔ Seeing which value is higher or lower.
- ✔ Determining whether a value entered by a user is different from what was expected (for example, letters instead of numbers).
- ✔ Taking a particular action based upon the value.

To compare two values to see whether they're equal, you use the equality operator, or == (that's two equal signs, not one). Table 9-1 gives the most commonly used comparison operators.

Table 9-1	Comparison Operators
Operator	*Function*
==	Equal to
!=	Not equal to
<	Less than
>	Greater than
<=	Less than or equal to
>=	Greater than or equal to

Of course, you'll have to perform some mathematical operations along the way. Table 9-2 shows the symbols you use to do them.

Table 9-2	Math Operators
Operator	*Function*
+	Addition
–	Subtraction
*	Multiplication
/	Division
++	Increment (add one to)
– –	Decrement (subtract one from)

In addition to the obvious numerical comparisons, you also need to manage logical comparisons, basically asking whether something is logically true or false. You form these comparisons by using three operators (shown in Table 9-3).

Table 9-3	Logical Operators
Operator	*Function*
&&	AND
||	OR
!	NOT

The AND operator compares two things and returns an answer of `true` if they're both true and `false` if one or both are different. The OR operator returns a value of `true` if either value is logically true. NOT, as you might imagine, tests whether the reverse of the value in question is true.

Branches

You really can't do much programming without branching. As the name implies, this is the point where the program flow can follow one path or another. It's a pretty simple situation, really. Let's say you're going to the grocery; you might intend to buy Cokes, but find that they're out of stock, so you buy 7-Up instead — that's branching. Here's what it looks like:

```
if (drinks==Cokes) {
buyThem;
}
else {
buy7Up;
}
```

Loops

A loop is pretty much what it sounds like — running around in circles. The reason for doing this is to wait for something to happen before proceeding with the rest of the steps in a program.

The following example sets up a loop that writes a number called count on a Web page, and then checks to see whether that number is less than or equal to 10. Since the variable count begins by being assigned a value of 1, the loop will continue to run until all the numbers from 1 to 10 have been written:

```
for (var count=1; count <=10; count++) {
document.write("count");
}
```

If you're not careful, you might end up creating an infinite loop. This is one from which there is no possible exit. The result is that your program won't do anything but run around that loop forever. For example, if the preceding code checked to see whether the variable count was a negative number, it would create an infinite loop because count would always be positive. Always, always, always make sure there's a way out of any loop you create.

Creating JavaScript Functions

Okay, if you've been following along in this chapter, you've had a good look at what makes a typical JavaScript work. But you still need to see how you start things off and finish them up.

Although HTML can't handle program instructions by itself, it gives you a way (as you might well imagine) to tell it to hand off control of the page to a JavaScript program. And it's probably no great shock that you do this neat trick by using the SCRIPT element.

As with most other HTML elements, this one has both opening and closing tags, so a typical JavaScript might be encompassed by HTML lines similar to these:

```
<HTML>

<HEAD>

<SCRIPT>
</SCRIPT>

</HEAD>

<BODY>
</BODY>

</HTML>
```

As you've doubtless noticed in the above code example, the SCRIPT element normally falls within the HEAD element. This is a very important fact — because the various declarations of values (as we discussed earlier) must happen before any action upon them is taken. In some rare circumstances, you might be able to get away with setting a JavaScript within the BODY element, but you'd be taking your chances, to put it mildly.

Whatever falls between the <SCRIPT> and </SCRIPT> tags is up to the JavaScript to handle. As the possibilities of such an interaction literally involve an entire programming language and everything it might accomplish in the minds of all the programmers who exist, they're inherently infinite.

You, whether or not you realize it at this time, are a part of that infinite interactive possibility. The decisions you make when designing your Web pages are perhaps only a small part of our global heritage, but each one of them reaches out to the whole Web as an example of what can be done.

Incorporating JavaScripts

JavaScript has a tremendous advantage over other methods of adding "beyond-HTML" features to your Web pages. It was designed for no other purpose, and it's so tightly integrated with HTML that it's a joy to use. The processing takes place in the visitors' Web browsers, so it's both fast for them and no problem for your Web server. You don't have to understand the language to add other people's scripts to your Web site. In many cases, no alterations to the code are needed. In some cases, you may have to change the filename or add some URLs to a list. Figure 9-1 shows the JavaScript Source at http://javascript.internet.com, one of the many places on the Web to get free JavaScript code.

Basic techniques

You need to add two things to your Web pages when you work with JavaScript: the script itself and something that triggers the script.

Figure 9-1:
The
JavaScript
Source
gives
you free
JavaScript
code.

The script

The script has to go in the HEAD element of your Web page, like this skeleton script named whatever:

```
<HEAD>
<Script Language="JavaScript">
/*
You will usually find comments here.
*/

function whatever()
{
Actual code is found here.
}
</Script>
</HEAD>
```

You can place scripts within the BODY element rather than the HEAD element, but that can be risky. A JavaScript has to be *interpreted* — translated by a Web browser from the human-readable code into something a computer can understand — before it runs. Scripts in the HEAD element are processed before the Web browser processes the elements within the BODY element.

That means these scripts are defined and ready to roll before anything shows up in the Web browser. If the script is in the BODY element, a visitor may possibly attempt to trigger it before it's defined, which begs for a malfunction. It's better to stick with the safer, usual approach.

The trigger

You need to add something to your Web page to trigger the script, which causes it to run. This goes within the BODY element. Many things can trigger a script, but you don't need to be concerned with all the possibilities. The script you add is most likely designed to have a particular trigger — say, a rollover image that changes whenever a visitor's mouse pointer is over the image. Or it may be intended to work after the Web page finishes loading into the browser. You can alter the trigger if you're familiar with JavaScript. (See Table 9-4 for a list of such trigger events.)

For a script that executes as soon as the Web page loads into the browser, use the onload attribute of the BODY element:

```
<BODY onload="whatever()">
```

Dealing with problems

Fortunately, practically any JavaScript you pick up is pretty much guaranteed to work — under the right conditions. But with JavaScript, zillions of things can go wrong. The biggest problem is that so many different versions of Web browsers are out there. Not only do Firefox and Internet Explorer handle scripts a little differently, but also different versions of the two major Web browsers don't work the same. That means that a script that works fine in the latest version may not work at all in an older one. Unfortunately, lots of older Web browsers are still out there — not everyone is in a hurry to tie up their systems by downloading the newest versions.

If one of your visitors is running some weird Web browser that doesn't recognize JavaScript, then your script won't run. There's no harm done, just a missed experience for the visitor.

Unless you want to put the time and effort into really mastering the language and doing your own debugging, your best bet is to simply try out the script you want to use. Test it in Firefox, Internet Explorer, and any other Web browser you think your target audience uses. If the script works well in all the browsers, you're home free. If it causes problems in any of them, you have to decide how important that segment of the audience is to you. For example, if your site is dedicated to Microsoft products and your script won't work in Firefox, you're probably pretty safe in going ahead with it anyway, because the vast majority of your visitors are likely to use Microsoft Internet Explorer.

The Document Object Model (DOM)

Most Web pages end up containing a large number of separate elements, and it can be a daunting task to keep them all in mind. Obviously, when it comes to combining the complex capabilities of DHTML with a sophisticated Web page, it would be really, really helpful to have some way of keeping track of everything that's on that page, some easy way you could reference all those elements in your programming.

That's where the Document Object Model (usually just called DOM for short) comes in. It establishes a hierarchy in which each and every element can be referenced by its nested position on the page.

For example, the Web page itself is an object called the *document*. The attributes of HTML elements are seen in the DOM as *properties*. Thus, if you wanted to reference the Web page's background color, you'd say `document.bgColor`. To reference the color of a table on the page, you'd use `document.tableName.bgColor`.

The whole process is a flow from top to bottom, not of the physical page, but of the nesting process. Recall that a Web page is composed of elements nested within other elements, and this form of notation is simply another way of looking at that nesting relationship. Thus every element nested within another element becomes, in the DOM, just another property of the higher element. The Web page itself, for instance, is a property of the Web browser (`window.document`).

I'll give you several examples of how to use this kind of referencing in your own JavaScript, but a full exposition of the DOM would take an entire book of its own. Fortunately, there's *Java & XML For Dummies* by Barry Burd (Wiley Publishing).

Making Choices with JavaScript Events

An *event* in JavaScript is, as you'd expect, when something happens. Either directly or indirectly, events are caused by users. When one of your site's visitors presses a key, for example, that generates a `KeyPress` event; when the visitor lets go of the key, it generates a subsequent `KeyUp` event.

This gives you a great deal of versatility in your programming efforts. Depending upon the situation, you can treat the same user action as various kinds of events.

Often, what seems to be a single action is actually a series of events — when someone clicks a link to another page, for example, doing so generates a Click event (clicking the mouse button) as well as an Unload event (leaving the Web page).

So how do you handle events? With *event handlers.* An event handler is simply any JavaScript that you write that reacts to a particular event. You use the prefix on to differentiate the event handler from the event; thus, you handle a Click event with an onClick event handler, a KeyPress event with an onKeyPress handler, and so on.

If all this sounds a little confusing, just hang in there and don't forget to consult the handy info in Tables 9-4, 9-5, and 9-6 if you need a little help when you're doing your own Web pages.

Table 9-4	Mouse-based JavaScript Event Handlers
Event Handler Name	*Handles This Action*
onClick	Click: When a user presses and releases the mouse button
onDblClick	DblClick: When a user presses and releases the mouse button twice
onMouseDown	MouseDown: When a user presses, but does not release, the mouse button
onMouseUp	MouseUp: When a user releases a previously pressed mouse button
onMouseOver	MouseOver: When a mouse pointer is over one of the Web page's elements
onMouseMove	MouseMove: When a mouse pointer moves
onMouseOut	MouseOut: When a mouse pointer moves off an element

Table 9-5	Keyboard-based JavaScript Event Handlers
Event Handler Name	*Handles This Action*
onKeyDown	KeyDown: When a user presses a key
onKeyUp	KeyUp: When a user releases a previously pressed key
onKeyPress	KeyPress: When a key is pressed and then immediately released

Table 9-6	Miscellaneous JavaScript Event Handlers
Event Handler Name	*Handles This Action*
onLoad	Load: The page opens in a Web browser.
onUnload	Unload: The Web browser goes to another Web page.
onSelect	Select: Text is highlighted by selecting it with the mouse.

Mouseovers and clicks

The two most common JavaScript events are the ones you might expect (and have probably used in your own Web surfing): mouseovers and clicks.

Mouseovers are commonly used to initiate some change in an element, such as substituting one image for another or altering either the foreground or background colors. The onMouseOver event handler is used to trigger a JavaScript when the mouse pointer moves over an element.

The corollary event is onMouseOut, which is used to execute scripts when a mouse pointer moves away from an element.

No matter what it looks like on the screen, an element is shaped like a rectangle — and a mouseover will take place when the pointer crosses the edge of that invisible box that surrounds the element, not when it reaches the visible part! Likewise, a MouseOut event won't happen until that invisible border is crossed.

For a script that requires the visitor to click an element — when they press and release the left mouse button — use the onClick event handler. This example uses the A element, but onClick is a ubiquitous attribute that you can use with just about anything:

```
<A onClick="whatever()">Click here for whatever.</A>
```

The documentation for a script normally specifies which trigger(s) it's intended to use. If you want to explore JavaScript, try *JavaScript For Dummies,* 4th Edition, by Emily A. Vander Veer (Wiley Publishing).

Keyboard input

Although the mouse is the most common method of Web interaction, you can also utilize the keyboard. An instruction to the user to "Press any key" enables you to treat that action as three different events, depending upon the requirements of your particular script.

When a user presses a key and releases it, that's called (as you might expect) a `KeyPress` event. This action can, if needed, be further broken down into a `KeyDown` event and a `KeyUp` event.

Adding Interactive Menus

Although it's nice to have a program that makes your page do something you wanted, one of the greatest things you can do with DHTML is to add *interactivity* to your Web pages — your users become active participants rather than merely watching some process over which they have no control.

Nearly every program you've ever used has some form of *menu* — a list of options you can choose from — and they're a pretty common sight on Web sites as well. You can choose from a variety of styles; the most common are either horizontal or vertical.

Making drop-down lists

A *drop-down list* (shown in Figure 9-2) is easy to add to your site. It's a form that contains a selection menu that helps visitors navigate your site. When a visitor makes a selection from the list, the form calls the appropriate JavaScript code and loads the selected page.

Figure 9-2:
A Java-
Script
drop-down
list menu.

To add this JavaScript to your Web page, first you put the script into your `HEAD` element so your code looks like this:

```
<HEAD>
<SCRIPT language="JavaScript">
function golinks(where) {
self.location = where;
}
</SCRIPT>
</HEAD>
```

Of course, you'll probably have some other stuff in the HEAD element, too (such as your title), but I'm focusing on the basics here.

Next, put the form into your BODY element:

```
<BODY>
<FORM>
<SELECT onchange="golinks(this.options[this.
    selectedIndex].value">
<OPTION value="http://www.dummies.com/">
    Dummies Press</OPTION>
<OPTION value="http://www.wiley.com/">
    Wiley Publishing</OPTION>
</SELECT>
</FORM>
</BODY>
```

Change the values of the OPTION elements to the URLs you want to link to. Of course, you'll want to change the descriptive content, too. To add more links to the list, just add more OPTION elements.

Making a menu with CoffeeCup

You don't have to tackle coding for all your forays into DHTML. There are lots of programs that give you a helping hand — including CoffeeCup HTML Editor, the one we've used in other chapters. Of course it allows you to edit JavaScript just as it does HTML, but it also lets you put together a DHTML menu quickly and easily. Just follow these steps:

1. **Choose Insert⇨CSS Menu Designer from the menu.**

   This brings up the Menu Designer, shown in Figure 9-3.

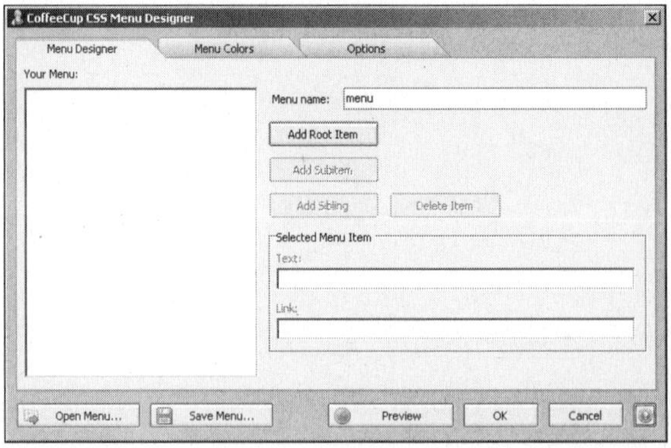

Figure 9-3:
The CSS
Menu
Designer.

2. **Under Menu name, type your own name over the default "menu."**

3. **Click the Add Root Item button.**

   In the options under Selected Menu Item, type the text you want to show in the menu for this choice. Also, enter the URL of the page you want to link to.

4. **Repeat Step 3 for all the menu items you want to add.**

   Figure 9-4 shows what the situation looks like when the same options are added that were used in the preceding JavaScript example.

Figure 9-4:
A basic menu struc-ture with two options.

5. **To add items beneath the root options in the menu's hierarchy, select the desired root item and then click the Add Subitem button.**

   You can only add three levels of subitems, as shown in Figure 9-5.

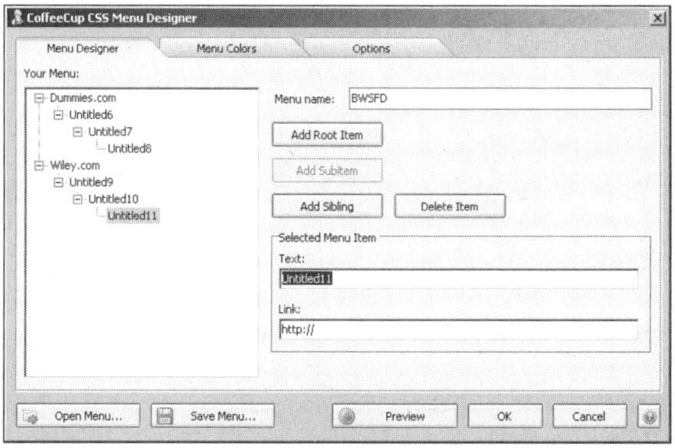

Figure 9-5:
Adding subitems.

6. **To delete a menu choice, select it and click the Delete Item button.**

7. **To add more items on the same level (rather than as subitems), select a menu option, then click the Add Sibling button (see Figure 9-6).**

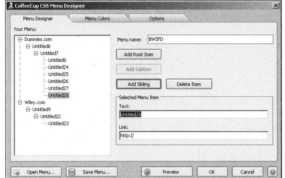

Figure 9-6:
Adding sib-
ling items.

8. **Click the Preview button to see how your efforts so far will look on a Web page (see Figure 9-7).**

Figure 9-7:
Previewing
the menu.

9. **To specify colors to use, click the Menu Colors tab, shown in Figure 9-8.**

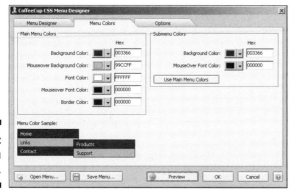

10. **Under Main Menu Colors, click the arrow to the right of the color box to access a color chart (see Figure 9-9).**

   These options let you set the colors for the menu items' background, border, and font. In addition, you can set the background and font colors that will be shown when a MouseOver event occurs.

   If you like, you can also simply type a hexadecimal color value into the text box to the right of any of the options.

Figure 9-9:
Selecting a
color.

11. **If the typical colors in the chart aren't to your liking, click the Custom Color box to access more (see Figure 9-10).**

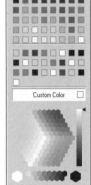

Figure 9-10:
Choosing
a custom
color.

12. **Under Submenu Colors, set the values of the background and MouseOver font colors.**

    If you don't want to specify different colors for the submenu items, just click the Use Main Menu Colors button.

    Use the Preview button any time you make a color change to make sure the results are exactly what you want.

13. **Click the Options tab (shown in Figure 9-11).**

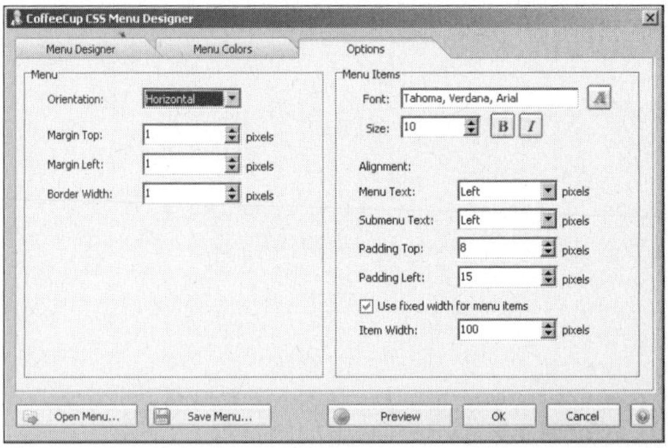

Figure 9-11:
The Options
tab.

14. **Under Orientation, select either Horizontal or Vertical.**

    Figure 9-12 shows the results of changing the example from the default horizontal orientation to a vertical one.

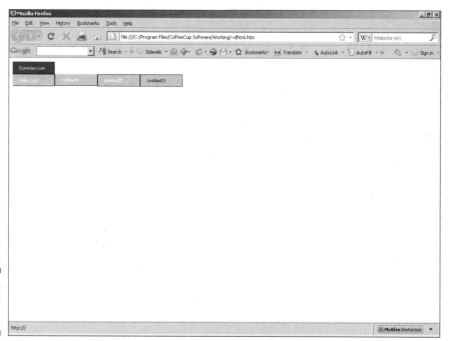

Figure 9-12:
A vertical
orientation.

15. **Set the margins (the distance between the edge of the menu and the top or edge of the Web page) by either typing directly into the text box to the right of Margin Top and Margin Left or using the arrows to scroll up and down.**

Although it's possible to enter negative numbers here, the results can be unattractive, moving portions of the menu out of sight.

16. **Set the Border Width the same way; you can only use values from 0 to 20 here.**

17. **Under Menu Items, click the A button to access a list of available fonts (see Figure 9-13).**

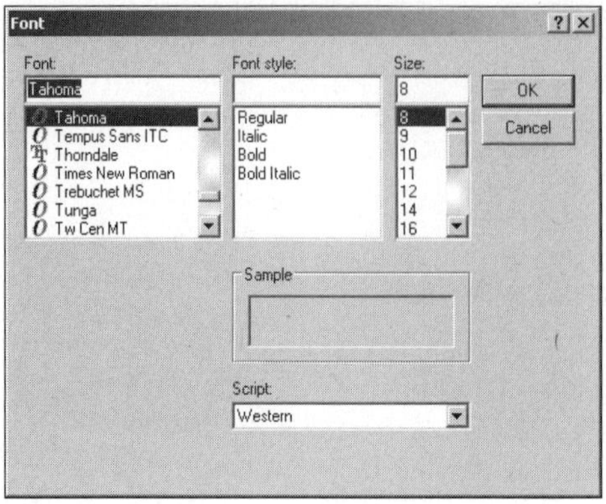

Figure 9-13:
Choosing a
font.

18. **Select a size for the font by scrolling. Click the B and I buttons to make the font bold and italic, respectively.**

19. **Under Alignment, select Left, Center, or Right for both the Menu Text and Submenu Text.**

20. **Set the amount of padding in pixels for both the top and left.**

    Just as with table cells (see Chapter 3), this specifies the amount of space between the edges of the menu item and the text it contains.

21. **If you want all menu items to be the same size regardless of their content, be sure to select the Use Fixed Width for Menu Items check box; then specify a size (in pixels) in the Item Width entry.**

    You'll want to use the Preview button to see whether this choice makes the menu unreadable!

22. **Click the OK button to complete your menu.**

Online Sources for JavaScript and DHTML

Table 9-7 lists some places on the World Wide Web where you can find more resources like the ones covered in this chapter.

Table 9-7   **Online Resources for JavaScript and DHTML**

Web Site Name	Web Address
JavaScript	`www.javascript.com`
JavaScript Source	`http://javascript.internet.com`
JavaScript Tutorial	`www.w3schools.com/js`
JavaScript Kit	`www.javascriptkit.com`
DHTML Tutorial	`www.w3schools.com/dhtml`
Dynamic Drive DHTML	`www.dynamicdrive.com`

Chapter 10

Adding Image-Based Buttons and Image Maps

Although it's true that you can do all kinds of stuff with just plain old textual methods — as detailed in the various chapters surrounding this one — there's nothing like an image to nail things down in the minds of your site's visitors.

It would be unimaginable to attempt to publish a newspaper or magazine with no photos or artwork — and it's a rare book indeed that goes to press without a single illustration of any kind. The reason for this is very simple — a picture is worth a thousand words. For Web pages, this old saying is true a million times over (so a Web image must be worth a billion words, right?). Higher math aside, you need to consider the graphical nature of your pages as well as their textual content if you want to succeed in the most competitive market the world has ever known.

When I speak of the graphical nature of your Web pages, I'm not just talking about tossing in a photo of the latest scandal-ridden celeb somewhere between a couple of paragraphs of text. What you need here is to focus, right from the git-go, on making your pages attractive to your visitors' visual needs. People have a natural response to symbols, shapes, and colors. Even something as simple as a stop sign has much more to it than that single word STOP — its shape and color also help define it. The same is true of the contents of your Web pages.

That means you need to give some serious thought to how you present (say) menu options and links. You could just take the easy way out and settle for some simple text that's blue and underlined, but your pages are going to look a whole lot better if you take the time to add some fancy-looking buttons instead. All by itself, that'll take you a long way, but this chapter also delves into the mysteries of using *image maps,* which are images that contain several links that are activated by clicking different parts of the image. Just like it sounds, they're often composed of traditional maps just like you'd find in any atlas, but you don't have to settle for any traditional approaches. Hey, this is the Web we're talking about, and anything goes — the only limit is your imagination.

So come along and get a look at the basics of how these things are done. Beyond that, let your creativity soar!

Creating Buttons

Two kinds of people make buttons for Web pages — professional artists and the rest of us. If you're the first kind, you've probably already dashed out a couple of dozen prototypes in a variety of styles while you were reading this paragraph. If you're the second kind, then you're not alone if you need a little help.

If you want some buttons fast (and your best efforts with programs like Photoshop leave a wee bit to be desired), try surfing over to CoolText.com at — you guessed it — www.cooltext.com. This Web site generates graphics, according to the options that you choose, while you wait. The process is simple and fun, and there's no limit to the number of logos you can experiment with.

Not only are its logos cool, but so are the site's legal requirements: none, zip, nada. There's no copyright issue to deal with, no ads stuck in the middle of things, and no fine print of any kind. As an act of gratitude for such a great service, you may want to add a link back to this site from yours, but even that's not required.

 Although CoolText.com doesn't hold a copyright on the logos you create, you probably do. I'm not a lawyer (and I don't even play one on TV), but it seems to me that the decisions you make during the course of designing the logos qualify them as artistic creations. Don't take my word for it, though. If this point is important for your situation, check with an attorney who really knows copyright law, or e-mail the U.S. Copyright Office at copyinfo@loc.gov.

To make a custom logo at CoolText.com, follow these steps:

1. **Go to** www.cooltext.com.

2. **Scroll down to Choose a Button Design at the bottom of the page and click any logo style, as shown in Figure 10-1.**

Figure 10-1: CoolText.com's logo page, showing the styles that you can use to create your own custom buttons — for free!

This takes you to the Design Your Button page, shown in Figure 10-2.

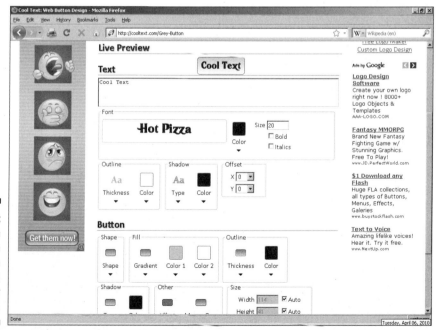

Figure 10-2: The Design Your Button page, where you choose options for your button.

Different styles offer different options. If you choose the first button, you end up with the options shown in Figure 10-3; if you choose any of the other three, you end up with those shown in Figure 10-4.

3. **For the first button type, type the text for your button in the text box.**

   If you need more than one line, you can put a new line symbol (\n) in the text, as in the following example:

   ```
   First Line\nSecond Line
   ```

4. **Click the font name (in this example, Hot Pizza), and then select a font category from the list that's presented. Finally, select the name of a particular font.**

   You're automatically returned to the design page.

5. **Click the Color box and then select a glow color from the resulting color picker. (See Figure 10-5.)**

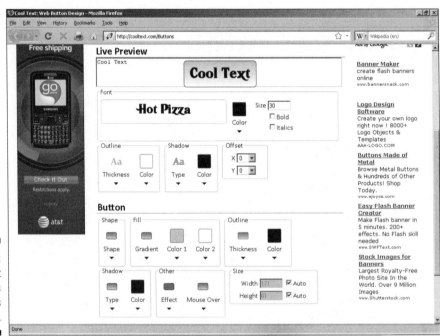

Figure 10-3: The first button's options page.

Figure 10-4:
The other
buttons'
options
page.

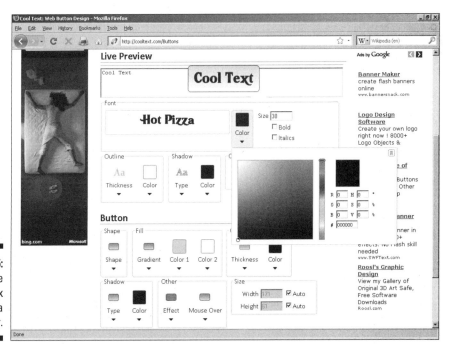

Figure 10-5:
Click in the
color box
to choose a
color.

6. **Enter a font size in the Size text box.**

7. **If desired, select the Bold and/or the Italics check box.**

8. **Select the thickness and color for the Outline.**

   The thickness options are None, Thin, Medium, Thick, and Huge. The colors work the same way as for the text.

9. **Select the type of shadow and its color.**

   The shadow options are None, Sharp, Soft, and Glow. The colors work the same way as for the text.

10. **Choose an offset (values range from –30 to 30 pixels).**

11. **Select a shape for the button.**

    Values are Rounded, Rectangle, Pill, Ellipse, and Circle.

12. **For Fill, select a type of gradient and two colors.**

    Gradient types are Flat, Vertical Gradient, Horizontal Gradient, Diagonal Down Gradient, Diagonal Up Gradient, and Radial Gradient. The colors work the same as before.

13. **Choose an outline thickness for the button.**

    This works just like the thickness for the text that you set in Step 8.

14. **Select the button's shadow type and color.**

    Shadow types are None, Drop, Glow, and Mirror. Colors are set the usual way.

15. **Under Other, choose an Effect of Flat, Glass, Gel, or 3D. For Mouse Over, choose from None, Bright, Spot, or Glow.**

    The Mouse Over options set how the button's appearance changes when a user places a mouse pointer over the button (see Chapter 9 for info on mouseovers).

16. **If you want to set a custom size for the button that is different from the one that the program automatically chooses (based on the text you entered back in Step 3), deselect the Auto check boxes and enter a specific size in pixels in the Width and Height text boxes.**

17. **Click the Render Button button to finish.**

If you chose one of the other three types of buttons, then you'll follow a similar set of options:

1. **Enter the text under Logo Text.**

2. **Click the Font name and choose the one you want.**

3. **Under Text Color, you have various ways to specify a color. If you click the blank box, you end up looking at a color picker like the one shown in Figure 10-6. Click anywhere to select the desired color, and then click the X in the upper-right corner to finish.**

   Alternatively, click the eyedropper icon to select a color from anywhere on your computer screen. You can also click the color chart icon on the right, which will give you a list of named colors as shown in Figure 10-7. Finally, you might enter a color value in RGB (red, green, blue) or hexadecimal values in the text boxes.

4. **Choose whether you want any of the three text effects: Outline Text, Bold, or Italics.**

5. **Under Text Shadow, choose None, Soft, or Crisp.**

6. **Select a text offset ranging from –50 to 50 pixels.**

7. **Under Shape Options, choose Rounded, Rectangle, Pill, Ellipse, or Circle.**

8. **Under Effect, select Flat, 3D Sharp, 3D Round, Bordered, Metal 3D, Gel, or Glass (see Figure 10-8).**

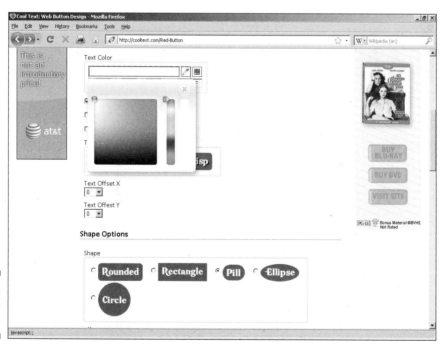

Figure 10-6:
Using the
color picker.

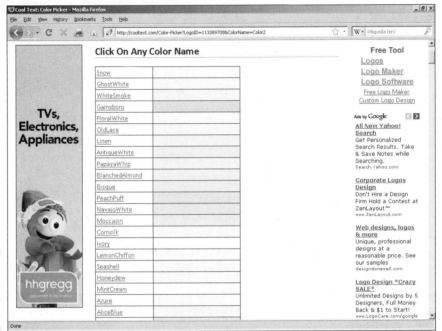

Figure 10-7:
Selecting a
color from
the list.

Figure 10-8:
Setting
Effect
values.

9. **Choose the Button Color the same way you chose text color in Step 3.**

10. **Select a Shadow value of None, Drop, Glow, or Mirror.**

11. **If you want exact values for width and height, deselect the Auto Width and Auto Height check boxes and enter specific dimensions.**

12. **For Mouse Over, choose from None, Bright, Spot, Glow, or Emboss.**

    The Mouse Over options set how the button's appearance changes when a user places a mouse pointer over the button.

13. **Choose a background color in the usual way.**

14. **Click the Render Button button to finish.**

Creating Image Maps

Although Chapter 2 introduces using links with images, you can also use a special kind of image link called an *image map*. If you use a normal image link, you're limited to a single link that goes with a single image. By using image mapping, however, you can add several links to a single image.

When you use an image-mapping program, you draw shapes over specific areas within an existing image. You then assign a particular URL to each of these areas. When visitors click the part of the image that links to that URL, they're sent to it immediately.

You may, for example, use a map of the world as your image map. When your visitors click England or Scotland, they go to a page about the United Kingdom. If they click Africa, they go to a page about that continent. And so on and so forth . . .

You don't need to stay purely geographical, either. You can just as easily take a diagram of the human body and set up an image map where users click the abdomen to go to a page about appendectomies or click the mouth to go to a page about dentistry. Any kind of logical connection you can come up with will work as an image map.

Many Web-design programs include image-mapping features; you get to try out the ones in CoffeeCup's HTML designer here (the same company has a stand-alone image program called Image Mapper as well). Many graphics programs, such as Fireworks, also include image-mapping capabilities. If you don't own one of those programs, you may want to check out some of the image-mapping programs listed in Table 10-1.

Here's how to add an image map to a page you're working on in CoffeeCup HTML Editor:

1. **Choose Tools⇨Image Map from the menu.**

2. **Make sure that Create a New Image Map is selected (see Figure 10-9), then click the Next button.**

Figure 10-9:
Starting a new image map.

3. **Click the Browse button, select the image you want to use as the basis for your image map (see Figure 10-10), and then click the Next button.**

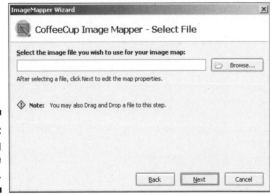

Figure 10-10:
Selecting the base file.

4. **If you want to change the name of the map, do so in the dialog box that appears now (see Figure 10-11); by default, the map name is the same as the filename.**

Optionally, you can enter a URL that will be accessed if a user clicks somewhere outside the defined areas you will create on the image map (you may or may not decide to create such an area). If you're using frames, select the frame in which you want to open the linked page. Click the Next button.

ImageMapper Wizard [x]

CoffeeCup Image Mapper - Edit Map Properties

Enter a name for your image map. This name is required to be unique if you use more than one map file in an HTML page. (Not available when opening an existing map file.)

Map Name: | states(bright)

Enter a default URL. If someone clicks outside a defined area, they will be directed to this URL. (Optional)

Default URL: |

Enter the frame to open the clicked area in. This is only required when using frames, and only if you want the clicked area to open a page in a different frame. (Optional)

Frame: | Page Default (None) ▼

[Back] [Next] [Cancel]

Figure 10-11:
First options.

---

5. **In the succeeding dialog box, click the Finish button. The image now opens in the Image Mapper, as shown in Figure 10-12.**

6. **Choose the type of geometric figure best suited to your image-mapping needs — rectangle, circle, or polygon — by clicking the appropriate icon on the upper-left side of the Image Mapper (see Figure 10-13).**

   Because the borders of the various United States can't be outlined as either a rectangle or a circle, I'm using the polygon tool, which lets me draw my own shapes.

7. **Click at a starting point, move the mouse pointer to the farthest point you can while following the border, and then click again. Continue to do so until you have outlined everything you want to make into a clickable area.**

   In this example, I clicked the northwestern corner of California first (where it meets Oregon at the Pacific Ocean), then the northeastern corner, down to the bend, and I continued clicking at each turn until I had returned to my starting point.

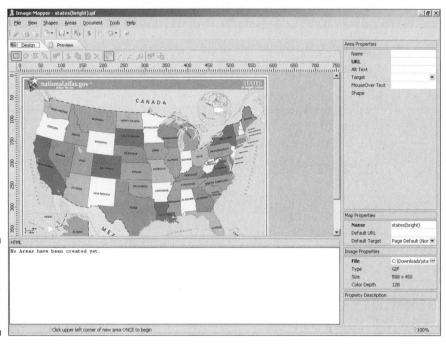

Rectangle tool

Circle tool

Polygon tool

Figure 10-13:
Selecting a
shape.

Click the magnifying-glass icon if you need to see more detail on the map you're working on.

8. **When you've completed the circuit, double-click to finish the area. You should now have something that looks like the image map shown in Figure 10-14.**

9. **Under Area Properties, enter a name for the area and the URL you want your visitors to go to when they click that area (see Figure 10-15).**

10. **Optionally, enter Alt Text that will show if the image map is unavailable.**

11. **If using frames, select the target frame from the drop-down list.**

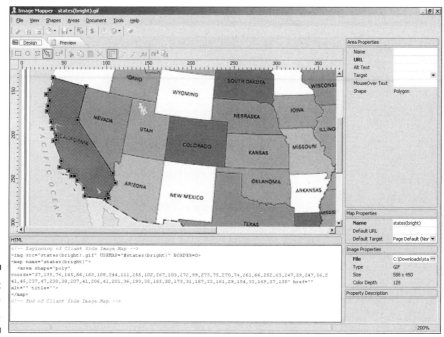

Figure 10-14:
The completed area.

Figure 10-15:
Specifying area properties.

12. **Enter text that will show up as a text bubble if a visitor places a mouse pointer over the area (see Chapter 9 for info on MouseOver events). Figure 10-16 shows the text bubble in action.**

Figure 10-16:
The
MouseOver
text.

13. **Repeat Steps 6–12 for all areas you want to create.**

14. **When you're finished, save the image map. You can do this via the Ctrl+S key combination, the File⇨Save menu option, or via the Save Items icon.**

Online Sources for Buttons and Image Maps

Table 10-1 lists some places on the World Wide Web where you can find more resources like the ones covered in this chapter.

Table 10-1	Online Resources for Buttons and Image Maps
Web Site Name	*Web Address*
Brilliant Button Maker	www.lucazappa.com/brilliantMaker/buttonImage.php
Free Menu Buttons	www.hscripts.com/freeimages/icons/menu-buttons/index.php
Freebuttons.com	www.freebuttons.com
Image Web Buttons	www.apycom.com/image-web-buttons
Mapedit	http://www.boutell.com/mapedit/
Trellian Image Mapper	www.trellian.com/imagemapper

Chapter 11

Web Sights and Sounds

In This Chapter

▶ Finding video and music to use on your site

▶ Avoiding legal hassles

▶ Understanding file formats

▶ Making files smaller

▶ Adding audio and video to your site

*W*eb pages don't just sit there anymore. They've come a long way since the early stages of just displaying text on your computer screen. New forms of multimedia experiences crop up all the time. Television and radio stations, for example, have broadcast on the Web for a long time, but most of them target only individual users; few of these broadcasters have realized the importance of allying with Webmasters to get more exposure for their signals. I dug up a few sites for you that are Web-based themselves, existing only on the Web instead of being traditional broadcast or cable stations — and they do understand how much you, the Webmaster, mean to them.

I also point you to plenty of sources for sound files that you can use on your Web site. Of course, as with any innovation, there's a certain amount of debate about the use of sound on Web pages. Aside from the carping of die-hard traditionalists who just plain insist that you shouldn't use it, there are some serious considerations. Sound doesn't necessarily go with every site. If you decide to use it, you need to match the mood of the music with the page's theme. The right song can add a new dimension; the wrong one can sound ridiculous — and maybe even make your site a bit of a joke.

 If you use sound, make sure that you give your visitors a way to turn it off. Embedded sound with no controls is an annoyance to many visitors. You may as well give them the option; otherwise they can simply turn off their speakers to get rid of the sound (or just leave your site in disgust, never to return).

Getting Music and Video

First things first: You gotta get hold of the music or whatever media content before you can add it to your Web site. Okay, grabbing music off the Web, off a newsgroup, through FTP, or just about any other way that data moves on the Internet is a pretty easy thing to do. However, you face two problems with taking just any old song that you can get your hands on — and the same goes for video. First, if you can snag it with no trouble, so can everyone else — and you presumably want your site to stand out from the crowd. Second, you face the question of copyright. The odds are pretty good that you have no idea who owns the copyright to a song or video that you snag from some Web site — or whether it's *in the public domain* (legally available for everyone to use) instead of under copyright.

You can avoid this copyright mess by following these few simple suggestions:

- ✔ Get your own custom music or video by hiring professionals to create it for you — totally new and completely unencumbered. That way, you won't have any legal hassles, and nobody else can use it legally on another site.
- ✔ Buy or download royalty-free music and video collections.
- ✔ Use public-domain music and video (if you don't mind everyone else using the same music or video on countless other Web sites, too).
- ✔ Create your own music or video.

The following sections describe how to get these different types of files for your site.

Finding music houses

Professional music suppliers can accommodate your desires to play unique music on your site, either by selling you custom compositions that they design to serve your particular needs or by providing you with music they already have on hand for you to buy or license. The exact deal you strike depends on the company's policy — and on how much money you're willing to part with. Some companies license you to use the music only in certain ways (sort of like the way software licenses say things like you can use a program on only a single computer). So when you talk to them, be sure to specify that the music will be used on Web pages. You shouldn't, however, have to pay any royalties — fees for every time you play the music — just the flat fee when you get the music.

LicenseMusic.com (shown in Figure 11-1) is one good source that sports a useful database of what's available. Table 11-1 lists some other good Web sites where you can find or order royalty-free music.

Figure 11-1:
License
Music.
com lets
you easily
search for
music.

Table 11-1	Royalty-Free Music Suppliers
Web Site Name	**Web Address**
Fresh Music Library	www.freshmusic.com
LicenseMusic	www.licensemusic.com
Music 2 Hues	www.music2hues.com
Music Bakery	www.musicbakery.com
Nash Music Server	www.nash.jp/
Partners In Rhyme	www.partnersinrhyme.com
PBTM Library	www.pbtm.com
SONOTON	www.productionmusic.com
Royalty Free Music	www.royaltyfree.com
Stock Music	www.stockmusic.com

Finding public-domain music and video

Not all music or video is currently under copyright. Music has been around a lot more than 80 years, so most of it's in the public domain — meaning that nobody holds the copyright to it. The reverse is true of video. Video is a more recent technology, and the massive proliferation of compact, lightweight video cameras means that most moving pictures have been created within the past few years.

Copyright can prove to be a tricky issue. If you make a mistake, you can end up in federal court, paying hundreds of thousands of dollars in fines. Rest assured, however, that very few copyright infringers ever go to prison, although the law provides for that eventuality. On the other hand, some of these copyright infringers find themselves spending all their time talking to lawyers — and paying lawyers. So before you add some public-domain music or video to your Web site, make absolutely sure that it *is* in the public domain.

Table 11-2 lists some good public-domain music and video sources.

Table 11-2	Public-Domain Music Sources
Web Site Name	**Web Address**
ChoralWiki	`www.cpdl.org/wiki/index.php/Main_Page`
Classical Piano Free Downloads	`www.sheetmusic1.com/new.great.music.html`
Musopen	`www.musopen.com`
PD Info	`www.pdinfo.com`
Public Domain Music	`http://pdmusic.org`
U.S. National Archives	`www.archives.gov/research/index.html`
Virtual Sheet Music	`www.virtualsheetmusic.com/Downloads.html`

Some public-domain music sites provide copies of sheet music that you can use to create new recordings of your own. Others have music files that you can download and use right away. There's a catch, however; a *recording* of a public-domain song is not, itself, in the public domain. The written music is, but the recording isn't. Yes, I'm repeating myself, but it's critical for you to remember that. The legal reasons are so convoluted that any two lawyers have three opinions about why it's so, but it's a fact. So unless the site specifically states that it's releasing its music files into the public domain, you probably have to pay for the download. Some sites that charge commercial sites to use their recordings are willing to let noncommercial sites use them for free.

Picking a File Format

Your main concern when choosing a file format for either Web audio or Web video is download time — the length of time it takes for a Web site visitor to be able to experience the music or movie. Most people won't be willing to go make a sandwich to pass the time waiting to hear a favorite song, and even your dearest friends may not be happy about spending all afternoon trying to see the video of your vacation.

Three main factors affect download time: the speed of the network connection, the file size, and whether the file has to completely download in order to start playing. No matter how fast your Web server's connection is, you have no control over the speed of your visitors' connections. Thus the only thing you can really do is modify either the file size or the manner in which the file is displayed.

I deal with file compression in the following section, so now I want to take a look at streaming versus regular files. With a regular file, such as the MP3 format that is so popular for reproducing music, the entire file must be downloaded and then played. With a streaming file, such as Real Audio, the user can hear the first part of the music while the rest of it is still on the way.

In theory, it sounds like a great idea. Sometimes, though, streaming files (whether with video or audio content) can be jerky and aesthetically deficient, especially with slower connections. So you have to decide whether speed of display is more important to you than smoothness of presentation.

Tables 11-3 and 11-4 show some commonly used video and audio file formats, a description of each, and whether each format is streamable.

Table 11-3	Video File Formats	
File Extension	**Description**	**Streamable**
`.avi`	Microsoft's Audio Video Interleave format can be problematic. Although it achieves good quality, various factors can yield a large file size, and it can't support full-screen movies.	Yes
`.flv`	Flash video is the standard format on YouTube and is also used by such providers as Google Video. It uses the Adobe Flash Player.	Yes
`.mov,` `.qt`	The Apple movie format for QuickTime is excellent and has great file compression.	Yes
`.mpeg`	The Motion Picture Experts Group format is as popular for video as its MP3 cousin is for audio. With both high file compression and excellent reproduction quality, this is the vehicle of choice for many Webmasters.	Yes
`.ram`	The Real Audio Movie format was the most common form of streaming video, but it lost popularity because it requires the use of a proprietary program, RealPlayer, which is often criticized for carrying too much advertising and being somewhat difficult to use.	Yes
`.wmv`	Windows Media Video tends to produce small files of good quality.	Yes

Table 11-4	Audio File Formats	
File Extension	**Description**	**Streamable**
`.aiff,` `.au`	These files are mainly used on Macintosh systems. Because the majority of computer users don't own Macs, think twice before committing to it because your other visitors may or may not be able to use it. File sizes tend to be large in these formats.	No

File Extension	Description	Streamable
.midi	The Musical Instrument Digital Interface is a venerable old music format. So many MIDI files are online that it is impossible to count them, and this format is supported by the vast majority of all music-creation programs. Nonetheless, it's mainly biased toward non-vocal music; thus, it may have only limited utility for Webmasters despite its small file size.	No
.mp3	This is the king of the audio files. Everybody has heard of — and probably has — songs in MP3 format. Although people may argue that other formats have technical advantages, MP3s are widely supported and are probably instantly playable on almost all your visitors' systems.	Yes
.ra	The Real Audio format (from the same folks who brought you streaming video) can create smaller files than many of the others, but at a serious cost in sound quality.	Yes
.wav	Waveform Audio files are good in that any computer with sound capabilities can play them, but they're notorious for their large file sizes.	No
.wma	Windows Media Audio files are often smaller than MP3s and have very good quality.	Yes

Compressing Files

Windows Movie Maker is a quick and painless way to familiarize yourself with the various factors that affect file size and the ways these factors can create a good or bad Web experience for your visitors. A full exploration of video preparation is outside the scope of this book, so if you're interested in delving more deeply into working with Web video, check out *Digital Video For Dummies,* 4th Edition, by Keith Underdahl (Wiley Publishing).

To experiment with various settings and see how they affect file size, follow these steps:

1. **In Windows Movie Maker, select a movie by clicking its icon. (See Figure 11-2.)**

2. **Click the Save to My Computer link on the left side of the screen.**

   The Save Movie Wizard appears, shown in Figure 11-3.

3. **Enter a filename for your movie in the first text box.**

4. **If you don't want to save your videos in the My Videos folder, the default setting in the second text box, click the Browse button and choose a different location.**

5. **Click the Next button.**

   On the next page, the default setting Best Quality for Playback on My Computer is selected, as shown in Figure 11-4.

6. **Before checking out the other options, take a moment to look over the values in Setting Details and note the estimated file sizes those settings generate.**

Figure 11-2:
Choosing
a movie in
Windows
Movie
Maker.

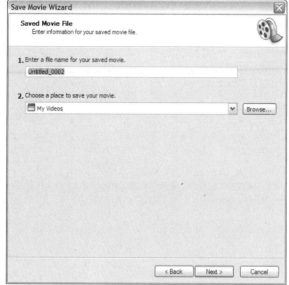

Figure 11-3:
The Save
Movie
Wizard
guides you
through the
process.

Figure 11-4:
The settings
determine
the file size.

7. **If you want to go with the default setting, skip ahead to Step 10. Otherwise, click the Show More Choices link to see additional options.**

8. **If you have a particular file size in mind as your target, select the Best Fit to File Size option button and then either enter the value or scroll up or down until you find it. You can set the target file size in either K (kilobytes) or MB (megabytes).**

   As you set different values for the target size, only one of the values in Setting Details changes: Bit Rate. This setting determines the amount of information included in the file. A lower bit rate means a lower quality of video and a smaller file size; a higher bit rate means the reverse.

9. **Select the Other Settings option button, as shown in Figure 11-5. From the drop-down list next to it, select various settings and observe the impact on the values in Setting Details.**

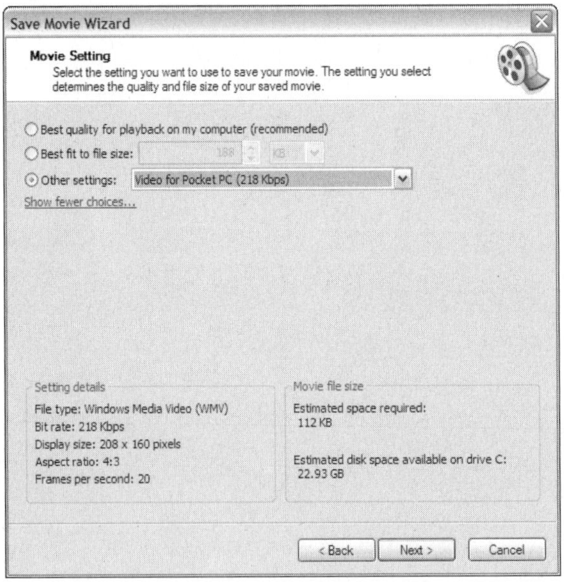

Figure 11-5:
Selecting
the Video
for Pocket
PC option.

The Video for Broadband option, for example, sets a bit rate of 512 Kbps, a display size of 320 x 240 pixels, and a replay rate of 30 frames per second, generating a 260K file. The Video for Dial-Up Access option, on the other hand, sets a bit rate of only 38 Kbps, a display size of 160 x 120 pixels, and a replay rate of 15 frames per second, resulting in a file that takes up only 20 kilobytes.

10. **After you've arranged the settings to your satisfaction, click the Next button.**

    The file is saved.

11. **Click the Finish button to close the Save Movie Wizard.**

Adding Audio and Video Files to Your Site

You put both audio and video files on your Web page in the same way — or ways, rather. The simplest way to do it is the same way you connect any file to a Web page. Just put in a link for visitors to click, something like this one:

```
<a href="videofile.mpg">Click here to see the
   vacation video.</a>
```

Depending upon a particular visitor's system and configuration, the link to the video or sound file will cause different responses when clicked. It may work right in the browser. It may have to launch an external application to play the file. It may prompt the visitor to download the file. And so on. The one thing that won't happen is the seamless integration of the file into your Web page.

If you'd like to make that happen, use the EMBED element. Here's the basic setup:

```
<embed src="musicfile.mid" width="300" height="100">
</embed>
```

You may want to pay attention to a few other attributes besides width and height. The most important of these is autostart, which does what you'd expect: It starts the music or video playing automatically. Just alter the code so it reads like this:

```
<embed src="musicfile.mid" width="300" height="100"
   autostart="true">
</embed>
```

The other useful attribute is loop, which specifies whether the file will play more than once and, if so, how many times. To set it to play over and over again, just enter this code:

```
<embed src="musicfile.mid" width="300" height="100"
   autostart="true" loop="true">
</embed>
```

To specify how many times to loop, just use the number instead of the word true. Here's an example:

```
<embed src="musicfile.mid" width="300" height="100"
   autostart="true" loop="3">
</embed>
```

Adding a Flash music player

When it comes to adding sound, you can get a lot more sophisticated than plain old HTML. Sound players based in Adobe Flash, for example, let you seamlessly integrate everything from your MP3s to your own recordings into your Web site.

What if you aren't a Flash wizard or you just don't want to spend that kind of money to get started? No problem — lots of programs let you create your own Flash-based players with little effort or no investment.

One of the tops on my list is the Website Music Player. Here's how easy it is to use:

1. **Go to** `http://download.cnet.com/Website-Music-Player/3000-2168_4-10512716.html?tag=mncol`, **download the Website Music Player, and unzip it.**

2. **Check with your Web service provider to make sure you have PHP available (that's a common Web scripting language, so you probably do).**

3. **Upload the files** `musicplayer.swf`, `playlist.php`, **and** `music-player.js` **to your Web site's main folder (the same place your home page is).**

4. **Make a folder named** `mp3` **in your main folder and upload your mp3 files into it.**

5. **Add the following HTML code to your Web page:**

```
<table align="center" border="0" cellspacing="0"cellpadding="0"><tbody><tr
        ><td>
<div align="center">
<script language='JavaScript' src='musicplayer.js' type='text/
        javascript'></script></div>
<tr><td><div align="center"><font face="Arial"
font size="1"><a href="http://www.websitemusicplayer.com"
target="_blank">website music player</a></font></div>
</td></tr></tbody></table>
```

Your Web page will now show the player as shown in Figure 11-6.

Figure 11-6:
The Website
Music
Player on a
Web page.

Table 11-5 gives the URLs of some other Flash sound player utilities.

Table 11-5	Flash Sound Player Utilities
Web Site Name	*Web Address*
Chameleon Flash Sound Player	`www.lucidflash.com`
Making a Simple Player	`www.lukamaras.com/tutorials/ sound/simple-mp3-loop-tune- player.html`
Oven Fresh Audio Player Maker	`http://www.ovenfreshweb.com/ software/`
soundPlayer Component	`www.hotscripts.com/ Detailed/53816.html`
soundPlayer Pro	`www.flashloaded.com/flash components/soundplayer`
xmp3Player	`http://allwebcodesign.com/setup/ addons-xmp3Player.htm`

Importing YouTube video

YouTube (www.youtube.com) is one of the hottest sources of videos on the Web. Although you can use some services such as keepvid.com or youtube catcher.com to download a video, it's easier to just either link to it or embed it. To link to it, simply copy the address in the URL text box and add it as a link in your site. (See the code samples in the "Adding Audio and Video Files to Your Site" section, earlier in this chapter.)

Fortunately, the embedding process is about as easy as it can possibly be. YouTube gives you the source code for it right next to every video. (See Figure 11-7.) All you have to do is click in the Embed text box, which automatically selects the whole thing, and then copy the code and paste it into your own Web page.

Figure 11-7:
The Embed text box contains the code you need.

The Embed text box

YouTube uses both the `<object>` and the `<embed>` elements for embedding video. This makes sure that the video will display in any Web browser.

Online Sources for Web Audio and Video

Table 11-6 lists some places on the World Wide Web where you can find more resources like the ones covered in this chapter.

Table 11-6	Online Resources for Web Audio and Video
Web Site Name	**Web Address**
Adobe Audition	www.adobe.com/products/audition
Anvil Studio	www.anvilstudio.com
Cakewalk	www.cakewalk.com
FinaleMusic	www.finalemusic.com
GoldWave Digital Audio Editor	www.goldwave.com
MAGIX	www.magix.net
PG Music	www.pgmusic.com/products_bb.htm
SimpleServer:Shout	www.analogx.com/contents/download/ network/ssshout.htm
Sonic Spot: Audio File Formats	www.sonicspot.com/guide/fileformat list.html

Chapter 12

Adding a Blog

*B*logs (or *'blogs,* if you want to get technical) are Web logs — essentially, a way for you to alter the content of your Web site at will. Blogs cover a wide range of content, from daily diaries to professional journalism, and their popularity seems to know no bounds.

You can use blogging technology to keep your site updated without having to get into coding — and you can make changes while you're on the road, away from your design computer. Just drop into an Internet café, go online, fill out an electronic form — and your site is updated right away.

Adding Blogger to Your Site

Blogger — another Google Web service — is perhaps the most popular Web log provider and one of the easiest to use. To get started, follow these steps:

1. **Go to** `www.blogger.com` **and click the Create A Blog button (see Figure 12-1).**

2. **You need to create a Google account to use Blogger.com; to do so, enter your e-mail address, your password twice, and the name you want as your blog signature. If you don't want to receive e-mails relating to Blogger, deselect the E-mail Notification check box. Enter your birthday and the Word Verification. Select the I Accept the Terms of Service check box, and click the Continue button (see Figure 12-2).**

3. **Click the Continue button.**

4. **Enter a name for your blog in the Blog Title box (see Figure 12-3). Enter a subdomain name in the Blog Address (URL) box. Also, do the word verification (this tells Google you're a human being).**

Figure 12-1:
Getting
started.

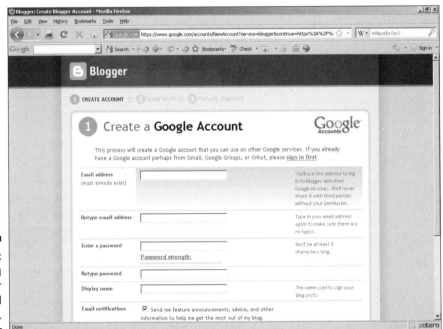

Figure 12-2:
Entering
your
personal
information.

This has nothing to do with the URL of your own Web site. It's to establish the URL on Blogger where your blog will be hosted on Google's servers. You'll get a chance to specify your own site's URL later on. If your blog is called, say, CelebNews, you'd enter that name as the subdomain on Google.

5. **Click the Continue button.**

   The Choose a Template page appears, as shown in Figure 12-4.

6. **Select the option button under the design you like best.**

   Regardless of which template you pick, you can change it later.

Figure 12-3:
Naming
your blog.

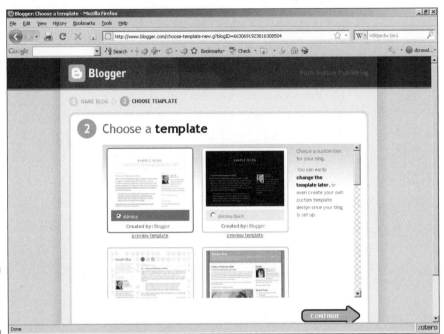

Figure 12-4:
Choosing a
template.

Figure 12-5:
Getting
to the
Advanced
Options.

7. **Click the Continue button.**

   Your new blog is created.

8. **Click the Advanced Setup Options link, which causes two new links to appear, as shown in Figure 12-5.**

9. **Click the Set Up a Custom Domain link.**

   This takes you to a page (see Figure 12-6) where Google offers to sell you a domain. As you already have one, click the link on the right that says Switch to Advanced Settings. The page now changes so it looks like Figure 12-7.

10. **Enter the URL of your domain, complete the word verification, and (finally) click the Save Settings button.**

    The Use a Missing Files Host option is used if you have two different sources for the files in your blog (which most people don't bother with, of course). If you're one of the rare ones, select this option and specify the location of your backup blog files.

    If everything went well, then you'll see a page showing your settings and saying at the top that Settings Were Saved Successfully.

11. **Click the Posting tab (see Figure 12-8) and you're ready to start blogging on your site. Enter either some prepared material or just any old thing that comes to mind.**

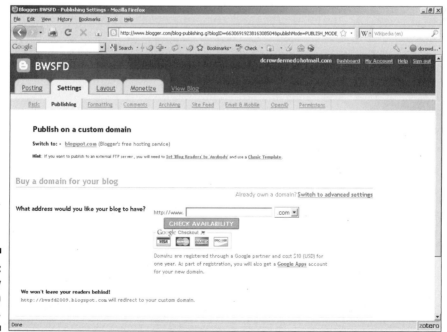

Figure 12-6:
The Buy
a Domain
page.

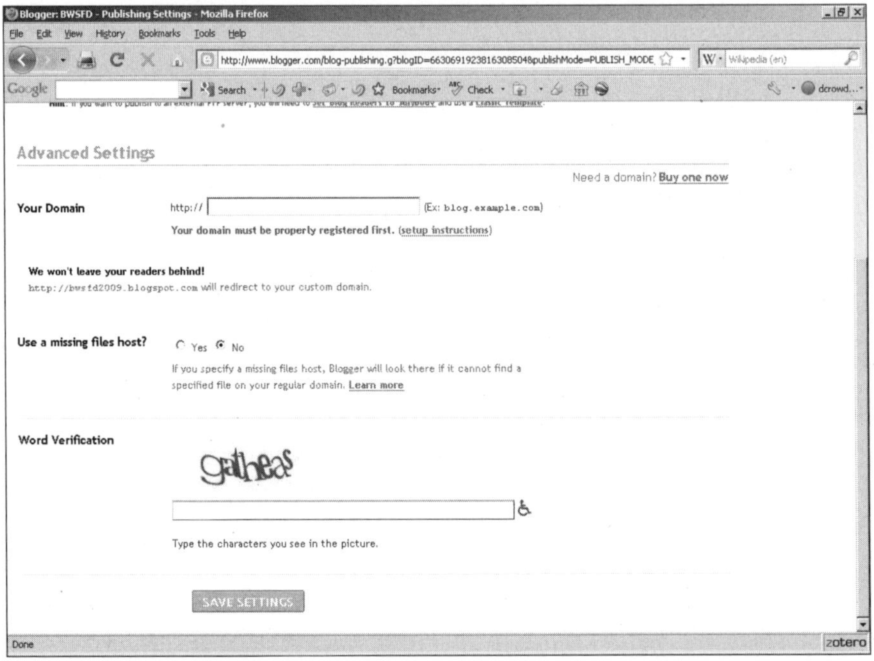

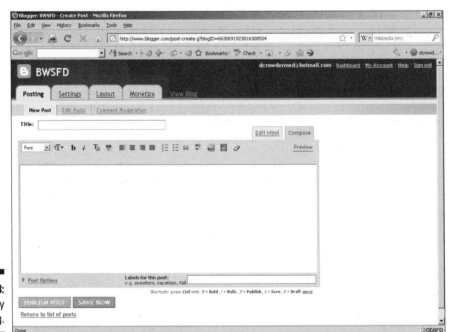

Figure 12-7:
The
Advanced
Settings
page.

Figure 12-8:
You're ready
to blog.

12. **Click the Preview link.**

13. **If you don't like what you see, you can click the Hide Preview link and go back to the drawing board. If you're satisfied, click the Publish Post button instead.**

    You're done.

Bloggin' with WordPress

Although Blogger (see the preceding section) is hosted on Google's servers, WordPress is an open-source blogging program that resides on your own Web server. There are pluses and minuses to both approaches. Of course, any software that runs on someone else's server is software that reduces the load on your own server, but it's also software that you have (of course) less control over. In such a case, you need to be sure that you can trust the provider to give you good service; with Google, however, you can count on one of the most reliable companies around.

The odds are very good that your Web service provider already has the prerequisite software needed to run WordPress, but you might want to double-check — before you commit to using it — that both PHP and MySQL are a part of your service.

Before you decide to install WordPress yourself, check with your Web provider. Your provider might do it for you as part of their basic service because it's such a popular program and they get a lot of requests for it. Many providers even offer automated installation of WordPress; check out the options on your Webmaster's control panel and see if that's included.

Here's the easy process for how to get and install WordPress:

1. **Go to** `wordpress.org` **and click the Download WordPress button. On the following page (believe it or not), click the same button again (gotta love redundancy).**

2. **Once the** `.zip` **file is downloaded, extract its contents into a folder.**

3. **Upload the folder's contents to your Web server.**

4. **Create a MySQL database on your Web server.**

    Normally, this is a simple matter of clicking a link or button on your Web service provider's control panel that says something along the lines of "Manage MySQL Databases," then another on a new page that says "Create MySQL Database." All you do then is to give it a name of your choice. If the situation is more complicated, you might want to consider changing providers!

If you have any doubts or hesitations about how to proceed or exactly what information is required on your system, check with your Web service provider. No matter how strange something may seem to you, they've probably dealt with it a thousand times; don't be too surprised if they get you the answer right away.

5. **Surf with your Web browser to the location where you've installed the WordPress files and open the `install.php` file (for example,** www.yourownsite.com/wp-admin/install.php**).**

6. **Enter the requested data (such as the name of the database you created in Step 4) and your MySQL user name, then click the Submit button.**

   Again, if you don't know these, just ask your provider.

7. **You're asked to enter a title for your blog and your e-mail address. When you've done so, click the Install WordPress button and you're done. Just log in to get started.**

When you've got WordPress installed on your system, you can modify things to suit your own particular needs. Figure 12-9 shows the WordPress "dashboard" from which you control things.

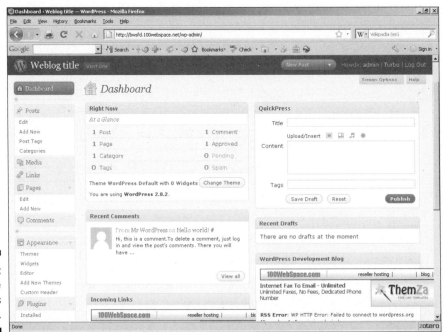

Figure 12-9:
The WordPress dashboard.

There's a default posting that you may want to view; if you want to read the whole thing, just click the View All button in that message. Otherwise, move your mouse pointer over it until a series of options appears below the posting and click the Delete link.

Adding a post in WordPress

The fastest way to add a new post is to use the QuickPress option on the upper-right side. To do so, follow these steps:

1. **Enter a title for your post in, of course, the Title box.**

2. **Type a message in the text area labeled Content.**

3. **If desired, you can add a *tag* — that is, a keyword. Although this isn't required, it gives potential readers a quick and easy way to see whether the content of your blog is their particular cup of tea.**

4. **If you want to send this post to your blog immediately, click the Publish button. To save it for later editing, click the Save Draft button instead.**

   If you choose the latter option, you can click the Preview Post link (which won't exist until you save a draft) to see what your post will look like, as shown in the example shown in Figure 12-10.

Figure 12-10: Previewing a draft.

You've also doubtless noted the series of Upload/Insert buttons above the Content area. These are for the purpose of adding multimedia content to your posts. There are four options: Add an Image, Add Video, Add Audio, and Add Media. Clicking any of these brings up a dialog box where you can select files residing on your own computer (via the From Computer tab, of course), from some site on the Web (via the From URL tab as shown in Figure 12-11), or from the Media Library tab (a listing of all the media you have so far accessed from whatever source).

Figure 12-11:
Adding an image from the Web.

Altering the General Settings

Of course, you'll probably want to monkey with your default blog settings in order to integrate your blog as properly as possible into your own Web site. To do so, click the General link in the Settings menu on the bottom left side of your screen.

You'll then see a page showing the current settings (see Figure 12-12). On this page, you can replace such generic values as "Weblog title" with something like "My Politics Blog," "I Don't Like Angry Walruses," or whatever suits your nature. You will probably also want to replace the default "Just another WordPress weblog" tagline text with something more applicable to your site's purposes.

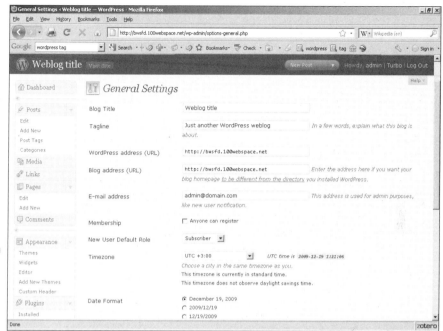

Don't even think about replacing the URLs in the WordPress address or Blog address settings! These are standardized and your blog won't work if you do.

As for the rest of the settings here, you'll probably want to click the Anyone Can Register check box under "Membership," as well as set the appropriate time zone (the default installation missed mine by two hours, for example). Feel free to set the date and time formats for whatever system you're most comfortable with and to reset the "Week Starts On" setting from the default of Monday to Sunday.

When you're done fiddling with these options, just click the Save Changes button to make them permanent.

Online Sources for Blogs

Table 12-1 lists some places on the World Wide Web where you can find more resources like the ones that are covered in this chapter. Most of the sites in the following table allow you to create your own blog for free.

Table 12-1	Online Sources for Blogs
Web Site Name	*Web Address*
40+ Free Blog Hosts	`http://mashable.com/2007/08/06/` `free-blog-hosts/`
Blog Perfume	`www.blogperfume.com`
Introduction to Blogging	`http://codex.wordpress.org/` `Introduction_to_Blogging`
LiveJournal	`www.livejournal.com`
TypePad	`www.typepad.com`

Part IV
Making Money

The 5th Wave   By Rich Tennant

"Just how accurately should my Web site reflect my place of business?"

In this part . . .

Here's where I take a look at how you can make money from your site. Chapter 13 covers getting your Web site listed in the search engines and establishing reciprocal links with other sites. Chapter 14 explodes the myths about Internet income and shows you how you can really make a profit. And Chapter 15 tells you how to set up a credit-card merchant account.

Chapter 13

Attracting an Audience: Publicizing Your Site

In This Chapter

▶ Choosing keywords wisely

▶ Getting listed with search engines

▶ Checking your search-engine ranking

▶ Trading links

▶ Using banner ads

Search sites (also called *search engines*) such as Google are a critical part of the World Wide Web. Without them, it's nearly impossible for most people to find what they're looking for. Therefore, if you're serious about your Web site (and I assume you are because you're reading this book), it's important to know as much about search sites as possible (such as by hands-on, real-life experiences). And you can't do much better than trying out the search sites yourself. You can find out which ones give helpful responses to your queries and which ones return nonsense. For even more info, check out *Search Engine Optimization For Dummies,* by Peter Kent (Wiley Publishing), which goes into very fine detail about what readers can do to get their sites listed in the search engines.

Table 13-1 lists the major search sites.

Table 13-1	Major Search Sites
Search Site	*Web Address*
AlltheWeb	www.alltheweb.com
AltaVista	www.altavista.com
Ask.com	www.ask.com
Bing	www.bing.com
Excite	www.excite.com
Google	www.google.com
Lycos	www.lycos.com
Metacrawler	www.metacrawler.com
WebCrawler	www.webcrawler.com
Yahoo!	www.yahoo.com

If you're tired of slow search response times, try AlltheWeb. It gives you answers so fast that your head spins.

To make sure that people know your Web site exists, you should have it listed in lots of search engines. How many you should list it in is a matter of opinion. There's certainly no harm in going for broke and listing your site with every search engine, but about a zillion of them are out there — and most of them aren't nearly as well known as Yahoo! or Google. In my opinion, after you're listed with all the ones in Table 13-1, any more effort runs into the law of diminishing returns. Yes, you will generate more visits by listing your site at even more search sites, but you don't get anywhere near as many visits from obscure search sites as you do from the more popular ones.

Speaking of popularity, the number one search engine is the oddly named but fantastically functional Google (www.google.com). Not that it needs the push, but I highly recommend it. If your site isn't listed on Google, you'll miss out on a lot of potential visitors.

There are many reasons for Google's success, but the main one is simply that it gives better results than many of its competitors. This is in large part due to its sophisticated page-analysis software, and you would do well to keep in mind what it looks for when you design your site's pages. Here are some tips on how to do that:

✔ Make sure that the important terms describing your site (the ones you think people will use as search terms when they're hunting for information on Google) appear in both your page title and in the first paragraph of your Web page.

✔ Use the same words at least a few times elsewhere on the page, but don't go hog wild — if you overdo it, you'll lower your ranking.

✔ Break up your page's text by using heading elements (H1, H2, and so on) that contain key phrases. Google pays more attention to these than to normal text.

✔ If, for some reason, your page design can't utilize heading elements, use the B (bold text) element to emphasize your keywords. (The STRONG element does the same thing.)

✔ Exchange links with other Webmasters, especially with those who already have a high Google ranking.

Using search sites isn't the only way of getting the word out. You can also work out reciprocal link arrangements with other Web sites, either on a personal level or through the agency of a banner-link exchange. (See the section "Investigating Reciprocal Linking," later in this chapter.)

Working Keywords into Your Pages

Search sites have different ways of gathering information on the content of Web sites:

✔ Some search sites are put together by human effort. People visit Web sites that have been submitted to the search site and then manually categorize those sites.

✔ Other search sites are fully automated. Programs called *robots* or *spiders* surf the Web, cataloging their findings and adding Web pages to the search site's database. Robots and spiders don't just note the URL of a page, though. They also index all the words on the page (except for words like *a, an, the, for,* and so on).

When someone runs a search, the search terms are compared with the indexed words. Links to whatever sites match the search terms are then shown to the person doing the searching.

In addition to the words in the text of your page (and sometimes in the alt text fields of images and other elements as well), search engines also index meta keywords.

The following sections give you the lowdown on incorporating keywords into your site.

Adding meta tags

META is one of the most versatile elements in HTML because it's one of the most poorly defined ones. Some would just say it doesn't have many limits. Its name and content attributes enable you to put many types of information into your HTML documents.

META always goes within the HEAD element, and it has no end tag.

You can have all the META elements you want, but only two of its uses matter to a search engine: as a page description and as a list of keywords. Neither one is essential. In fact, despite the frenzy about META keywords, your page description and TITLE element are actually more useful for search engines. (Google, the most successful search engine, doesn't even look at META keywords.)

Page description

When someone performs a search that returns a hit to your site, the response usually shows your page title and a blurb of text from the beginning of your page. This response underscores the importance of a good title. If the first sentence of your page doesn't describe all its contents, that may not be the best possible enticement for someone to visit it. If your page has a META description, however, the search engine will use that description to — you guessed it — describe your page.

Imagine that you have a page titled "The Love Letters of Grover Cleveland." Well, that title may not mean much to a lot of folks, and if the first sentence is something like a tame quotation from one of those letters, you're not doing too well. But a good description like this can fix that:

```
<META name="description" content="The secret life of the
        24th President">
```

List of keywords

You add keywords in much the same way that you add a description:

```
<META name="keywords" content="Grover Cleveland, 24th
        President, Buffalo, New York, Mugwumps">
```

Mugwumps? Trust me — it's a Grover Cleveland thing.

The META keywords aren't that important because the content of the page itself should already have the important terms in it. And some search engines don't even look at META keywords. Where keywords are useful is in a special situation that you can't easily accommodate in the visible page content without looking silly: You need to intentionally misspell words.

It's a fact: Lots of people have trouble spelling or typing or both. Therefore you should also add common spelling errors to your list of keywords. For example, if you list *flying saucers* and someone's looking for *flying sossers,* that person won't be able to find your site. (Well, okay, you may not want that person to find you, but I'm not going to get into that.) You should also cover yourself for any legitimate spelling variants. For example, if you sell tires and don't want to miss out on the British market, you should also list *tyres* among your keywords.

When it comes to choosing keywords, don't neglect synonyms. One person may look for *car parts* while another searches for *automotive accessories.*

Incorporating keywords in the content

The actual content of your Web pages is much more important than META keywords. In fact, it's critical — to both your search-engine ranking and visitor retention. When you write the copy for your pages, make sure that you throw in as many terms as possible that accurately describe your topic. As far as the search engines are concerned, the more often you can reasonably include relevant keywords, the better. After all, search engines rank your Web site by how well the contents of your pages match up with the search term that someone enters.

When it comes to the human visitors to your pages, as opposed to the robotic visitors, you need to write in a way that entertains your audience. As a professional writer, I always try to avoid using the same phrase too often. When I need to refer to the same thing or action over and over again, I strive to find new ways to say it. I practically live for synonyms and pronouns.

It can be a difficult balancing act to satisfy your human visitors while at the same time catering to the search engines' needs. You don't want to bore your readers by endlessly repeating the same terms, but you do want to nail down the ranking you deserve. Here are some general steps on how to do this:

1. **To start with, make up a list of terms that you think people might use if they search for your page.**

2. **Go ahead and write your content without paying any attention to your list.**

   Writing your content first is important because if you stare at your list of terms while you're working, you may stifle your creativity.

3. **After you've finished writing your page, look over the list and mark down how many times you've used each of the terms on the page.**

4. **Go over your page and see where you can work in the words that you** *didn't* **use. Then for words that you** *did* **use, look for places you might use them again without screwing up the flow of the writing.**

After you've done these things, toss the list in the trash and reread your page. If it's still good, go with it. If it doesn't read well, you may have to sacrifice some of the terms to make the text more reader-friendly.

Avoiding keyword trickery

Lots of the get-rich-quick sites advise you to raise your ratings with the search engines by stacking the deck. Typically, this involves using the same phrase over and over again in your meta tags, like this:

```
<META name="keywords" content="computer books, computer
        books, computer books, computer books, computer
        books, computer books, computer books">
```

Another common trick is to put content like that into the text of the page itself. Often, Webmasters hide this bogus text from their human readers by setting its color to the same as the page's background color or by making the text so small that it's barely visible — or both.

Avoiding traps

The traps, in this case, are some of the perfectly normal Web site design approaches. If you use frames or image maps, you're asking for trouble with the search engines. Why? Because many of the search engines don't navigate frames properly, and none of them can read the text in an image map. The same problem crops up when people use images containing text as a part of the image itself — your human visitors can read it, but a search engine's robot won't even know it exists.

Does that mean you can't do things like putting text-filled images in a table for layout purposes? No — and you don't have to give up on frames or image maps, either. But you do have to provide a plain old text-link-alternative approach to these fancier methods. Lots of Web designers do so anyway to accommodate old or off-brand Web browsers.

This common trick is not the same thing as legitimately using the same terms and phrases several times in different places within the real context of your Web page. If you run a site that deals with airports, for example, the word *runway* may show up hundreds of times on one page, and anyone searching for that term will rightly find your page.

So why not use the trick method? Well, for starters, it doesn't work. Playing these kinds of games with keywords is a fast way to get dropped from the major search engines altogether. The people who run search engines aren't stupid, and they're fully aware of this type of stunt. They don't care for sites that try to stack the deck, because they're in the business of providing good results, and tricks like these skew the results. You don't want to make enemies of the search-engine folks; it's much better to keep on their good side.

Even if you do manage to find a workable trick that artificially boosts your ranking, you're not doing yourself any favors. What if you end up number one on every search, but your actual content isn't what you said it was (it's all just a clever use of keywords)? Do you think that the people who drop in to check out your site will be coming back? After they find out that you're not delivering what you promised, they'll be off to other destinations before you can blink, and they won't pay any attention to your listing after that, even if it does turn up on top in their next search.

Some of the Web sites that come up on the first page of search results turn out to be dead links. If those sites had paid more attention to site-design fundamentals than to search-engine rankings, they might still be around.

Analyzing keywords that other sites are using

Taking a look at what other people are doing with keywords can be instructive. You can find out just what people are searching for plenty of ways; if some of those terms fit in with what you're doing, you may want to work them in. Here are some ways to analyze keywords:

> ✔ **Keyword Analysis Tool:** One of the best sites you can visit is Keyword Analysis Tool, shown in Figure 13-1. It runs a check on sites you specify

to see what keywords they're using. You can download it for free from `http://www.webmaster-toolkit.com/keyword-analysis-tool.shtml`. Try it. You'll like it.

✔ **Keyword Extractor:** Check out Keyword Extractor, a useful freebie from AnalogX (see Figure 13-2). You can find it at `http://www.analogx.com/contents/download/Network/keyex/Freeware.htm`. Keyword Extractor lets you analyze Web pages just like search engines do. It indexes all the words on the page and assigns weights to them depending on their frequency of use and position on the page. One of the best ways to use this program is to perform a search at one of the major search sites, follow the links to the top-ranked pages, and run Keyword Extractor on each of those pages. Study the results to see how those pages earned their ranks.

Figure 13-1:
The Keyword Analysis Tool site (note British spelling) lets you see what the most common keywords are on a site.

Figure 13-2:
Keyword
Extractor
is a stand-
alone
program
that lets
you check
out the
keywords
people are
using on
their pages.

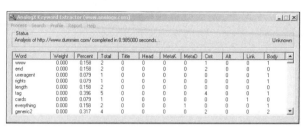

Don't just toss in popular search terms in an attempt to generate bogus hits.
Adding *sex* and *MP3* to a site that's about walrus migration patterns won't
bring you the kind of visitors you're looking for.

Keyword advertising

Analysis of your site's keywords is also important in the multifaceted world
of *keyword advertising,* such as the use of Google AdSense to place targeted
ads on Web sites and in search results. The flip side of this process is Google
AdWords (http://adwords.google.com), which is where the advertise-
ments come from.

The nice thing about Google AdSense is that it pays you to use it. With
programs such as Google AdWords or Yahoo! Search Marketing (http://
searchmarketing.yahoo.com), however, you'll be getting a bill rather
than a check. If you've always thought of Google, Yahoo!, and such Web sta-
ples as free, think again — this is where they make their money. Just like TV
or radio, it's the advertisers who pay for it all. Advertisers do this by buying
space on a search engine's results page (see Figure 13-3). Which results page,
though, and where? That depends upon the keyword the user entered and
several other factors. All other things being equal, the advertiser who pays
the most gets the top slot. The ad might also be limited to display in certain
geographical regions.

If you're still with me, don't worry — the bill can fit within almost any type of budget. Perhaps the most important limitation you can specify is the most money you're willing to spend in a month. Although you can officially get started with pocket change (at this writing, Google AdWords has a mere $5 registration fee), it's important to manage your advertising budget carefully. Fortunately, prompt feedback is a normal feature of these advertising programs. If you'd like to start advertising with Google AdWords, be sure to check out *AdWords For Dummies,* by Howie Jacobson (Wiley Publishing).

Figure 13-3: Yahoo! has sponsored ads — just like Google.

Submitting to the Search Sites

You can just sit around and wait for a spider or robot to trip over your site. Sooner or later, that'll probably happen all by itself — the search engines are always hungry for more sites to add. But being proactive and making certain that your site is listed is a lot smarter. You can submit your site on your own, or you can use services that do it for you.

Doing it yourself

Why bother doing it yourself when you can pay someone else to do it for you? Well, there's the obvious advantage of saving money. If you're on a shoestring budget, that can matter. If not, you're likely going to say something like this: "It's more cost-effective for me to pay someone to get my site submitted to search engines than for me to take time away from actually running the business." There's something to be said for that reasoning too.

But there's nothing like making sure the job gets done right. And it's a wise Webmaster who gets thoroughly familiar with the many variations on how the search engines want Web page URLs to be submitted. I strongly recommend that you try submitting to at least a few of them yourself. Table 13-2 gives the URLs of the submission pages for several major search sites.

Table 13-2	Search-Site Submission Pages
Submission Page	*Web Address*
AlltheWeb	www.alltheweb.com/help/webmaster/ submit_site
Ask.com	http://www.ineedhits.com/paid-inclusion/ ask-jeeves-search-engine.aspx
Bing	www.bing.com/webmaster/SubmitSitePage. aspx
Google	www.google.com/addurl.html
Yahoo! (commercial sites)	http://add.yahoo.com/fast/ add?+Business
Yahoo! (noncommercial sites)	https://siteexplorer.search.yahoo.com/ submit/

Some search engines charge for adding your site to their listings, and more may do so. Yahoo! offers unpaid listings only for noncommercial sites. Make sure that you find out whether it's free before you submit.

Most search engines accept submissions in pretty much the same way, and the process is pretty simple. With Google, for example, you simply go to www.google.com/addurl.html (see Figure 13-4), enter your URL, and click the Add URL button.

Yahoo! works the same way. Just go to https://siteexplorer.search. yahoo.com/submit/ and enter the URL of your home page, then click the Submit URL button.

Figure 13-4:
Google is
the one
search site
you must list
with.

Using submission services

You get what you pay for, you know? When it comes to Web site submission services, that saying really hits home. Very few of the free services submit your URL to anywhere near as many search sites as the paid ones do. Although the paid services submit your info to many more search engines, you don't get much payback from listing in all the obscure ones.

Many Web site submission services fall into a gray area, offering limited free services but charging more for anything extra. The paid services may or may not be worthwhile, depending on how well they know their stuff. If you're going to part with your hard-earned bucks, you have the right to ask them a few questions first. Make sure that the people you're dealing with understand the differences among the search engines. If they can't tell you (for example) which ones accept HTML coding in their listings or how long a description is acceptable at a particular search site, you may not be getting much bang for your buck. You may be better off doing it yourself.

ProBoost (www.proboost.com), shown in Figure 13-5, is one classy example of folks who know what search engines are all about. With ProBoost, you don't just fill out a form. You can actually work with real, live people who are committed to your success. ProBoost has free telephone support and a chat room, too.

Figure 13-5:
ProBoost offers excellent service and support for your Web page submission effort.

Keeping out of the search sites

Not everybody wants all their pages indexed and offered to the general public at a search site; you may, for instance, want to share things with family or a small circle of friends, but not the entire world. There are two methods you can use to keep a search engine's robot from indexing your site. One may require the assistance of your network administrator or Internet service provider. The other you can do yourself.

Getting outside assistance

For a long time, the only way to lock a search engine out was to use a file called `robots.txt`. This file, located in the top-level domain directory (the same one your home page goes into), lists all banned search bots as well as directories that can't be searched. The reason you may need some professional help here is that unless you run your own dedicated server, you may not have access to the top-level domain directory. Putting `robots.txt` anywhere else doesn't do you any good. If your Web site is housed on your ISP's server or on a virtual server, it's really in a subdirectory of a dedicated Web server. What you need to do, in this case, is to let the people who run your HTTP server know which directories you don't want searched. They'll take care of the rest — which consists of simply listing those directories in a text file.

The following example shows how to block all search bots from searching two sample directories:

```
User-agent: *
Disallow: /~mine/private/
Disallow: /~mine/personal/
```

Someone who wants to pry into your site can get a good start by looking at the contents of your `robots.txt` file. After all, it contains a list of all the directories and files you don't want the world to see. If you have anything confidential in those areas, `robots.txt` is a road map pointing straight to it.

Doing it yourself

If you want to grab control yourself, or if you just want to avoid using `robots.txt`, you can turn to that good old friend, the `META` tag. Remember that I said that tag is versatile. Well, this is another useful application for it. By assigning the `name` attribute a value of `robots` and adding one or more variables to the `content` attribute, you can specify your desires about the page it's in.

By default, a search robot will not only index your page (adding the words in it to the search site's database), but also follow all the links on the page. If you want to disallow both of these behaviors, add the following HTML code in the `HEAD` element of your file:

```
<META name="robots" content="noindex,nofollow">
```

You can accomplish the same thing by using a value of `none`:

```
<META name="robots" content="none">
```

Technically, you could do the opposite — that is, allow both options — by using a value of `all`, but there's no point in doing that. If you want both options working, just don't do anything.

To allow the indexing, but keep robots from following your links, use this line of code:

```
<META name="robots" content="nofollow">
```

Remember that the robot's indexing and following of links are default behaviors, so you don't need to specify either one if you're allowing it. Thus, the preceding code doesn't mention indexing at all. You could, if you want to be pedantic about it, say the same thing like this:

```
<META name="robots" content="index,nofollow">
```

The situation would have to be unusual, but you may wish for a robot to follow the links in a particular directory without adding the pages in it to a search engine. To allow a robot to follow your links, but deny it from indexing, use this code:

```
<META name="robots" content="noindex">
```

Checking Your Search Site Position

You need to follow up on your submissions to make sure you're listed (different search sites react on different timetables) as well as to find out where you land in the rankings when your keywords are used in a search.

Obviously, the fastest way to find out both of these things is to log on to the search engines you've submitted to and check. First, enter the name of your site and see if it comes up. If it doesn't come up, and more time has elapsed than the search engine is supposed to take, you may want to resubmit your site.

This is also a great way to find out which other Web sites have links to yours, because any page with your site's name on it will show up in the search results. (See the next section "Investigating Reciprocal Linking.")

If your site does come up, you'll want to enter the keywords from your site as search terms. This quickly shows you where you fall in the rankings. Assuming that some other sites show up on top of your own, it's worthwhile to take a look at their source code to see what keywords they use. Also, don't forget to look over their pages carefully. This is one of those rare instances where your competitors' techniques are literally an open book.

Investigating Reciprocal Linking

Reciprocal linking is the Web's equivalent of "You scratch my back, and I'll scratch yours." The way it works looks like this: You put in a link on your page to another Web site, and the other Web site returns the favor by putting in a link to yours. Even directly competing sites can benefit from linking to one another, just as two restaurants can happily exist side by side.

Finding sites to link to

So whom do you want to link with? Well, the simple answer is "anybody and everybody." The smart answer, though, is "the best and most popular sites in my category." What's best is a matter of opinion, but it's pretty easy to find the most popular ones, and you can use this technique to piggyback on their success.

What you need to do is to spend some time working the search engines. Here's the drill:

1. **Enter the keywords you think people would use to find your site.**

2. **Follow the links in the results to the other sites that are similar to your own.**

All search engines will return at least some poor responses, so don't automatically assume that all the results would be good sources of reciprocal links for your Web site. Use your own judgment.

3. **Look for an e-mail link to the site's owner.**

Typically, you can find this type of link at the bottom of the page, but it may be anywhere.

4. **Click the e-mail link and send the site's Webmaster a message politely suggesting that you both link up.**

It may be helpful to put in a link to the other site first. That way you can say something like, "I've linked to your site and would appreciate a return link from yours." This takes the discussion out of the realm of the hypothetical and puts the other site's Webmaster under an obligation to respond in kind. There are no guarantees, but most people do reciprocate.

Sometimes you can't find any contact info on a Web site, no matter how hard you look. If that's the case and you really want to set up a reciprocal link with that site, you can run a search on the site's domain name by using a WhoIs service. WhoIs identifies the administrative, billing, and technical contacts for a domain. The best known one is at Network Solutions (`www.network solutions.com/whois/index.jsp`). Or you can run a search from your own system with software such as WhoIs ULTRA from AnalogX (`www. analogx.com/contents/download/network/whois.htm`).

Another worthwhile program you may want to check out is Link Trader. You use Link Trader to create a database of all the people you've set up recipro-cal links with, and it checks those sites to verify that the link back to you still exists. Keep the database up to date and run the program on a regular basis, and you can quickly spot any sites that drop your link. Then you can e-mail the Webmasters and ask them to put the link back in. You can download Link Trader Pro at `www.homebizfactory.com/Link_Trader_Pro.html`.

Many search engines (Google, for example) consider the number of other sites with links to yours when determining how high you rank. This means that of two sites, with everything else being equal, the one with more links leading to it from other sites shows up before the other one in search results. Reciprocal linking is a powerful tool that you can use to legitimately boost your own site's rankings.

Joining Web rings

Web rings are a kind of super-size reciprocal link arrangement. Instead of making a reciprocal link between two sites, you make it with an entire group of similar sites at one time. You can find Web rings on just about any topic you can think of, and many such rings are listed at `http://dir.webring.com/rw` or `www.ringsurf.com`. (See Figure 13-6.) You can also start your own Web ring if you want.

Figure 13-6: RingSurf is a good source for Web rings.

The weakness of Web rings is that they link in a ring. In other words, each one links to the previous one in the list and the next one in the list. If any site drops out of the ring, that messes up the whole thing, just as if you broke a link in a chain.

Joining a banner exchange

In a *banner exchange,* each member creates a banner ad and submits it to a central site. That site, the exchange itself, automates the process of displaying all the members' ads on all the other members' Web sites. A banner exchange sounds like a great idea, but in practice, few banner exchanges survive for very long. If you're considering joining one, make sure that you ask how long it's been in operation. Also make it a point to contact current members and see how satisfied they are with the exchange.

That said, joining a banner exchange is an easy task. You fill out a simple application form on the exchange's Web site; then you send the exchange your banner and place some HTML code on your site. That's all there is to it — the exchange handles everything else. Several reputable banner exchanges are listed in Table 13-3.

Online Sources for Getting the Word Out about Your Site

Table 13-3 lists some places on the World Wide Web where you can find more information on the topics covered in this chapter.

Table 13-3	Online Resources for Publicizing Your Site
Web Site Name	*Web Address*
Add Me.com	www.addme.com
Apex Pacific	www.edynamicsoft.com
Guerilla Marketing Online	www.gmarketing.com
HitExchange	www.hitx.net
LinkBuddies	www.linkbuddies.com
Search Engine Watch	www.searchenginewatch.com
Wordtracker	www.wordtracker.com

Chapter 14

Designing for Internet Commerce

· ·

· ·

More pure bull hockey is floating around about Internet commerce than about practically any other topic in the world. If you haven't found thousands of e-commerce Web sites promising you the moon — and a moon made of gold and platinum at that — you aren't looking.

According to these self-proclaimed gurus of e-commerce, all you need to do is put up a Web page — not even a site, just a page — and the money comes rolling in. You can vacation in Acapulco this weekend and sun yourself on the Riviera by Monday. The secret to this success? Well, of course, they can't just *tell* you what it is. That kind of information is worth some real money, you know.

This "get-rich-quick-over-the-Internet" scheme reminds me of an ad that used to run in the backs of cheap magazines many, many years ago. For 25¢, the ad promised, you could discover how to make a fortune fast. After you sent in your quarter, you got back a pamphlet that, boiled down to its basics, told you to put an ad in a magazine asking people to send you a quarter. Today's get-rich-quick schemes are no more solid than that one, even if they're draped in the latest finery of high technology.

So is there any truth at all to the glowing promise of Internet commerce? Yes, there is. The Internet represents the greatest market that's ever existed, and the opportunity is very real. You *can* make a fortune in e-commerce, just as you can make a fortune in any other kind of commerce. But success takes a combination of brains, toughness, marketing savvy, luck, and — most of all — determination to succeed. In this chapter, I show you how to become a real Internet marketer.

Learning the Real Secret to Internet Success

Are you ready for the real secret of success in any business? Here it is:

Put the right product or service in front of the right audience at the right time for the right price.

There ya go. That's all you need to do to succeed. Well, okay, implementing this advice isn't always easy. And when it comes to e-commerce, there are some special considerations.

Developing the right attitude

If you go into Internet commerce figuring that you don't need to do any real work — that it's just something that you can dabble in between football games or pay attention to if you happen to feel like it — then you're better off going fishing. At least that way you may end up with food on your table.

To win in any kind of business, you need a different attitude from what you need just to hold down a job. Let's face it: The whole point of most jobs is merely to keep a paycheck coming in. Most people work in jobs they don't care all that much about — or even in jobs they hate. They stick with their jobs solely because they have bills to pay. (Honestly, would you show up for work if you won the lottery? No? Neither would most people.)

If you run your own business, though, work is different. If you're sick and tired of rush hour, wearing suits and ties or high heels, and having bosses stand over your shoulder demanding that you work harder than they do, the Internet may be your ticket to financial independence. But you must pay a certain price. To run your own business, you must work harder than you ever have before. And you need to take a good, hard look at who you really are.

Notice that I'm not saying "what you really want" but "who you really are." There's a good reason for that. If you're going to win in business, you win, not because you're doing some particular thing, but because you're being yourself. In my own case, if I won the lottery, I'd take a few days off to meet with my attorneys and accountants and get everything in order, but I'd go back to work as soon as possible. I can't help it because I'm a book person. Winning enough money to afford even more books can't change that fact.

What do you love most in the world? Whatever is your true passion is also your natural business. If you do anything else with your life, you can't give it the same kind of energy. That's plain old human nature. Who can give 100 percent all the time if they don't care about the outcome? If you're stuck in a job at a desk in a cubicle and the company you work for experiences a crisis, what you do usually doesn't matter. The situation isn't your doing, and you're not in charge anyway. Even if you do manage, by superhuman effort, to overcome the situation and save the day, you know you probably won't even get a raise out of it. After all, you're just doing your duty.

If you want to make a break from the traditional working world, you must make a clean break from the employee attitude, too. An Internet business is different — it's yours. It's a part of you, and if you listen to your inner voice, it's a natural extension of yourself. It's not what you do — it's who you are.

Focusing on your business

Many people believe that you can sell anything on the Internet. After all, zillions of people are on it, so anything you create is sure to appeal to someone. Well, that belief is more or less true, but it doesn't mean you can make money automatically from your creation.

If you're serious about making money, you must remember the key factor in a Web site's appeal: focus, focus, focus. If you run your site as a hobby or a public service, you can afford to drift a bit, but if you depend on it for your living, you must stay on target. Any drifting off the mark costs you money.

What I'm talking about here is *specialization*. When it comes to general merchandise, the Internet is pretty much already lost to you. Why? Because it's got JCPenney and Kmart and Wal-Mart (see Figure 14-1) and all those other well-established companies with very deep pockets. You're not going to put those companies out of business in a physical shopping mall, and you're not going to take them out on the Internet either. They already enjoy the kind of name recognition that takes a long time to build. And they can spend more money on one ad than the average online business has in its annual budget.

Even if you do have the kind of bucks that it takes to go up against the big outfits, I advise you to put your money into specialized stores. The future of e-commerce lies in smaller companies that can focus all their energies on a relatively small market. Here's where the size of the Internet really comes into play for you — a relatively small market on the Internet is much larger than it would be even in a large city.

Figure 14-1:
The major
general
retailers
effectively
dominate
their
markets, on
and off the
Internet.

Reaching customers all over the globe is the Internet's greatest strength. Like the telephone and air travel before it, the Net is making the world — especially the world of commerce — much smaller than it was even ten years ago. By targeting a particular submarket, you can tightly focus your business efforts and still reach more people than you ever could reach by running a local business. And a functional Web site is much cheaper than even a small physical store. You can indeed start successful businesses on a shoestring if you use the Net.

Even if you do need some kind of physical facilities for your operation, such as storage space for your products, you don't need to concern yourself with the appearance and attractiveness of those facilities. For most online businesses, a small warehouse space does just as well as a fancy, glitzy store in a major shopping mall. In many cases, you can start with a spare room in your house. If you end up needing more room to handle all the merchandise that people are ordering . . . well, we should all have such problems, right?

Getting supplies flowing

Okay, so now you know what your online business is all about. If you choose wisely, you probably already know plenty about the field. You know all the major suppliers, your competition, and all sorts of little tidbits that outsiders know nothing about. You know what other companies in the industry have tried, what worked and what didn't, and how your potential customers feel about it all.

Depending on your field, either you create your product or you line up some good, low-cost suppliers. If you create your own product or market your own service, you're already there. If you rely on outsiders, though, you must do some research. Even if you already have a supplier in mind, you'll probably be able to find a better deal (or get more or better services) if you ask around.

Identifying potential suppliers

Track down everyone who makes what you want to sell. Use search engines to find their Web sites and then print out some of those companies' Web pages. Make folders for each company (the manila kind, not the hard-drive kind) and arrange the hard copies neatly so you can refer to them at a moment's notice.

If a site you're researching offers a Contacts link, follow it to see whether its information is useful to you. Different companies provide different amounts of contact data. Some companies have confusing and relatively worthless listings or nothing significant at all. Others provide fully detailed breakdowns of their operations by department and by significant personnel, including everything from phone numbers, to e-mail and snail-mail addresses, to descriptions of people's job functions. You're looking for the director of sales and marketing. In the unlikely event that one isn't listed, go for the shipping manager.

The Contacts link may say something different, such as About Our Company or Regional Offices. Be creative and explore the site exhaustively when you're looking for contact info.

If you can't find the information you're looking for on the company's Web site, you can turn to one of the many business-phone-number databases on the Web. I list some for you in Table 14-1.

Table 14-1	Online Sources of Business Phone Numbers
Web Site Name	**Web Address**
BigBook	www.bigbook.com
Infobel World Telephone Directories	www.infobel.com
InfoSpace Yellow Pages	www.infospace.com/home/yellow-pages
Switchboard.com	www.switchboard.com
Yahoo! Local Yellow Pages	http://yp.yahoo.com

Try the AT&T AnyWho Online Directory that's listed in Table 14-1 before you spend any money on long-distance calls. This directory is a source of toll-free business phone numbers. Even if the company you're looking at doesn't list a toll-free number on its own site, it may still have one that shows up in the AT&T listings.

After you get a phone number and/or e-mail address, check with the supplier to find out whether it uses drop-shipping. (*Drop-shipping* is an arrangement in which you gather the orders and submit them to the supplier; the supplier then sends the merchandise directly to the customer and puts your return address on it. You, of course, must pay the supplier for the merchandise, but you pay a wholesale rate and keep the rest for your profit.)

If the supplier doesn't drop-ship, find out the minimum order you can place — and what kind of discount (if any) you get for different sizes of orders. In either case, make sure that you find out how long the company normally takes to fulfill your orders. You need to know this information so you can quote an expected delivery time to your customers. (Now you know why so many order forms say something like "Allow 4 to 6 weeks for delivery.")

Choosing a shipping company

If you get stuck with delivering the product to your customers yourself, you need to establish a business account with at least one shipping company. Most companies traditionally use UPS for shipping merchandise, although offering several alternatives to your customers doesn't hurt. You can also use the U.S. Postal Service, and FedEx is making a serious effort to compete with UPS these days on its own turf. Table 14-2 lists the URLs for some of the major shipping companies' Web sites.

Table 14-2	Major Shipping Companies
Web Site Name	*Web Address*
DHL	www.dhl.com
FedEx	www.fedex.com
Purolator Courier Ltd.	www.purolator.com
United Parcel Service	www.ups.com
United States Postal Service	www.usps.com

Be sure to find out from your shipping company whether you can get discounts for volume shipping.

Designing for E-Commerce

You may understand Web site design in general, but designing an online store requires some special considerations. Face the fact — if you're building a shopping mall in the real world, do you want an architect who specializes in houses or an architect who's built stores all his life?

Yes, your Web site must display a pretty face. Yes, it must perform all the functions you need to show your wares and process orders. But the key point to Web design is this one rule:

It must be simple to use.

If customers face any kind of hitch in the process, you're going to lose money. That's guaranteed — 100 percent. As you plan the site design for an e-commerce store, you must approach it from the buyer's viewpoint and concentrate on making the store easy to navigate and the buying process painless. Regardless of what you sell, here are some ways to satisfy your potential buyers' needs:

✔ **Include a picture of the product.** If you sell some type of merchandise, make sure that you include at least one picture.

Use thumbnail images instead of full-sized ones so that the basic product page doesn't take too long to load. (Customers may lose interest if they must wait too long for the site to load.)

✔ **Give detailed information, if appropriate.** How much information you give depends on what you're selling. With many products, you can easily fit all the necessary information about the product into the product's description. However, providing additional information gives you an opportunity to sing the product's praises at length, even if the extra info isn't totally necessary.

✔ **Clearly state the cost.** Put the price right out in the open where everyone can see it. You'd be surprised how often you can follow link after link on e-commerce sites without ever finding the price clearly stated.

✔ **Make it easy for customers to buy the product.** If you're using shopping-cart software for multiple products, make sure that it's easy to use and doesn't require a bunch of back-and-forth steps to work. If you sell a single product or service, make sure that your site can quickly accommodate the customer's decision to buy. Here are a few ways to do that:

> • *Put a Buy This Now link at the top of the page — and put one at the bottom, too.*
>
> • *Don't ask a bunch of extra questions on the order form. Stick with the basics, such as name, address, payment method, and shipping options.*
>
> • *If you want to add a survey, add it after the entire sales process is complete, not as an impediment to the ongoing sale.*

Adding a Search Function

Unless your site consists of just a single Web page, you need a search engine for it. Sites that don't offer search functions are at a real disadvantage compared with those that do have them. Put yourself in a visitor's shoes and ask, "Do I want to spend hours browsing this site in the hope that I may stumble across the information I want? Or do I want to spend a few seconds running a search to get the information I need right away?"

All the search options described in the following sections have their own strengths and weaknesses. Similar programs and services offer varying features. The importance of each feature is a matter for you to decide. I recommend checking out all of them. Because none of them requires much effort to install and use, you may as well road-test every one to see which you like best.

Using Google Site Search

Google Site Search is one of the best of the zillions of valuable tools that Google provides to the Web. You just slap a search box into your Web pages and bam! Your users can search every page in your site — or the whole Web, if you want — using the powerful Google search engine.

Before you can use it, though, you have to get a Google account. No worries — this is a no-obligation situation; you're just getting one more username.

There are lots of Google tools that require this account first, so even if you don't end up using Google Site Search, you'll probably still want to get the account.

Getting the account

To sign up for your Google account, follow these steps:

1. **Go to** `www.google.com/accounts/NewAccount` **in your Web browser. (See Figure 14-2.)**

2. **Enter your e-mail address.**

3. **Enter your desired password twice (once in each password text box).**

4. **Scroll down and select your location. (See Figure 14-3.)**

5. **Under Word Verification, type the characters that are shown above the text box.**

   This is a measure designed to defeat automated account piracy. Humans can read the graphics characters; computers can't.

6. **Click the button that says, I Accept. Create My Account.**

   Google will e-mail you a confirmation at the address you entered back in Step 2.

7. **Click the link in that message to complete the creation of your account.**

Figure 14-2:
Entering
your
information.

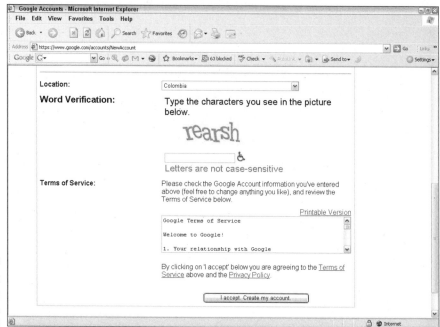

Figure 14-3:
Completing
the form.

Starting your (site-search) engine

Now that you've got your Google account, you're ready to go for your own personal site-search engine. Here's how you do it:

1. **Go to** `www.google.com/coop/cse` **in your Web browser.**

2. **Click the Create a Custom Search Engine button.**

3. **On the resulting login page, enter your e-mail address and password that you used for your Google account creation.**

4. **Click the Sign In button.**

   If this is a new Google account, you're taken to a page where you need to enter your first name and last name before you can continue.

5. **On the Create a Custom Search Engine page, shown in Figure 14-4, enter a name and description for your search engine.**

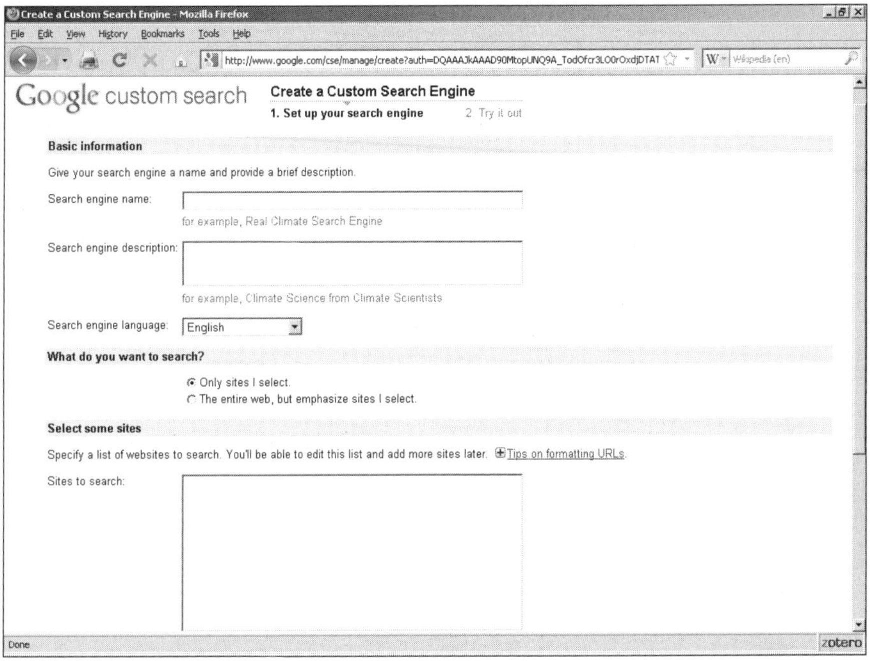

Figure 14-4:
Entering
basic data.

6. **Select the language for the search engine from the drop-down list.**

7. **Under What Do You Want to Search?, select one of the options:**

   • **Only Sites I Select:** Enables you to limit the search to your own site (or any specific others you want to add).

   • **The Entire Web, But Emphasize Sites I Select:** Searches everything, but puts your sites at the top of the list.

8. **Scroll down and enter the URLs of the sites you want to search in the text area.**

   Click on the Tips on formatting URLs link to get info on using wildcards, specifying individual pages, and the like.

9. **Under Select an edition, shown in Figure 14-5, select either the Standard (free, but with ads) or the Business version ($100 a year and up, without ads).**

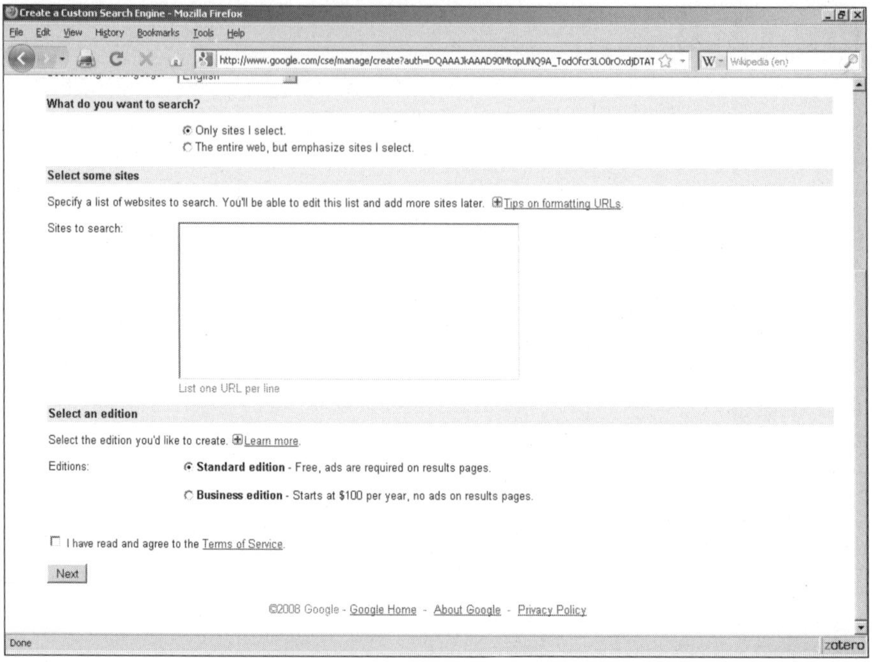

Figure 14-5:
Choosing
free or paid
service.

10. **Select the I Have Read and Agree to the Terms of Service check box.**

11. **Click the Next button.**

12. **On the resulting page, click the Finish button.**

    After doing so, you can perform some sample queries.

13. **On the next page, click the Control Panel link. (See Figure 14-6.)**

14. **On the Control Panel page, shown in Figure 14-7, click the Get Code link on the left.**

15. **On the next page (see Figure 14-8), select the HTML code in the text area, copy it, and paste it into your own Web page.**

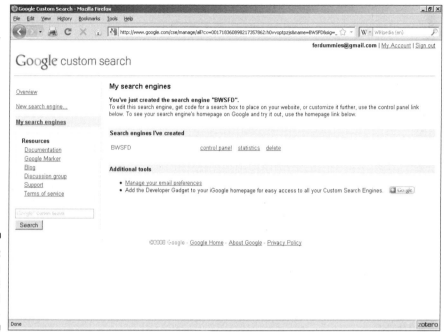

Figure 14-6:
The search
engine has
been
created.

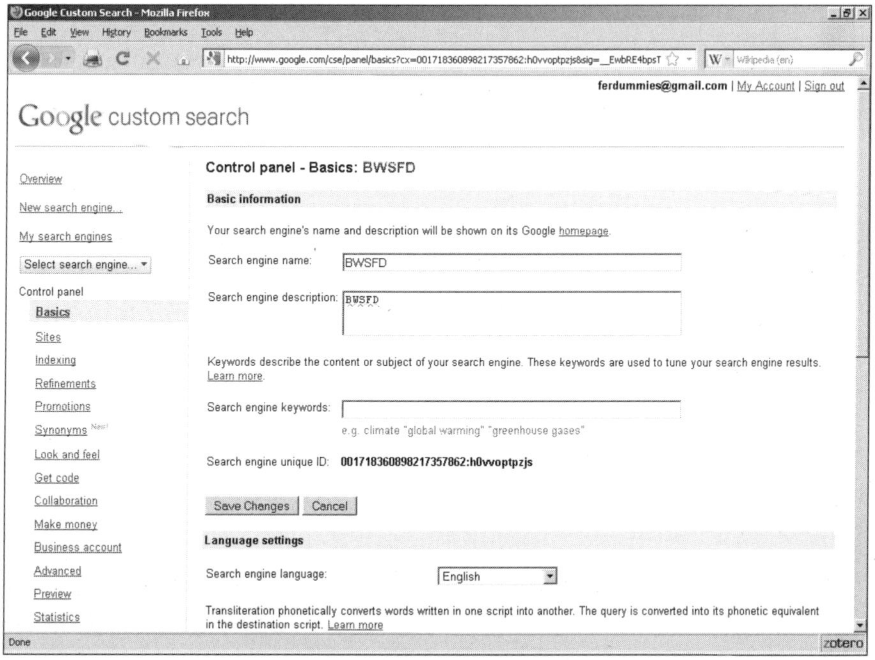

Figure 14-7:
The Control
Panel.

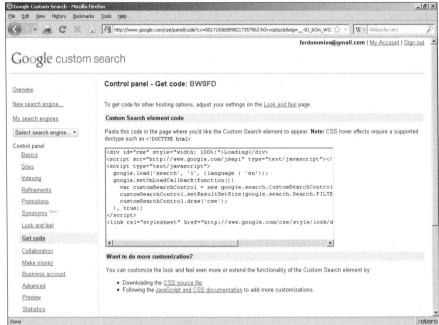

Figure 14-8:
Getting the
code.

Getting a free search engine with FreeFind

After you take a look at the capabilities of FreeFind's search engine (www. freefind.com), you may not bother to look at anything else (except that I describe another one that's worth a peek, too). It's a beautifully designed, full-featured, honey of a search feature that you can add to your site in just a few minutes. It's customizable, creates a site map for you, keeps an up-to-date What's New list that shows visitors what you've added lately, gives you extensive reports on what people are looking for, and does pretty near everything else you can ask for, except fry your eggs for breakfast. The cost? Nothing.

After you finish drooling over the search engine, you may ask, "What's the catch?" Advertising supports it — which means that an ad banner appears at the top of the search page on your site. If your site also has its own advertisers, you can't show any of your ads in competition with FreeFind's ads on that page.

On most sites, an advertising banner is a pretty small point to consider. Even if you have your own sponsors, you can still place their ads on every page on your site that doesn't have FreeFind, and FreeFind helps your visitors get to all those other pages more easily. FreeFind imposes a site limit of about 2,000 Web pages (32MB), but a polite e-mail message to the FreeFind folks generally gets them to raise the limit.

You do face one other restriction with FreeFind: FreeFind doesn't allow anyone to use its search engine on adults-only sites, because its advertisers don't want to appear on such sites.

Still with me? Okay, FreeFind's search engine runs on its servers, not on yours, so tons of people can use it simultaneously without tying up all your server resources.

You can set up FreeFind to search just your site, just the World Wide Web outside your site, or both your site and the Web in the same search. You can modify the search form, and FreeFind makes the job extremely easy for you by providing online wizards that help you make custom choices, such as designating link colors (either by name or hexadecimal value).

Joining FreeFind

To sign up for FreeFind, all you need to do is to fill out a simple form, as the following steps describe:

1. **Go to FreeFind's home page (**www.freefind.com**) and enter your Web site address and your e-mail address in the appropriate text boxes. (See Figure 14-9.)**

   FreeFind keeps your e-mail address confidential, so your address won't be sold to anyone.

2. **Click the Instant Sign-Up button.**

   FreeFind sends you an e-mail confirmation message right away. The message contains your password, site ID, and all the links you need to use its service.

3. **Click the link in the e-mail confirmation message to go to the FreeFind Control Center (**www.freefind.com/control.html**).**

4. **In the form on that page, enter your Web site address, e-mail address, and the password from the e-mail confirmation message; then click the Login button.**

   The Select Account Type page appears.

5. **Click the Select link next to Free Account.**

   Of course, if you're the adventurous type who wants to skip the "try before you buy" approach, you can always click one of the paid service links instead.

   You only have to complete this step the first time you sign in to FreeFind.

6. **On the main Control Center page, click the Build Index tab (shown in Figure 14-10).**

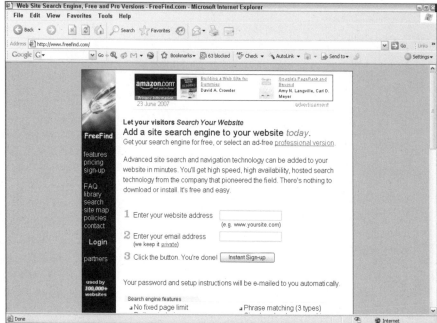

Figure 14-9:
Signing up for FreeFind's free search engine on FreeFind's home page.

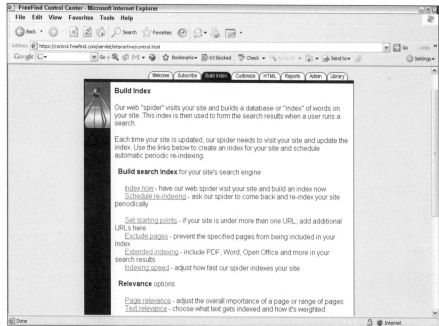

Figure 14-10:
The Build Index tab of FreeFind's Control Center, where you tell the search engine to start indexing your site.

7. **Click the Index Now link.**

8. **In the dialog box that appears, click the Finish button to have FreeFind index your site.**

FreeFind starts indexing your site and e-mails you when it's finished. At the same time it does the indexing, FreeFind also creates a site map and a What's New page for your Web site.

Adding the search engine

FreeFind gives you the HTML code for a basic search panel you can add to your pages. All you need to do is copy and paste the version you want (either from the e-mail message or the attachment) onto the Web page on which you want to use it, and then upload the page to your site, and your search engine will be fully functional.

You can't use the search engine until FreeFind finishes indexing your site. If you try to use it before FreeFind is finished indexing, you receive an e-mail message saying that the spider's indexing of your site isn't complete, and you get a Web page reminding you to wait.

Here's how to go to the goodies page and get your free code (if you're already in the FreeFind Control Center from the previous steps, you can skip straight to Step 3 here):

1. **Go to the FreeFind Control Center at** www.freefind.com/control.html.

2. **Enter your Web site address, e-mail address, and password, and then click the Login button.**

3. **On the main Control Center page, click the HTML tab (shown in Figure 14-11).**

4. **Scroll down the screen and view the different types of search panels that are available.**

   You can also click the links at the top of the page to jump to particular kinds of panels, such as ones that search your site only, as opposed to those that search the Web and your site.

5. **When you find a search panel you want, click inside the text area underneath it, which contains the HTML code, and select the code.**

6. **Copy the code and paste it into your own Web page code.**

If you want to customize and pretty up the search page, go to the Control Center page and click the Customize tab. You can specify background colors and images, the type of logo that appears, the positioning of the search results, and many other options. The choices that you make there also affect your site map so that both the search page and the site map share the same look.

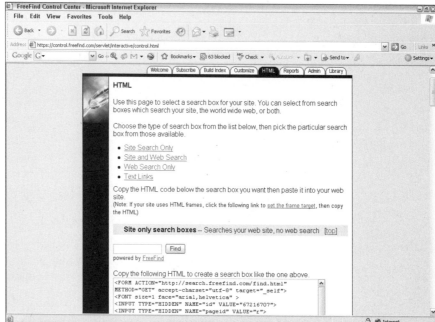

Figure 14-11:
You find the
code for
different
search
panels you
can use
by adding
FreeFind's
search
engine to
your site
on the
HTML tab.

Dropping in Perl CGI scripts such as Simple Search

If you're a go-it-alone type who doesn't want to rely on outside servers to process your site searches, you can drop in a Perl CGI script instead. (See Chapter 8 for more on scripts.) It requires a bit more technical skill than some tasks, or a little bit of help from your ISP or network administrator, but it's definitely doable, even if you don't know anything about CGI. One of the best and easiest CGI scripts to use is Simple Search. Written by Matt Wright, one of CGI's greats, Simple Search has been a venerable mainstay of many Web sites. Figure 14-12 shows Simple Search on a Web page.

You can download Simple Search from Matt's Script Archive at `world widemart.com/scripts/search.shtml`. To add Simple Search to your site, you first need to uncompress (unzip) the main file for the program (`simple.zip`, `simple.tar`, or whatever) and then make a few alterations in the enclosed sample files.

You need to change a few settings in the script to make it work on your site. Make sure that you follow the exact format of what appears in these settings as you replace the sample values in the script with the information for your site, or the script won't work. This mostly means you must leave all quotation marks and semicolons in place just as they appear in the following examples. Don't replace single quotes with double quotes or vice versa. Keeping a hard copy of the file handy while working on it may help you to remember what to do — and what not to do.

Figure 14-12:
Simple
Search adds
keyword-
searching
capabilities
to your site.

To prepare the Simple Search's Perl script for use, follow these steps:

1. **Go to** `http://worldwidemart.com/scripts/search.shtml` **and open the file** `search.pl` **in a text editor.**

2. **Scroll down until you reach the section with the heading** `# Define Variables.`

3. **Replace the** `$basedir` **value with the base directory path of your own site.**

   For example, in the following script line, the sample value for this variable is `/mnt/web/guide/worldwidemart/scripts/`. Remember to replace only the value itself, not the variable (`$basedir`) or any punctuation marks.

   ```
   $basedir = '/mnt/web/guide/worldwidemart/scripts/';
   ```

   The *base directory path* is the path on your Web server, not your Web site's URL, which you add in the following step. If you don't know this value, ask your ISP or network administrator. Make sure that you include the trailing slash at the end (`/`).

4. **Replace the** $baseurl **value with the base URL of your site.**

   The value you need to supply for the $baseurl variable is the URL of the directory where your site's main page resides. The base URL for Dummies.com, for example, is http://www.dummies.com/. And using both http:// and the trailing slash is important here, too, even if you're not accustomed to using both in Web addresses. In the following line from the script, the value you need to replace is http://world widemart.com/scripts/:

   ```
   $baseurl = 'http://worldwidemart.com/scripts/';
   ```

5. **Replace the sample values for the** @files **variable with the paths and files that you want Simple Search to process as part of its search.**

   In the following line from the script, the values you need to replace are *.shtml, demos/links/*.html, and demos/guest/*.html:

   ```
   @files = ('*.shtml','demos/links/*.html',
       'demos/guest/*.html');
   ```

   This is one of the easiest places to create a typographical error that keeps the script from working because the @files variable can have more than one value. Each value is surrounded by single quotation marks, as usual, but it's also separated from the other values by a comma. If you use more than one value here, pay careful attention to the sample code's syntax.

   If you want to search only HTML files in the main directory, for example, enter the value that the following example shows:

   ```
   @files = ('*.html');
   ```

   To search both HTML and SHTML files in the main directory, use the following example instead:

   ```
   @files = ('*.html','*.shtml');
   ```

   To search for HTML and SHTML files in a subdirectory called fauna as well, use the following example:

   ```
   @files = ('*.html','*.shtml','*/fauna.*html',
       '/fauna/*.shtml');
   ```

6. **Replace the value of the** $title **variable with the name of your site. In the following line from the script, the sample value you need to replace is** Matt's Script Archive.

   ```
   $title = "Matt's Script Archive";
   ```

   This value appears along with the search results, and the next step makes the text into a text link.

7. **Replace the value of the** `$titleurl` **variable with the Web address of your main page. In the following line from the script, the value you need to replace is** `http://worldwidemart.com/scripts/.`

   ```
   $title_url = 'http://worldwidemart.com/scripts/';
   ```

   This value is usually the same as the `$baseurl` value (see Step 4), although you may want to add the page's filename as well. For example, if your `$baseurl` value is `http://www.mysite.com/` and your main page is `index.html`, you can use either `http://www.mysite.com/` or `http://www.mysite.com/index.html` as the value for `$titleurl`.

8. **Replace the** `$searchurl` **value with the Web address of your search page. In the following line from the script, the part you need to replace is** `http://worldwidemart.com/scripts/demos/search/search.html.`

   ```
   $search_url = 'http://worldwidemart.com/scripts/demos/
       search/search.html';
   ```

9. **Save the file.**

To prepare the HTML search page for use, follow these steps:

1. **Open the file** `search.html` **in a text editor.**

2. **Change the** `action` **attribute of the** `FORM` **element to the URL where you're locating the Perl script on your Web server.**

   In the following line from the `search.html` file, the value you need to replace is `http://worldwidemart.com/scripts/cgi-bin/demos/search.cgi.`

   ```
   <form method=POST action="http://worldwidemart.com/
       scripts/cgi-bin/demos/search.cgi">
   ```

3. **Save the file.**

Now upload both files to your server. Make sure that you send `search.pl` in ASCII form and that you put it in your `cgi-bin` directory. Send `search.html` in ASCII form and put it in your Web page directory.

You have two options when uploading files. Your FTP program will send a file as either ASCII or binary. ASCII treats the file as text, binary is used for graphics, and so on.

Okay, remember I told you this one took a bit more tech savvy than most? This is where that hint comes into play. You need to set permissions for the files so they'll work on your Web server. If you don't know what that means, don't worry about it. Just ask your ISP or network administrator to do it for you. Tell them you need to "chmod `search.pl` to 755 and to chmod `search.html` to 744." They'll know what you mean, and they can take care of it in about ten seconds.

There are various opinions on how to pronounce "chmod." Most folks say "chuh-mod," but others say "shmod" or "see-aich-mod."

Adding a FAQ

FAQ is Internet-ese for "Frequently Asked Questions." Just like it sounds, this is a list of the questions that most users ask most often. Including one can save you lots of time when it comes to providing tech support to your visitors. That's why you usually see a link at the top of any support page asking users to view the FAQ before contacting the site's support team.

You can try to invent a FAQ before you ever go live with your Web site, but you're probably going to have to wait a while until users actually do ask enough questions before the content of your FAQ actually justifies the name.

If you do decide to go with the first option, the best technique is to ask friends and members of your family to surf your nascent site and write down anything that they find problematic. You can then take all their comments and work up a set of responses to create your preliminary FAQ so that you don't have to go live with nothing.

Online Sources for Internet Commerce

Table 14-3 lists some places on the World Wide Web where you can find more information about the topics covered in this chapter.

Table 14-3	Online Resources for Internet Commerce
Web Site Name	*Web Address*
Freightworld	`www.freightworld.com/exp_geo.html`
How to Redesign Your Website to Play to Your Audience, from *CIO Magazine*	`www.cio.com/archive/111503/play.html`
Package Tracking Links, from Copresco	`www.copresco.com/pkgtrack.htm`
TeleTransport Shipping Tracking	`www.teletransport.it/newweb/eng/pagine/servizi-ship.asp`
track-trace	`www.track-trace.com`

Chapter 15

Checking Out Online Payment Methods

. . . .

. . . .

*I*f you're operating a regular store, taking in money from customers is a pretty easy matter. Cash, checks, credit cards, debit cards — you name it, and some well-established process is in place to handle it. From night-deposit drops to armored car pickups, the bricks-and-mortar merchant is already well covered when it comes to getting paid.

You won't find any cash registers online, though, so you need to look at other options. The major approach is to take credit cards. You can, however, arrange to be paid in other ways, such as accepting checks by phone or using digital money. So far, however, none of the other ways can really compete with the power of plastic.

Checking Out Online Payment Methods

Credit cards are king. If you do nothing but take MasterCard and VISA, you're pretty thoroughly covered. Nearly everyone who can afford a computer has one or both of them. Toss in American Express for the high-end customer and the business client, and you're all set. But some alternatives are out there, and you may want to add some or all of them to your setup.

PayPal

When it comes to online payments, one very impressive option is PayPal, now part of the eBay empire. PayPal takes a slightly different approach to online payments, and it's worth a good look. With PayPal, you can accept credit card payments without having a merchant account, and your customers can pay you directly from their bank accounts.

What do you have to do? Not much. Just sign up for an account at `www.paypal.com`. (See Figure 15-1.) What does it cost? Nothing, unless you actually make some sales. In that case, you pay $0.30 per transaction and anywhere from 1.9 to 2.9 percent of the selling price on top of that. Rates can be higher for international sales.

PayPal offers a complete payment system for you to use at no extra cost. You can integrate its free Web tools into your site's pages easily. Throw in a thorough payment-reporting system — which PayPal does — and you couldn't ask for a better setup for a startup business — or even an established one.

Figure 15-1: PayPal provides easy shopping and payment facilities.

Google Checkout

Google Checkout is an exciting new opportunity for the online entrepreneur. Part of Google's ever-expanding variety of services, it may be the easiest way yet to set up the most important part of your store: the part where you actually get paid.

It's not very different from using PayPal; you simply place a Google Checkout button on your site. When your buyers click it, they're taken to an order form like the one in Figure 15-2. Except for the specific information from your store (item, price, and so on), it's the same form for all Google Checkout customers. This familiarity helps to create a high degree of comfort in your buyers.

Considering the vast user base that Google brings to the fray, this is a sales tool you can't do without, especially considering the prices — ranging from 1.9% to 2.9% plus 30 cents for each transaction.

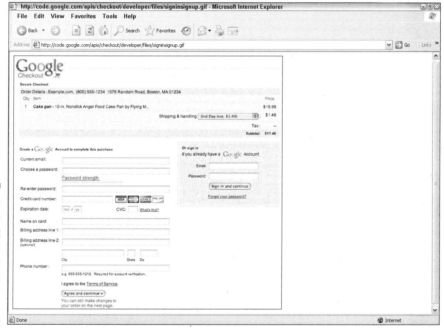

Figure 15-2: Google Checkout presents your buyers with a familiar order form.

To sign up for the program, point your browser to:

```
https://checkout.google.com/sell
```

Once there, sign in via your Google account. If you don't have one, see Chapter 14 for the details on how to get one.

Cash alternatives

E-cash. Digital wallets. Sounds cool. Nice, easy-to-understand metaphor. You use digitally signed certificates online just as you'd use cash in the non-Net world. But it really hasn't worked out. There's no standard yet, although something called *ECML* — the Electronic Commerce Modeling Language — seems to be the first fitful attempt at one.

The most telling thing, though, is that no one's telling. What I mean is that when you ask the folks who are trying to market e-cash exactly how many customers they have, exactly how many merchants are using their systems, and exactly how profitable this all is, they clam up real fast. This is not a good sign. When people are winning, they generally like to trumpet it to the world. But e-cash has nothing to show so far but hype and broken promises.

Phone checks currently offer a more accepted alternative. Here's the scenario: You print checks with other people's account numbers on them, take them to your bank and deposit them, and then watch the money roll in. It's not some kind of criminal operation, either. It's a perfectly legitimate business practice — as long as you have permission from your customers to do it.

The way it works is that your customers give you authorization to create a *draft* on their accounts. A draft is a check. You ask your customers to give you the information off their checks — bank name, check number, those little bank and account numbers across the bottom, and so on — and then you enter that information into a check-writing program. Next, you toss some special *safety paper* into your printer — that's the kind of paper checks are printed on — print those checks, and you've gotten paid just as if you had received a check in the mail.

Figure 15-3 shows a sample screen for creating a draft with Draft Creator from www.advancemeants.com/draft. See Table 15-4, at the end of this chapter, for more sources.

This is one of those systems you really should have in place. It has only two drawbacks. One is that few people are familiar with this system, but that situation is changing rapidly. The other is not a problem for you, but some of your more savvy customers may object that they're paying the full amount up front (whereas with a credit card, they can repay the purchase price over time in small amounts).

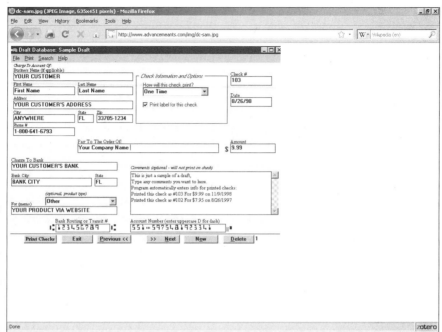

Figure 15-3:
You can
use a paper
draft in
place of
a normal
check.

There's one thing you just can't beat about this payment approach: All you pay for is the software and the paper (which you can get at any good office supply company). You have no monthly fee, no minimum charges, no discount rate, no nothin' that you've gotta put up with when you deal with credit card companies.

Phones, faxes, and snail mail

You should always give your customers some way to purchase from you offline. Even if you've got a fully secure system, plenty of people are still uncomfortable with entering their financial information online. If you can have someone answering the phone (at least during normal business hours), put that phone number on the order form. If you have a fax, put your fax number on there, too. And don't forget to add a physical address. That way anyone who wants to order, but fears online security gaps, can still do so in the old, traditional ways.

If you work from your home and don't want to give out your home address, you can easily get an office address by renting a private mailbox for about a buck a day at most package-shipping companies (not the big ones like UPS that drive trucks around, but the small storefront operations, like Pak Mail or Mail Boxes Etc., which wrap and send packages for you). Many of them will even forward your mail to anywhere in the world. Table 15-1 gives the URLs of several private mailbox companies.

Table 15-1	Mailbox Rental Sources
Mailbox Company	**Web Address**
Box4me.com	www.box4me.com
Mail Boxes Etc.	www.mbe.com
Pak Mail	www.pakmail.com
Postal Connections	www.postalconnections.com
PostalAnnex+	www.postalannex.com

Getting a Merchant Account

You know that old line of Groucho Marx's? The one that went something like, "I wouldn't want to join any club that would have someone like me as a member." Well, if you're just getting started and don't have any kind of business or financial track record, you may have to settle for a credit card merchant account — giving you the ability to accept credit cards — that doesn't necessarily give you the best deal.

Even if you're really good at what you do and you're going into all this with your eyes wide open, the odds are pretty good that a financial analyst will classify you right alongside the starry-eyed dreamers who don't have a chance — unless you have a solid business plan, a proven staff, and some serious money behind your operation. That doesn't necessarily mean you can't get a merchant account; after all, some credit card companies will give merchant accounts to businesses that they consider high-risk clients, just as there are loan companies that will give a loan to someone with poor credit. But it probably means you'll end up paying more for the privilege than a well-established firm would. Maybe lots more.

So what do you need to do to get established? And what are the pitfalls you have to guard against?

Choosing which acquirers to sign up with

If you think that you have a good relationship with your local bank, going into e-commerce might make you think again. Bankers are notoriously conservative. This is a good trait, of course, in people whom you need to trust with your money. But that conservative streak isn't so nice when you find out that the conservatism means that they don't get the whole e-commerce idea.

Even if your bank isn't Internet-friendly, you still have tons of other places you can turn to — although you can't get accepted directly by MasterCard or VISA. For those, you have to go through some kind of intermediary, called a *merchant account acquirer,* along the way. Acquirers just take applications and pass them on to the banks that set up the merchant accounts and do the actual transaction processing. To find out whom you can talk to about getting set up as an Internet merchant, check out these official Web sites:

- ✔ **MasterCard:** Check out `http://www.mastercard.com/cgi-bin/ acqdir/merchantReg.cgi`. Type the information about your company into the form there (see Figure 15-4), and MasterCard will take care of the rest. If you'd rather go outside the company, you can try `www. infomerchant.net/merchantaccounts/mastercard_acquirers. html` for an outside view.

- ✔ **VISA:** You can find a list of recommended companies at `http://usa. visa.com/merchants/new_acceptance/acquirer_list.html`.

- ✔ **American Express:** American Express is refreshingly simple — you apply directly to American Express. Drop in to `https://home.american express.com/homepage/merchant_ne.shtml` and go at it. If you prefer to keep everything under one roof, you can usually also sign up with American Express through the same merchant account provider you use for MasterCard and VISA. Or check out both approaches and see which method gives you the best deal.

The American Express Web site is one fine example of design. It's both functional and attractive. Anyone can learn a lot about Web design and structure from studying it.

In addition to the official Web sites, there are so many acquirers online that it'll make your head spin. Go to any good search engine and type the phrase *accept credit cards.* You should get millions of results. Even allowing for duplicate listings and bad links, that's a lot to dig through. I've pared the list down a bit for you, though. Check out Table 15-4 for some of the major acquirers.

Deciding which cards to take

So which card should you take? Or which cards? Well, the obvious answer is this: all of them. But the obvious answer isn't always the best. MasterCard and VISA for sure. They're the real biggies that almost everyone has. Beyond that, each card that you sign up for usually adds to your expenses. Most credit card firms charge you for the ability to accept the cards, even if you never process a single transaction with them. American Express doesn't. Well, actually, American Express has two plans. With the first one, you don't pay American Express any monthly fee, but you do pay the company a percentage of the take. The second plan is just the opposite — American Express doesn't get a cut, but you pay a flat fee every month. The choice is up to you.

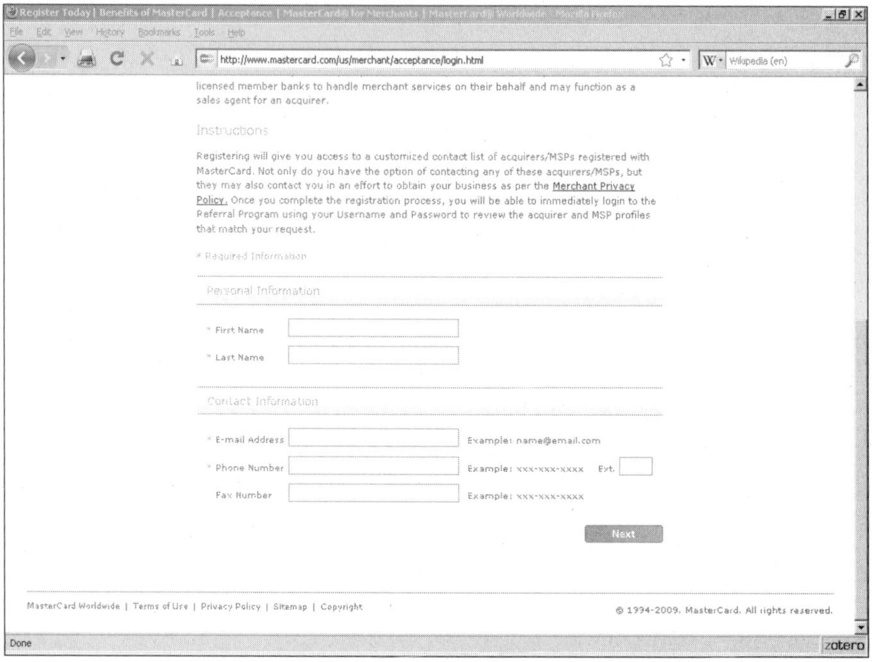

Figure 15-4:
Starting things with MasterCard.

If you're dealing with the general public, American Express is mostly useful for high-end purchases. If you're dealing with the business market, though, it's another story. Zillions of businesses have corporate American Express cards, and you can lose a significant amount of money if you can't take orders with these corporate cards, even for low-priced items. When it comes to the smaller cards, such as Discover and Diner's Club, you should probably take them only if you're a really big company that does millions of dollars in sales. It's just not worth it for a typical small business to accept Discover or Diner's Club. Fortunately, most customers who have those cards will also have VISA, MasterCard, or American Express.

Signing up

After you decide which acquirers you want to sign up with, contact them and ask for an application. From that point, the exact details vary somewhat from one company to the next — make sure that you ask each company about the process before you get involved so you'll have everything ready ahead of time — but the basic procedure goes something like this:

✔ **Fill out application forms.** Tons of sheets of them. And those forms are always too long to photocopy the whole sheet at once, so you'll have to keep turning them around and shooting them again to make a copy of the whole thing. You'll also need a magnifying glass to read some parts of the forms. These people take fine print seriously.

Most merchant-account providers now have an online application form. You fill it out and submit it online; then the provider mails a printed copy to you for your signature.

When you're getting ready to fill out the forms, don't neglect to have the information handy about where the credit card company should send the money you make — your bank name, business account number, and ABA routing code. (Ask your bank.)

Some merchant-account providers require you to open an account in a bank of their choosing. Run, don't walk, away from this kind of arrangement. It's a lot easier to handle your money if it's in your own bank.

✔ **Provide copies of your business documentation.** This may include a business license, corporate papers, or a partnership agreement, licenses to perform various services, or even copies of tax returns. Remember that merchant accounts are issued to companies, not individuals. Even if you're running a one-person shop, you have to do whatever your locality requires to be a legal business.

✔ **Estimate how many credit card orders you will process each month and how much money those orders will involve.** This is rough with a start-up business, but it's important because the merchant account provider will set a limit on how much you can submit for processing. If you end up making more than you thought, you have to ask the provider's permission to submit more orders than you signed up for. Most people deliberately overestimate the number of orders and the amount of money they expect, just to avoid this problem, but that can mean you end up paying more than you're required.

✔ **Have an on-site inspection.** That's right. Even though your business may not have a physical location and may exist only in cyberspace, you may have to put up with someone coming out to your house to look at it. These folks may even take a picture of your computer as your "place of business" for the record. This is nothing but a bit of red tape left over from the days before e-commerce.

Watching out for fees

At the top of the list of things to watch out for are fees. Merchants pay for the privilege of taking credit card orders, and the credit card companies have all sorts of little ways of sticking it to you. Here's a sampling:

✔ **Application fee:** This is pure gravy for the bank or — more likely — the sales agents, for whom it may be the main source of income. Double-check whether the application fee will be refunded if you don't get account approval — but take the answer with a grain of salt. Get it in writing. Better yet, stay away from companies that charge one. Plenty of companies out there don't charge you just for looking at your application.

✔ **Setup fee for starting the account:** Again, lots of companies will set you up for nothing. Try to avoid the ones that charge you for the simple act of becoming a customer.

✔ **Monthly statement fee:** This is a charge that the credit card companies levy on you because they have to keep track of how much money they're making from you. You'd think they'd be glad to do this for nothing, but that's not the case.

✔ **Percentage of each sale:** This is called the *discount rate*.

✔ **Transaction fee:** Yes, you're already paying a percentage. But the company still wants a few more cents.

✔ **Minimum monthly charge:** If you don't make enough sales for the credit card company's cut to meet a certain minimum amount, you have to pay the minimum amount anyway. Hey, the company isn't going to lose money just because you might. American Express has a refreshing difference — it doesn't have a monthly minimum.

✔ **Equipment charges:** If you're strictly online, you don't need any kind of equipment. Don't get suckered into buying a point-of-sale system or anything else you're not going to use.

Leaving off equipment, because it's unnecessary and wildly variable in cost, Table 15-2 shows the lowest costs typically associated with these fees. A lot of places claim to offer lower costs, but those firms must be running charities because these are the minimums that MasterCard and VISA charge Internet companies. (They do offer lower rates for more "stable" traditional bricks-and-mortar firms, however.)

Table 15-2	Low Internet Company Fees	
Fee	*Amount*	*When Paid*
Application	$0	One-time
Setup	$0	One-time
Statement	$9	Monthly
Discount rate	2.30%	Per transaction
Transaction	$0.30	Per transaction
Monthly minimum*	$20	Monthly

* If company's income from your transactions doesn't reach this amount

How do you pay all this and still make a profit? The same way every other merchant does: You raise your prices and pass the increase on to the consumer. However, a number of factors can make it hard to figure out exactly how much it costs you to accept credit cards. Sales that include the *CVV number* (the three-digit code on the signature strip on the back of the credit card) usually qualify for lower rates than sales that don't include it, for example. And if you're in a specialty business (about 30 types of businesses fit this category, including adult entertainment, credit repair, jewelry, and airlines), the rate you pay will be about double the standard rate for other types of businesses.

Some companies, of course, actually care about your business and have nice, helpful people working for them. The best way to find out whom you're dealing with — before you sign up for a merchant account with any company — is to talk to some of its current customers. You can ask the company for references, but its employees will likely steer you only to people they know will say nice things about the company. Think about the references on your résumé. You don't include the boss who thought you were a turkey or the coworker who always tried to take the credit for your work, do you? The credit card companies don't want to send you to the people who are mad at them either.

Well, it's kind of hard to track down the clients of a company without asking someone at the company, so why not do it the other way around? Every Web site that takes credit cards has to be doing business with an acquirer. And almost all sites have an e-mail link to the Webmaster. Just surf the Web and keep leaving messages. "Who do you use? How do you like them? Have you had any problems with them?" (That kind of thing.) Pretty soon, you'll start to build up a consensus about which companies are currently the best to do business with.

Protecting against credit card fraud

The worst problem is credit card fraud. So what happens if you get a bad order? The answer's simple — you don't get paid. It's called a *chargeback* — the folks who handle your account issue a debit instead of a credit, and the amount of the bad charge is deducted from your business bank account. The same thing happens if a customer complains to the credit card company, saying that you didn't fulfill your duties (say, if the customer never received the order or the product didn't work). And if you get too many chargebacks, you can lose your merchant account. Worse, you can get charged big-time fees. That's right — more fees. Not only do you lose the money from the sale, but also if more than 1 percent of your sales in one month come back as chargebacks, the credit card companies jack up your discount rate, which means your profit on future sales shrinks.

Even if you successfully dispute the chargeback, you still have to pay a processing fee to cover the credit card company's expenses in falsely accusing you. Then comes the ultimate "insult to injury" stunt: If you keep getting lots of chargebacks, the company charges you to review your account. And that review can run into many thousands of dollars — MasterCard chargeback fees can even go up to $100,000 in a single month for repeat offenders. Not many Internet companies can afford that kind of expense.

The problem here is that Internet companies — like those that specialize in mail order or telephone orders — have no way of ever seeing the credit card or the person who uses it. Normal fraud-prevention wisdom (such as watching to see whether the credit card comes out of a wallet or a pocket) can't work. Nor, except in rare cases where people mail in Web pages they printed out, can Internet companies get a signature on an order form. All the company can do is accept a credit card number. There's no way to prove who provided that number. That's the nature of the Net. No doubt this will be resolved in some manner someday, but for now, that's the way it is. Credit card companies have a phrase for this: *high risk.* That's right: MasterCard and VISA consider every company on the Internet to be a high risk. Well . . . not every company. If you're successful enough to make zillions of dollars, they pretend that you're not in the same boat as everyone else on the Net, even though nothing but the amount of profit is any different. Short of that, though, they've got the entire e-commerce world in their sights.

Make sure that the software you're using to process credit cards has an antifraud feature called *address verification.* Because the credit card's issuer knows where it sends the bill, the address on the order can be checked against the issuer's records. If the address isn't the same, you may not want to fulfill that order. Some companies, such as florists and fruit shippers, pretty well have to handle such orders because many of their products get ordered by one person to be sent to another person at another address. If you decide to take a risk like that, at least have two address areas on your form. One should be for the address to ship to, and the other one should be for the purchaser's home address if it's different from the address the item's being shipped to. It's not perfect protection, but it's a step in the right direction. And always make sure to require a signature for delivery. That way you can prove the item reached the right address — assuming you ship a physical product, anyway.

Building on a Business Platform

If building your whole business from scratch while designing a Web site to boot seems like a big task, you might want to consider using an existing business platform to build on. There are malls online just as there are in suburbia, and they provide you with a ready stream of traffic — the same reason stores cluster in malls in the real world. Many online malls also provide merchant-account services (such as Yahoo! Merchant Solutions from Yahoo! Stores, as shown in Figure 15-5). And most of the virtual and dedicated server providers (see Chapter 5) have some sort of shopping-cart software available as well. If you're looking for an all-in-one solution to your e-commerce needs, you should check out some of the sites in Table 15-3.

Table 15-3	Online Malls and Shopping Carts
Mall	*Web Address*
Americart Shopping Cart Service	`www.americart.com`
Clockwatchers	`www.clockwatchers.com/ shopping.html`
Code9 Software	`http://www.code9software.com/ fastecart-shopping-cart.html`
Coreave	`www.coreave.com`
Electronic Merchant Systems	`www.emscorporate.com`
StoreFront	`www.storefront.net`
Verio	`http://www.verio.com/products/ web-hosting/`
Yahoo! Merchant Services	`http://smallbusiness.yahoo. com/merchant`

Figure 15-5: Yahoo! Merchant Solutions presents a complete selection of options for e-commerce.

Many of the malls offer complete e-commerce solutions — Web sites, merchant services, integrated shopping carts, and so on — and have some pretty sophisticated antifraud capabilities. In fact, they may be better options for many small companies than going the traditional route.

Converting Currencies

Whatever you're up to with e-commerce, your audience is global. Even if that's not your intent, you're going to have potential customers who aren't necessarily familiar with the current value of the U.S. dollar. Is there a solution? Oh, yeah. A really good one.

The Universal Currency Converter (UCC) from XE.com is a must-have for any commercial site that expects to handle international business. Like most free services, it has a banner ad built into it, but you can negotiate with XE.com to remove it for a fee. The converter lets anyone convert any amount in any currency to the equivalent amount in any other currency.

The basic module has only the major world currencies in it. Don't sweat it, though; if you need to include others, it doesn't cost you anything. This limitation is only for practical reasons. After all, nearly every transaction takes place in one of the top currencies, and the more options you add, the slower things get. Really, how often do you need to figure out how many Seborga luiginos are equal to 800 Uzbekistan soms?

Adding the converter to your Web page

To add the converter to your Web page, follow these steps:

1. **Go to** www.xe.net/ucc/customize.php.

2. **Read through the terms of use.**

3. **Fill out the required form with your URL and contact information.**

   Notice that the URL must be the address of the Web page on which you will actually put the converter, not just the general URL of your domain.

4. **Click the Go! button.**

   You need to register each page you use the converter on.

5. **On the resulting page, click the Fast Track Instructions button.**

   Now, you're back on the earlier page, right below the form you filled out. Yes, it's a roundabout way to get there, but the registration process is legally required if you want to use the converter.

From here, you have two options. Both of them work fine, so it's just a matter of how you like to do things.

6. **Use one of the following methods to get the code for the converter:**

    • Download the compressed file for either Windows or Mac. You then need to unzip it and load the resulting HTML page into an editor before you can use the code.

    • Click the Click Here to See the Raw HTML link and just copy the code off your browser screen.

If you download the file, you see that the enclosed Web page, `samp-ucc.htm`, has none of the usual elements you're used to — HTML, HEAD, and BODY. Yet it will still load into any browser and will work just fine. That's because, as useful as those elements are for envisioning the structure of your Web page, they're not technically required under the HTML standard. I'm not recommending that you leave them out of your pages, and I'm sure that XE.com did it just because the purpose of that page is only to hold the code for you to copy and paste. But it's a decent bit of tech trivia you can use to amaze and amuse your friends.

7. **Whichever way you get your hands on the code, paste it into your Web page and save the file.**

8. **Upload the page to your Web server and try it out.**

    Figure 15-6 shows the converter on a Web page.

Figure 15-6: The UCC enables your visitors to convert an amount in one currency to the equivalent amount in another.

Customizing the converter

Now, this is one fine service as is. But you can customize it, too. XE.com will change practically anything about the currency converter for a fee, but the company has also built plenty of options into it that you can use on your own.

Changing the default currencies

If you know the country from which most of your foreign customers come, you may want to set the converter so it's ready to convert from your customers' currency to yours right away. Say, for example, that you're in the United States and you know that almost every one of your overseas customers is from the United Kingdom. You'd probably do well to set the conversion to default values of dollars to pounds in that case. This won't prevent anyone from another country from using the converter in the normal way. All it does is set which currencies are selected at the start; visitors can still choose other currencies if they want.

This is what you need to do to set the default currencies in the converter:

1. **Go into the HTML source code and find the** SELECT **elements.**

   The one whose name attribute has a value of From is — you guessed it — the currency to convert from. The one whose name attribute has a value of To is the currency to convert to.

   One of the OPTION elements in each has the selected attribute. In the original version, the default From currency is the euro, and the default To currency is the U.S. dollar.

2. **To change the default, just delete the word** selected **from the** OPTION **elements for the current currency and add it to the ones you want to use.**

   Simple, ain't it?

Setting the default amount

Now, what if you have only one product, or what if all your products are the same price? For example, suppose you have a price of USD $49.95 that most people will want to convert to some other currency. Having already set the From currency to U.S. dollars, you can now set the default amount to 49.95. This default makes it really easy on your customers — all they have to do is pick their native currency, and they're off and running. To set the default amount, look for the following code line near the beginning of the form:

```
<INPUT type="text" name="Amount" value="1" SIZE=10><BR>
```

Just change the value of the value attribute. To set it to 49.95, change the code to this:

```
<INPUT type="text" name="Amount" value="49.95"
        SIZE=10><BR>
```

Users can still change the default value to anything they want by simply typing over it, just as they can select different currencies by selecting something other than the default selections.

If you want to change the order of the currency choices from alphabetical to some other method — such as placing the most likely currencies on the top of the list — all you have to do is to cut and paste the OPTION elements that reflect the currency values in the listings. Remove them from their current positions and paste them into their new positions. That's all there is to it.

If, for some reason, you don't want to give your users any choice in these things, UCC accommodates your wishes through the use of hidden variables. To do this, you add some INPUT type="hidden" elements right after the <FORM> tag and just before the <TABLE> tag.

To set the From currency so it can't be changed, use the following code:

```
<INPUT type="hidden" name="From" value="xyz">
```

Replace the placeholder xyz with the three-digit code for the currency — such as USD for U.S. dollars or GBP for United Kingdom (or Great Britain) pounds.

To set the To currency, you do the same thing, but the line reads as follows:

```
<INPUT type="hidden" name="To" value="xyz">
```

To set the value so it can't be altered (which prevents people from using your version of the UCC for test purposes unrelated to your site), add the following line of code:

```
<INPUT type="hidden" name="Amount" value="xyz">
```

Replace the placeholder xyz with the amount to be converted (for example, 49.95).

Adding and deleting currencies

If you want to add more currencies, check out the Full Universal Currency Converter at www.xe.net/ucc/full.shtml and copy and paste the appropriate currency to your version. Just add a new OPTION element under the To and/or From SELECT element for each new currency.

If you want to delete currencies from the listings, you need to delete the entire line for that currency, beginning with the <OPTION> tag and ending with the </OPTION> tag.

Customizing the results page

If you want to customize the default results page that appears after a currency conversion calculation, as shown in Figure 15-7, you need to go a bit deeper. Customizing the results page requires creating not only an element or an attribute, but also a *header* and a *footer*. The header contains HTML that specifies what is displayed before the calculation results appear, and the code in the footer goes in after them.

Figure 15-7:
The UCC
results
page.

To set up the header and footer, think about your HTML code ahead of time, as well as consider the variations that the UCC demands of you. The header has to go right after the line with the <FORM> tag and has to include the [HTML], [HEAD], [/HEAD], and [BODY] tags. Notice anything weird about these? Yeah, the brackets aren't the regular angle braces; they're regular brackets. This way, a Web browser that reads this code won't get confused by encountering two identical tags such as <HTML> in the same page. You put these odd-looking quasi-HTML elements in as values of a hidden INPUT element, and the UCC software reinterprets the square brackets just as though they were angle braces when it comes time to create the results page.

So if you wanted to put in the following regular HTML code as your header . . .

```
<HTML>
<HEAD>
<TITLE>
This is a currency converter.
</TITLE>
</HEAD>
<BODY>
```

. . . you'd add it to the line in the currency converter code, like this:

```
<INPUT type="hidden" name="Header" value="[HTML][HEAD]
        [TITLE]This is a currency converter.[/TITLE][/
        HEAD][BODY]">
```

Then comes the regular output of the converter. After that comes the footer. If you wanted to add the following HTML code to it . . .

```
<B>Thanks for using the converter!</B>
</BODY>
</HTML>
```

. . . you'd do it like this:

```
<INPUT type="hidden" name="Footer" value="[B]Thanks for
            using the converter![/B][/BODY]">
```

The Shopper's Currency Converter (www.xe.net/ecc/shoppers) provides the same functionality as the UCC.

Online Sources for Merchant Services

Table 15-4 lists some places on the World Wide Web where you can find more information on the topics covered in this chapter.

Table 15-4	Online Resources for Merchant Services
Web Site Name	**Web Address**
AIS Media	www.aismerchantservices.com
AMS Merchant Account Services	www.merchant-accounts.com
ClickBank	www.clickbank.com
ePayment Solutions	www.epaymentsolutions.com
Instant Check	www.easydesksoftware.com/check.htm
Merchant Systems	www.merchant-systems.com
MerchantAccount.com	www.merchantaccount.com
Network Solutions Merchant Accounts	http://merchantaccounts.networksolutions.com
Paymentech	www.paymentech.com
Skipjack Financial Services	www.skipjack.com
Total Merchant Services	www.totalmerchantservices.com

Part V
The Part of Tens

The 5th Wave — By Rich Tennant

"What do you mean you're updating our Web page?"

In this part . . .

Well, it just wouldn't be a *For Dummies* book without the Part of Tens. Chapter 16 shows you where to go when you need to find answers to everything from business and legal issues to grammar questions. Chapter 17 is a guide to some of the best things an e-commerce site can add. And Chapter 18 is a potpourri of ten more great add-ins.

Chapter 16

Ten Great Web Sites to Get Advice

⋯⋯⋯⋯⋯⋯⋯⋯⋯⋯⋯⋯⋯⋯⋯⋯⋯⋯⋯⋯⋯⋯⋯⋯⋯

*W*e all need advice from time to time. Even if you're terribly independent, as nearly self-sufficient as can be, there are times when you need to turn to others for assistance. Well, here are ten Web sites where you can go if you feel the need to ask for help. Each site has its own special feel and particular set of standards. But somewhere in this chapter, you're gonna find a few places that you'll be so happy to know about that you'll just burst with joy.

Bizy Moms

Despite its name, Bizy Moms appeals to both the mother and the father who want to work from home while raising a family. The site hosts live chats on issues such as "The Internet, Money, and You" or "Business on a Shoestring." Bizy Moms is the best place to go if you want to know about free postage, Internet marketing, or just about anything else of interest to the work-at-home parent.

Toss in the advice on time management and paperwork control from those who've been there, and you're just beginning to explore this site.

The Bizy Moms site (`www.bizymoms.com`) is shown in Figure 16-1.

Figure 16-1:
Bizy Moms
is a fabulous
resource for
the work-
at-home
crowd.

Cozahost Newsletter

The Cozahost newsletter is an e-commerce e-zine with a difference: It's actually worth reading, packed full of useful information written by people who know what they're talking about. Granted, it doesn't have as many neat links as are packed into this book, but against competition like that, who stands a chance? (For the humor-impaired, that's a joke — consider yourself officially notified.)

Seriously, folks, the links in the Cozahost newsletter, although fewer than you find on some sites that have a lot less to offer, are premium. It's worth your time to follow them. If they're internal links, they lead to good articles on Web work; if they're external, they lead to decent tools that you should consider adding to your own repertoire.

You can check out the Cozahost newsletter, shown in Figure 16-2, at www. cozahost.com/news.

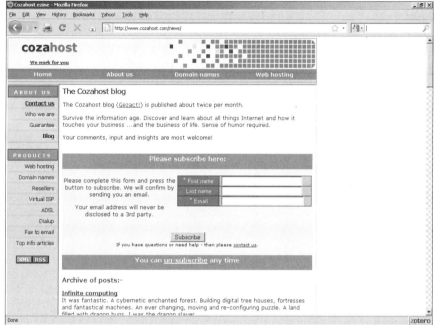

Figure 16-2:
The
Cozahost
newsletter
is a great
e-commerce
e-zine.

Geek/Talk Forums for Webmasters

Ah, fellow geeks! Geek/Talk is the place where you can let it all hang out. The Geek/Talk bulletin board (see Figure 16-3) is for those of us who just *love* technical stuff, who absolutely live for the last bit that we can squeeze out of HTML, who . . . well, you get the idea. Actually, you're welcome to pop in and ask the simplest questions in the world. Even if you don't know the first thing about HTML, this site is the place to ask your dumbest questions and expect a civil answer.

This wonderland is a great place to visit. Here you'll find folks who are interested in all the same things you are, from Web design to e-commerce. And you can find a different BBS (bulletin-board service) for just about any topic you want to discuss.

The Geek/Talk Forums site (www.geekvillage.com/forums) is shown in Figure 16-3.

Figure 16-3:
The Geek/
Talk
Webmaster
forums.

grammarNOW!

Do your participles dangle embarrassingly? Are your diphthongs out of style? If you ever stay awake wondering about these mighty questions, grammarNOW! is your kind of site. This site is one place where you can get free answers to those embarrassing questions with complete confidentiality. The folks who run this site e-mail you an answer without showing the world that you don't know what to do about the ablative absolute.

If you're really out on a limb, you'll be happy to know that not only can you get a quick answer for free, but you can actually hire the brains behind this site to go over your Web site with a fine-toothed comb and clear up any grammatical problems on it. And the site's list of grammar links is well worth exploring on its own.

Figure 16-4 shows the grammarNOW! site (www.grammarnow.com).

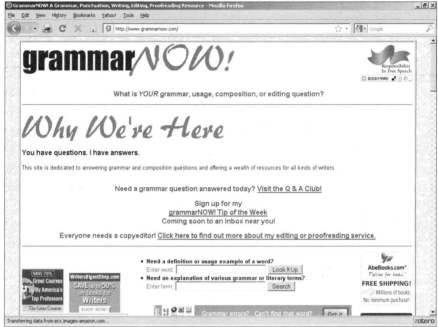

Figure 16-4:
At grammar NOW! you can get answers to your grammatical questions.

LivePerson

LivePerson is a great place to get answers on a wide variety of topics, ranging from businesses to computers. It's also a great source of information on lots of things that Web people need to know. Interested in starting a home-based business? Want to know about tax liabilities? Or about e-commerce or Web design? Ask LivePerson.

LivePerson has the people who know all the answers, and they'll get back to you quickly with good, solid information.

The LivePerson site (www.liveperson.com/) is shown in Figure 16-5.

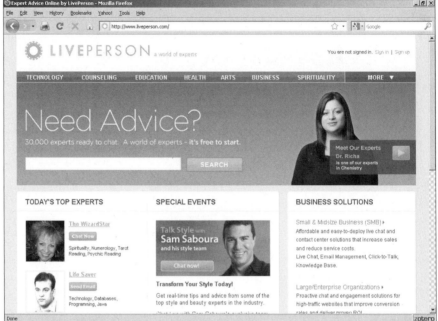

LawGuru.com

LawGuru.com is a nice source for legal research. At this site, you can check out everything from the latest U.S. Code revisions to that money you forgot you were owed.

This site has a huge database of legal questions and answers — and if you can't find what you're looking for in it, you can submit your own questions to the LawGuru folks. They've also got chat rooms for both attorneys and normal people, as well as a no-nonsense FAQ (Frequently Asked Questions) page about copyright.

Figure 16-6 shows the LawGuru.com site (`www.lawguru.com`).

Figure 16-6:
LawGuru.
com is a
great legal
resource.

webmaster-talk.com

If you're interested in Web design, webmaster-talk.com is just what it sounds like — a meeting place for people who run Web sites. This site is a pretty nice place to stop in and absorb all kinds of Web savvy. It even has its own Webmaster forums, including Web site critiques and discussions about topics such as e-commerce and Web-site programming techniques.

You can find articles on e-commerce, marketing, and Web design, just to name a few of the features of this premier site.

The webmaster-talk.com site (www.webmaster-talk.com/) is shown in Figure 16-7.

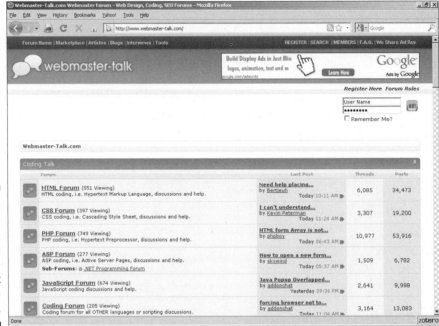

Figure 16-7:
Tips on
everything
about Web
develop-
ment live at
webmaster-
talk.com.

The Small Business Advisor

The Small Business Advisor is one handy little resource for those of you who are thinking about opening your own business. This site covers everything from taxes to insurance and has business news that actually makes sense to small business people (and tall ones, too). Its free e-mail newsletter is a prime source of savvy advice, useful information, and links that you'll want to click.

The site's various checklists alone are worth the visit — they cover everything from choosing a business partner or a bank to working with an attorney. Lists of business-oriented newsgroups, Internet-specific business commentary, and state-specific contact information are just a few of the tidbits that this site offers.

The Small Business Advisor site (www.isquare.com) is shown in Figure 16-8.

Figure 16-8:
The Small
Business
Advisor
has tons of
information
for commer-
cial Web
sites.

Web Developer's Journal

What is there to say about a site that's just chock-full of so many goodies? The Web Developer's Journal lives up to its name, providing tons of material on every aspect of life — at least as far as it affects the Web. Really. Everything from setting up forms to animation.

Figure 16-9 shows the Web Developer's Journal site (`www.webdevelopers journal.com`).

Website Tips

If you're looking for one place to find information on everything from accessibility to XML, it's hard to beat Website Tips. You're talking several thousand listings here: handheld wireless devices, JavaScript, e-commerce, legal considerations — all calculated to increase your Web-design IQ.

The Website Tips site (`www.websitetips.com`) is shown in Figure 16-10.

Figure 16-9:
Web
Developer's
Journal
is a great
source of
information.

Figure 16-10:
Website
Tips offers
great advice
on Internet
design and
more than
2,000 worth-
while links
to explore.

Chapter 17

Ten Fabulous Tools for E-Commerce

· ·

*Y*ou simply must try this blend of programs, add-ins, and services if you're into e-commerce. Even if you're not, some of the items in this chapter, such as HumanClick, MapQuest, or the Direct Marketing Association's Privacy Policy Generator, may come in handy. Some of these items are freebies, some cost serious money, and others offer a combination in which you can get a lesser version at no charge.

CafePress.com

Got some great ideas for T-shirts, coffee mugs, or mouse pads? If you don't want to spend lots of money for bulky and dangerous equipment, drop in to CafePress.com. It's not just another place that'll iron an image onto a mouse pad for a fee. It's a whole e-commerce setup that costs you nothing.

You can set up a store at the site with no investment except your image files. Just upload those files to CafePress.com, and it takes care of everything. Not only does it do the manufacturing and shipping for you, but you don't even have to get a credit card merchant account; it'll process your credit card orders, too.

The CafePress.com site (`www.cafepress.com`) is shown in Figure 17-1.

Figure 17-1: CafePress.com makes it easy to get into the art business.

DMA Privacy Policy Generator

The Direct Marketing Association (DMA) assists you in creating a privacy statement with its free DMA Privacy Policy Generator, a simple, easy-to-use online form. By filling out the form and selecting the check boxes that apply to your company's situation, you provide the basic material for your privacy statement. When you finish, you can have the completed statement e-mailed to you as plain text or as a ready-to-use Web page that you can drop into your site.

The DMA site is shown in Figure 17-2. The DMA Privacy Policy Generator site (www.dmaresponsibility.org/PPG/) is shown in Figure 17-3.

Figure 17-2:
The Direct Marketing Association site.

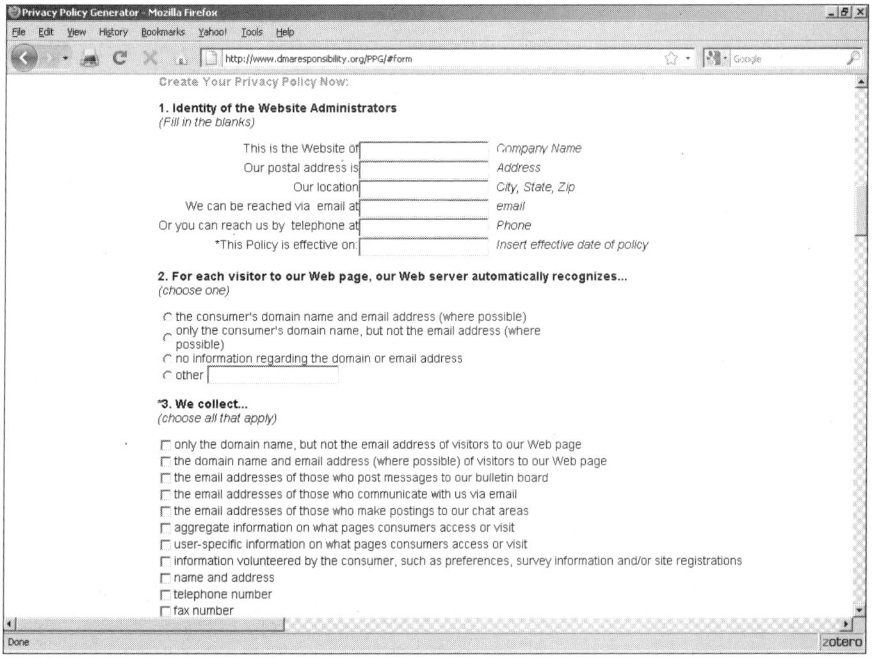

Figure 17-3:
The DMA Privacy Policy Generator helps you develop a privacy statement for your Web site.

ECommerce Guide

The ECommerce Guide is an e-zine that's a truly valuable resource for anyone involved in e-commerce. It's got reviews of online store software, the latest news for e-sales, and some really, really good columns. If you're not checking out this site, you're missing out on a lot of useful information.

Figure 17-4 shows the ECommerce Guide site (`www.ecommerce-guide.com`).

HumanClick

HumanClick is a fantastic way to add a human touch to your Web site. It's a service that enables you to respond instantly to your customers' needs. Imagine: You're looking at a page on someone's site, and you have some questions about the products you see. An icon there reads Click for a Real Person. You do so, and you go into a chat with someone who can answer your questions. Pretty nice, eh? Yep, this one's a must-have. Drop everything and go to this Web site. Click the Free Trial link and think about how nice having this feature on your site would be.

This service is definitely something you want on your Web site — and you don't even need to keep your people available 24 hours a day to use it. During the times that nobody's around to answer questions, you just tell the HumanClick client program on your computer that you're unavailable, and the icon on your site changes to read Leave a Message.

As if all that's not enough, the service places no burden on your customers because HumanClick is JavaScript that's embedded in your pages. It works with every major Web browser, and your visitors don't need to download anything to make it work.

The HumanClick site (`www.humanclick.com`) is shown in Figure 17-5.

MapQuest

The MapQuest site at `www.mapquest.com` (shown in Figure 17-6) is well known for helping you find your way, but MapQuest is also a fabulous place to get maps for your site. No kidding — maps. But not just plain old road maps. These beauties are customized maps that you can create for helping people find your location, for example, or showing them how to get from the hotel to a tourist attraction.

Figure 17-4:
The
ECommerce
Guide
provides
useful
information
about
e-sales,
online store
software,
and so on.

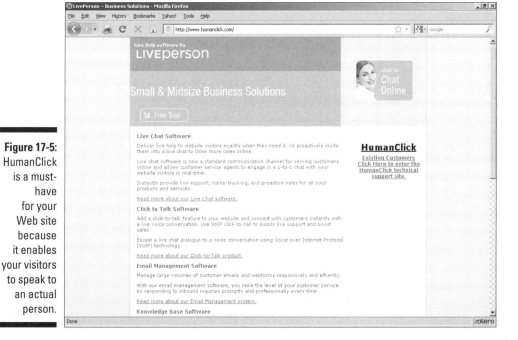

Figure 17-5:
HumanClick
is a must-
have
for your
Web site
because
it enables
your visitors
to speak to
an actual
person.

Figure 17-6:
MapQuest's
main page
is used by
zillions of
people.

Although MapQuest charges for plenty of things on its site, it also offers a free service that you may want to take a look at: LinkFree. LinkFree links your site to the main MapQuest site so that your users can take advantage of its cartography services.

To access the MapQuest free services page, shown in Figure 17-7, go to `http://www.mapquest.com/features/lf_main`.

osCommerce

osCommerce has a deal that's hard to refuse — you can download its osCommerce software for zero dollars with no limits, no time constraints, no nothing. Using this package is a worthwhile way to get your store up and running. It handles everything from creating product pages to managing shipping and just about anything that you can imagine in between. It's easy to use, too.

It's open-source software, which means that not only is it free, but you also get to play with the source code and change it to suit yourself. Ah, yes, that's the catch. If you're not a PHP programmer or don't have one on staff, you may get in a bit over your head with this software; if you are, or do, however, you can download this software.

Figure 17-8 shows the osCommerce site (`www.oscommerce.com`).

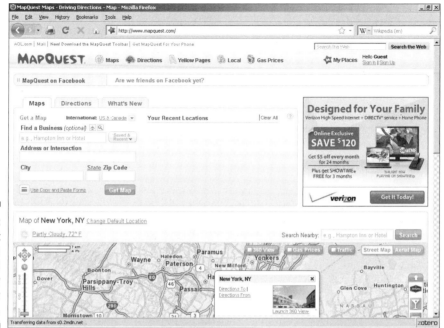

Figure 17-7:
MapQuest
gives you
professional
cartography
services for
free.

Figure 17-8:
osCom-
merce
software
makes it
easy to
manage
an e-com-
merce site.

S&H greenpoints

Ah, remember how you used to collect S&H Green Stamps? Okay, ask your parents about it. Or maybe your grandparents. At any rate, someone you know will remember. It used to be that you'd go to the grocery, fill your cart, and pay for your purchases. Then, along with your change, you'd get a certain number of stamps from the cashier, depending on how much money you'd just spent. You'd toss the stamps in the grocery bag along with your receipt and trot on home. You'd put the stamps in a kitchen drawer until you had so many that you couldn't open the drawer any more without stamps spilling out all over the floor.

When things reached that stage, you'd have to face the odious task of licking all the stamps and pasting them into the books that you also picked up at the grocery. When you had a whole bunch of books filled, you'd sit down with the S&H catalog and go on a shopping spree. Now the Internet is reviving this grand old piece of Americana. But this time around, you don't have to lick all those stamps! Now, it's S&H greenpoints, a new form of digital reward — kind of like the Web equivalent of frequent-flyer miles.

I have a major hunch that this arrangement is going to work out well for both online shoppers and e-merchants. If you're into any kind of e-commerce, look into this site.

The S&H greenpoints site (www.greenpoints.com) is shown in Figure 17-9.

SYSTRAN Translation Software

One of the hottest sites on the Web is AltaVista's Babel Fish translation page. It works with SYSTRAN translation software, and you can go right to the source and set up your very own translation system. Anyone who's serious about e-commerce must deal with the fact that the World Wide Web is just that — a global setup. Your storefront is an international business, and although English is widely spoken, it's hardly the only language in the world.

With SYSTRAN translation software working on your site, visitors quickly translate your pages among more than half a dozen major Western languages: Dutch, English, French, German, Greek, Italian, Portuguese, and Spanish. And SYSTRAN doesn't stop there. The service also includes Chinese, Japanese, Korean, and Russian. So hurry up already and pop into SYSTRAN's Web site. The whole world is waiting. Run — don't walk — to SYSTRAN's site.

Figure 17-10 shows the SYSTRAN Translation Software site (www.systran soft.com).

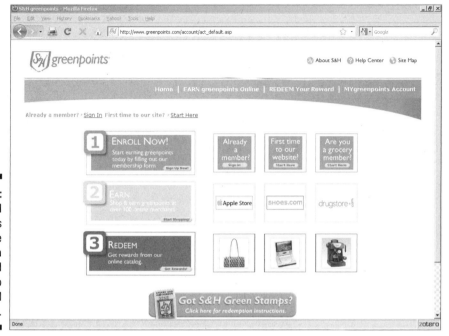

Figure 17-9:
The S&H greenpoints home page brings a grand old tradition to new digital life.

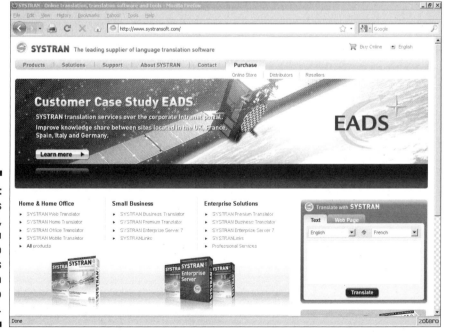

Figure 17-10:
SYSTRAN's home page, where you can sign up to add its translation service to your site.

TRUSTe

Using this site is kind of an open question. What question is that? Well, whether it's worth the price to your organization to pay hundreds or even thousands of dollars to an outside group to certify that your privacy policy means what it says. To solidly quantify how much a trustmark such as the TRUSTe seal means in terms of extra sales is impossible, just as it is with things such as Chamber of Commerce or Better Business Bureau logos in a store window. Nonetheless, major outfits from MSN to eBay have jumped onto the TRUSTe bandwagon.

If you collect any kind of potentially embarrassing personal information, such as criminal records or health status, getting TRUSTe certification is probably worth the cost. Without it, people may be reluctant to provide honest answers to such questions. Still, unless you're in the employment or insurance business (or something similar), you're not likely to gather any kind of information other than names, addresses, phone numbers, credit card numbers, and so on.

Visit the TRUSTe site and read over all the materials there to decide for yourself whether its service is right for your situation. You also find valuable advice there on creating a privacy statement.

The TRUSTe site (www.truste.com) is shown in Figure 17-11.

WorldPay

When it comes to finding a financial partner for an online business, you can't do much better than WorldPay. Unlike so many banks, the WorldPay folks "get it" — the Internet, that is. They truly understand that a Web business is a global business.

Let's face it — how many merchant account providers are comfortable dealing with payments via both American Express and Lastschriften? How many of them can help you comprehend payments in dollars and euros and yen? WorldPay also supports deferred payments, allowing you to let your customers spread their buying power over time.

On top of this, the WorldPay folks are happy to work with companies large and small, and they have a refreshingly simple application process for merchant accounts. So what are you waiting for?

The WorldPay site (www.rbsworldpay.com/) is shown in Figure 17-12.

Figure 17-11:
TRUSTe
provides
Web sites
with privacy
policy
certification.

Figure 17-12:
WorldPay is
geared for
e-commerce.

Chapter 18

Ten More Great Add-Ins

*W*ell, you just know that every book has to have a final chapter. I'd like to keep on going forever, but I can't, so I'm using these last few pages to point you toward some more great Web site add-ins and services.

@watch

If you have deep pockets and need a detailed analysis of your Web server's downtimes and uptimes, you may want to take a look at @watch.

@watch offers three program levels: @watch Advanced ($14.99 and up per month), @watch Pro ($29.99 and up per month), and @watch Enterprise ($39.99 and up per month). Prices decrease if you sign up for a year at a time, and you get volume discounts for multiple URLs.

The @watch site (www.atwatch.com) is shown in Figure 18-1.

Crossword Compiler

If you want to add a crossword puzzle as a feature on your Web page, you need the right software — a program that understands what a Web designer wants, not just what someone with a pencil and paper does. Crossword Compiler is such a program. You'll be thrilled about how easy it is to use and the utility of its Java-enabled Web page connection. Prices range from $49 for a single-user license all the way up to $1,900 for a multiuser package with all the bells and whistles.

Figure 18-2 shows the Crossword Compiler site (www.crossword-compiler.com).

Figure 18-1:
@watch generates reports on your server's availability.

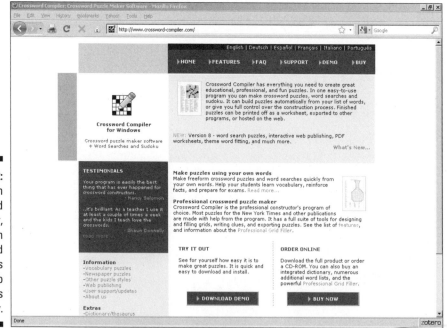

Figure 18-2:
With Crossword Compiler, you can create and add puzzles to your Web pages easily.

Everyone.net

You would like to offer your visitors an e-mail service, but you don't have much in the way of mailboxes available. You may have a handful that came along with your Web service, but they won't stretch very far. So you turn to Everyone.net to save the day with their free service.

Just fill out a simple application and then eagerly count the hours until the e-mail message with all the details arrives. In it, you will discover the wondrous secrets of giving your users free 25MB mailboxes (not bad). Set your course for `http://www.everyone.net/private-label-email/offer-free-email.html`.

The Everyone.net site (`www.everyone.net`) is shown in Figure 18-3.

GeoPhrase

It is *so* nice when you run across some people who really understand what the Internet is. And the first thing it is, is global. The visitor logging on to your home page right now could be sitting anywhere from Tulsa, Oklahoma, to Tokyo, Japan. It makes no difference to your Web server, but it probably makes a difference to the visitor.

That's where GeoPhrase, a technology from Geobytes, comes in. It checks where your visitors come from and, depending on their location, offers a different greeting to them. And all you have to do is paste some HTML code into your Web page.

And that's just the beginning. You can customize the whole shebang, and GeoPhase will even help you do it. Oh, did I mention that all this is free? Fire up your Web browser and check it out!.

The GeoPhrase site (`www.geobytes.com/GeoPhrase.htm`) is shown in Figure 18-4.

Figure 18-3:
Everyone.
net adds
regular mail
service to
your site.

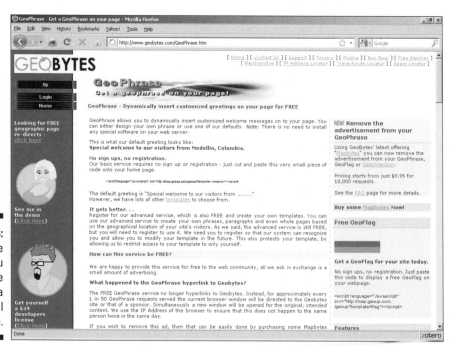

Figure 18-4:
GeoPhrase
lets you
personalize
things for a
global
audience.

VFM Leonardo

VFM Leonardo is a must for anyone in the travel industry. But even if your site isn't travel-oriented — if you just need some great content about tourist destinations around the world — you must see this site. It's like going on a shopping spree in a chocolate boutique.

One person's vacation spot is another person's banking center or technology Mecca . . . or whatever.

These folks provide photos, recordings, video, and just about anything else you can imagine. Drop in, sign up, and take a look around at the stuff shown in Figure 18-5.

localendar

This calendar is one of the best add-ons you can have on your site — period. Aside from the fact that it's something you're likely to want to use yourself, localendar is an incredible facility to offer your Web site visitors. You don't even have to put up with hosting some banners on your calendar site — just the little localendar link icon. And all for free!

You can set up localendar in a variety of displays such as a daily, weekly, or monthly format, and you can set it up to blend in well with your site's layout.

The localendar site (www.localendar.com) is shown in Figure 18-6.

Merriam-Webster Online

As you probably expect, Merriam-Webster offers dictionary and thesaurus services, and you just know from the nature of this book that you can latch onto those services for your own site, right? You can just go to the Merriam-Webster site and fill out a simple form. Then you choose from among a selection of search boxes and paste the code into your Web page. What could be simpler? Check it out at www.merriamwebster.com/searchbox/index.htm. (See Figure 18-7.)

Figure 18-5:
You can get images, sounds, and so on of everything from cruise lines to car rentals at VFM Leonardo.

Figure 18-6:
localendar puts a calendar on your site.

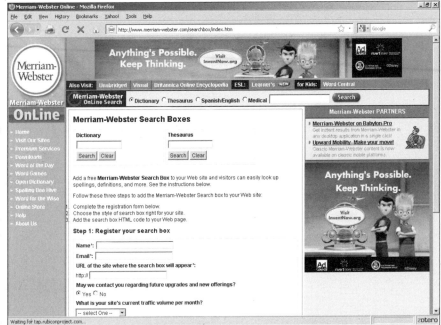

SuperStats

If you want nothing more than a simple, visual page counter — or if you just gotta have the most detailed reports of page hits possible — what do you do? You head for the same place: SuperStats. It's part of Network Solutions, a name that will be instantly familiar to you as the big-name domain registrar.

These folks know just about everything there is to know about Web sites, and they're a good thing to have on your side. They've got a variety of plans that cover the needs of Web sites both large and small.

The SuperStats site (`http://counter.superstats.com`) is shown in Figure 18-8.

Figure 18-8:
SuperStats
is Network
Solutions'
Web-traffic
monitoring
service.

Google Friend Connect

If you envy social networking sites like Facebook but thought you had to hire a whole team of programmers to set one up, then you're going to love what Google has done.

Just head to `www.google.com/friendconnect/home/overview` and click the Setup a New Site link. If you don't already have a Google account (such as Gmail), you'll need to sign up (it's free and easy — just fill out a simple form). When that's done, just copy and paste the provided code into your own Web page and you'll be up and running in minutes!

If you're tech-minded and want to expand on the basic offerings, Google offers an API (application programming interface) that lets you do just about whatever you want. Check it out at `http://code.google.com/apis/friendconnect/`.

This marvelous new service from the folks at Google (`http://www.google.com/friendconnect/`) is shown in Figure 18-9.

Figure 18-9:
Google
Friend
Connect
lets you
add social
networking
to your Web
site.

theFinancials.com

theFinancials.com is one of the most incredible sites for economic content that you can find anywhere. I kid you not, if you want to know something financial — or, more important, you want your site visitors to know it — then drop everything and head on over!

You'll find Pacific Rim market reports, tickers, crude oil prices, mortgage rates . . . you name it. Just click the link for the report you want and then click the Send Me the Code for This link.

Figure 18-10 shows theFinacials.com site's main page for free content (`www.thefinancials.com/mfr_free.html`).

Figure 18-10: theFinancials.com offers a bewildering array of free reports for your Web site.

Glossary

· ·

aardvark: A type of anteater — its name means "earth pig."

above the fold: The material at the top portion of the Web page that shows when it first loads into the browser. See also *below the fold*.

acceptable use policy: A policy that sets forth the type of user behavior that is accepted by the management of a Web site.

acquirer: See *merchant account*.

Acrobat: See *Portable Document Format (PDF)*.

active link: See *link*.

Active Server Page (ASP): A Web page created with HTML and either VBScript or JScript (Microsoft's name for JavaScript) or both. Commands on Active Server Pages are processed via the ActiveX engine. See also *HTML, VBScript, JavaScript,* and *ActiveX.*

ActiveX: A system developed by Microsoft to enable a Web page utilizing ActiveX controls to interface with the Windows operating system.

Address Verification System (AVS): An antifraud feature for credit card transactions in which the address of the credit card holder is compared to the address on an order form. If the two addresses aren't the same, the probability of fraud is higher.

AJAX: Short for Asynchronous JavaScript and XML, a version of DHTML (Dynamic HTML).

alt text: Text that is shown in place of a figure when the figure cannot be displayed.

anonymizer: A Web server that strips identifying information from a visitor's Web browser, thus preventing any Web page that the user visits from gathering data about the user. It does this by reissuing the user's request for a Web page instead of simply passing it along. The reissued request contains only the identifying information of the anonymizing server itself, not the identifying information about the user.

applet: Major programs are known as *applications.* Short programs, especially those written in the Java programming language for use on the Web, are called by the diminutive *applet.*

ARPANET: The original test bed for the Internet, a computer network developed by the Advanced Research Projects Agency.

ASCII (American Standard Code for Information Interchange): A common method for representing textual characters.

ASP: See *Active Server Page.*

attachment: A file that is sent along with an e-mail message. Most e-mail client programs place an attachment into a separate directory from the one in which they store the e-mail messages. E-mail attachments are one of the primary means of spreading viruses.

authentication: Verifying the identity of a person or service, usually through digital IDs.

autoresponder: A program that responds automatically to an e-mail message by sending back a preprogrammed e-mail message of its own. Autoresponders are useful for providing price lists, back issues of newsletters, and so on.

AVS: See *Address Verification System.*

axis: In three-dimensional (3D) graphics, each of the three directions is indicated by an axis. The typical coordinate system uses an x-axis that runs horizontally, a y-axis that runs vertically, and a z-axis that runs, essentially, between the front and back of the monitor.

B2B: Business to business e-commerce, such as sales of photocopiers.

B2C: Business to consumer e-commerce — general products or services not related to business.

bandwidth: The total amount of data that a particular network connection can handle. The higher the bandwidth, the more data that can be sent in the same amount of time.

banner: An image link that appears on a Web page (generally at the top of the page) and contains advertising for a sponsor.

below the fold: The portion of the Web page that is out of sight when the page first loads into a browser, which the viewer must scroll down to see. See also *above the fold.*

binary file: A program file. In transferring files through FTP, you must be careful to send program files as binary files rather than as text files because text files have a different format.

blog: A shortening of *web log.* A personal diary on the World Wide Web.

blogosphere: The sum of all the blogs in the world.

breadcrumb: A listing of the trail followed to reach a particular Web page on a site. Like the breadcrumbs in the Hansel and Gretel fairy tale, this trail can be followed backward by clicking the links.

bricks-and-mortar: A normal, physical store as opposed to an online store.

broadband: Internet service capable of carrying a greater amount of information than earlier methods such as a modem/telephone connection.

browser: See *Web browser.*

cable modem: A broadband device supplied in conjunction with cable television service.

Cascading Style Sheet (CSS): A method of specifying the layout and appearance of a Web page that gives greater control than HTML at the cost of greater complexity.

cat: A creature that deigns to permit humans to inhabit the same planet.

CFML: See *ColdFusion Markup Language.*

CGI: See *Common Gateway Interface.*

chargeback: A debit issued against your merchant account by a credit card company because of a dispute over the validity of a transaction.

chat room: A place where people meet online and exchange messages in real time.

click-through: The action of a site visitor in clicking an advertising link to visit the advertiser's site.

client/server: A networking system in which one computer provides resources to other computers over a network. The main computer provides a network service and is known as a *server.* Computers that use the services of a server are *clients.* You also use the term *server* to refer to the software that provides the service. The software that accesses the server is also known as the *client* or *client agent.*

ColdFusion Markup Language (CFML): A proprietary Adobe markup language that provides Web designers with the capability to easily create Web-based database query forms and the Web pages that present their responses. See also *markup language.*

colocation: Similar to leasing a dedicated server; the server is located at a site that provides technical services to you (such as network monitoring), but you own the server instead of leasing it. You may provide your own equipment or purchase it from the colocation firm.

Common Gateway Interface (CGI): A program that can take information gathered from users in a Web page form and pass that information to other programs for processing.

compile: The source code that you create with languages, such as Java or C, is run through a *compiler* that prepares a stand-alone, ready-to-run program.

configuration: The particular arrangement of practically anything having to do with computing. Configuration, for example, may refer to how many and what types of peripherals are connected to a computer. It may also refer to the settings in the "preferences" section of a program.

cookie: A text file that a Web site places on a visitor's computer. Cookies typically contain information such as an identification code, the date of last visit, visitor preferences, and so on.

copyright: The right to make copies. The creators of works such as books, paintings, songs, or computer programs own the copyrights to those works unless they transfer their rights to another person or company.

CSS: See *Cascading Style Sheet.*

dedicated server: A computer that is reserved for the use of a single person, company, or organization. See also *virtual server.*

default: Failure to pay bills. Okay, seriously, defaults are the normal settings for software and hardware as they come from the manufacturers. In most cases, you can change the default settings to suit yourself.

demographics: Information that you gather from visitors to your site. Commonly, demographics include such things as the computer systems that visitors use, their income levels, and any other information that you require to understand your audience. Be careful about gathering data on age, race, sex, ethnicity, religious persuasion, and such — because this may lead to discrimination charges. Make sure that, if you do ask for this type of information, you make clear that such disclosures are purely optional. And never, never, *never* make any of this information available to anyone else, except as a lump-sum total that doesn't name names. You need to keep the individual input absolutely confidential.

Denmark: A country in northern Europe, of which about 75 percent is composed of farms.

DHTML: See *Dynamic HTML.*

digital ID: An encrypted identifier that you keep on file at a central repository known as a *Certificate Authority.* It certifies that you *are* who you say you are (just in case you're wondering).

Digital Subscriber Line (DSL): A popular method of high-speed Internet access that utilizes existing telephone lines. Normal telephone operation is also possible on the same line, so you can use phones and fax machines while the DSL connection is active. The DSL connection doesn't interfere with normal phone signals because it goes out at a different frequency.

discount rate: A percentage of each sale that you pay to the bank that processes credit card transactions.

DNS: See *Domain Name System.*

domain extension: See *top-level domain.*

Domain Name System (DNS): A system to translate the human-readable domain names, such as `www.dummies.com`, into the numerical IP addresses that computers understand (in this case, 38.170.216.18).

dot com (or dotcom): Colloquial expression meaning an Internet-based company.

download: Transferring a file to your computer from another computer. Also refers to the file that you download. See also *upload.*

downtime: The time during which a server or connection fails to function.

draft: A check that you print to draw funds from another person's account after the person provides you with account information and authorization.

drop-shipping: An arrangement by which you gather orders and submit them to another company; that company then sends its merchandise to your customer with your return address on it. You pay the company a wholesale rate and keep the difference as profit.

DSL: See *Digital Subscriber Line.*

Dynamic HTML (DHTML): The combination of HTML along with JavaScript and Cascading Style Sheets to create a Web page with dynamic elements. See also *JavaScript* and *Cascading Style Sheet.*

e-commerce: Business conducted on the World Wide Web or via intranets. Although some elements of e-commerce may contain traditional bricks-and-mortar aspects such as mailed order forms, it takes place primarily via the Internet or some similar network system.

e-mail: The sending and receiving of written messages via computer networks such as the Internet.

Emerald City: The home base of the Wizard of Oz.

emoticon: A symbol used to express the emotion of the writer, such as a *smiley* like :-) to indicate pleasure or harmless intent, or a wink like ;-) to show the writer's words are intended as a joke.

encryption: The encoding of data (such as e-mail messages or personal information entered into online order forms) so it can't be read by anyone who does not have the key to the code.

end tag: See *tag.*

eXtensible HyperText Markup Language (XHTML): A version of HTML that follows the XML specification. See *HyperText Markup Language* and *eXtensible Markup Language.*

eXtensible Markup Language (XML): A markup language that allows users to create custom tags, allowing them (in effect) to create their own personalized markup languages. See also *markup language* and *tag.*

eXtensible Style Language (XSL): A language for adding style sheets to XML documents. The relationship between XML and XSL is the same as between HTML and CSS. See also *eXtensible Markup Language, HyperText Markup Language,* and *Cascading Style Sheet.*

FAQ: A listing of Frequently Asked Questions and their answers.

Fargo: A city in North Dakota.

feed: The transmission of information from a server to either its clients or another server.

feed reader: A program for deciphering RSS feeds.

File Transfer Protocol (FTP): A method for transferring files from one computer to another across a network or the Internet.

flame: A message that contains insults or inflammatory material.

flame war: An extended exchange of messages containing flames. Flame wars disrupt the normal process of communication in mailing lists, newsgroups, message boards, and chat rooms.

font: A complete set of letters, numbers, punctuation, and special characters that all have a particular look and shape. For example, this is in the Arial font, whereas `this` is in the Courier New font.

frame/frameset: A method enabling you to display multiple Web pages on a single browser screen. Framesets set off different areas of the screen. Each area is known as a *frame,* and each frame contains its own Web page.

FTP: See *File Transfer Protocol.*

GIF: An image file that follows the standards of the Graphics Interchange Format. You commonly use GIFs for limited animation.

guillemot: A type of sea bird famous for waddling.

hardcopy: A printed version of a Web page as opposed to the electronic version seen in a browser.

high-risk: The category into which credit card companies place businesses that they believe are particularly prone to suffering from fraudulent transactions.

hit: A single access of a Web page.

home page: The main Web page from which all other pages in the site branch out. It is commonly called `index.html`, although this is not a requirement. In fact, any name will work — though if you use another name, visitors may see a listing of available files instead of instantly viewing your home page. The users then have to figure out which file among those listed is the home page.

Other common names include `index.htm` and `default.htm`. (The difference between the `.htm` and `.html` extensions is practically nonexistent, by the way, going back to the days when the early DOS operating system recognized only three-letter extensions.) All modern operating systems are capable of recognizing longer file-type extensions, and few professionals limit themselves to the old DOS conventions anymore.

horizontal rule: A line across a Web page that you use to separate one section of a page visually from another. The HR element in HTML creates a horizontal rule.

HTML: See *HyperText Markup Language.*

HTML editor: Text editor with special features designed to assist you in creating Web pages.

HTTP: See *HyperText Transfer Protocol.*

hyperlink: See *link.*

hypertext: Text on a computer that includes links to other text, images, sound, and so on.

HyperText Markup Language (HTML): The native language of the World Wide Web, which you use to construct Web pages.

HyperText Transfer Protocol (HTTP): System for transferring files across the World Wide Web.

ICANN: See *Internet Corporation for Assigned Names and Numbers.*

image: General term for any picture or artwork on a Web page. Web images are usually stored in GIF, JPEG, or PNG formats.

image map: An image that contains multiple links. Users viewing an image map select different links by moving the mouse pointer to different parts of the image and clicking. You must carefully design the images you use in image maps to provide visual clues to the links that they contain.

image repository: A Web site that contains a large amount of digital art, mostly simple icons. Image repositories typically gather these files without paying attention to whether they're violating copyrights and trademarks.

InterBank: An organization that processes merchant credit card transactions for its member banks.

Internet: Short for *Internetwork.* The Internet consists of several different computer networks that all link together into a network of networks.

Internet access: The capability to connect to the Internet, usually provided by an ISP.

Internet Corporation for Assigned Names and Numbers (ICANN): The organization that accredits domain-name registrars.

Internet service provider (ISP): Company that provides Internet access, usually by dial-up connections, although many also offer high-speed dedicated connections.

interpret: To "translate" source code written in languages such as JavaScript or Perl into usable instructions. A Web browser or Web server will interpret incoming code before carrying out the instructions it contains. See also ***compile.***

intranet: A network, usually private, consisting of several computer networks linked together. Unlike the Internet, access to an intranet is limited to its membership. Intranets are commonly used in B2B e-commerce situations.

IP address: The numerical equivalent of a domain name.

Isopoda: A type of crustacean with a small head.

ISP: See ***Internet service provider.***

Java: A programming language that is often used to create applets for the Web. See also ***applet.***

JavaScript: A simple but powerful programming language that programmers use to create scripts for Web pages. See also ***script.***

JPEG: Also known as JPG. An image file that follows the standards of the Joint Photographic Experts Group. JPEG files are generally smaller than graphic files in other formats but maintain high-quality images nonetheless.

John of Lancaster: Admiral of the British fleet in 1422.

JPG: See ***JPEG.***

keyword: A word or phrase that search engines use to locate Web pages containing matching terms.

link (hyperlink): A connection between a Web page and another Internet resource. Usually a link contains the URL (Internet address) of another Web page, but it can also connect the user to other resources, such as images. By convention, a link appears as blue underlined text that, after you activate it (usually by a mouse click), causes a Web browser to load the linked resource. You also often use images as links. An *active link* is one that you're currently clicking; a *visited link* is one that you activated previously.

link farm: A Web site that has no useful content of its own, but merely contains a group of links to other sites.

list owner: The person who manages a mailing list. Usually the list owner is the person who conceives of — and launches — the list. This person is also known as a *list manager* and may be the *moderator* of the list as well. See also *moderator.*

list server: A program that processes the e-mail messages that comprise a mailing list. The list server usually also handles such routine administrative matters as subscribing and unsubscribing list members if they send it a message containing the appropriate commands.

locomotive: A specialized type of railroad car, also known as an *engine,* that propels other railroad cars along the track.

log file: A file that records activity. A Web server log file, for example, records the origin of anyone who looks at a Web page, the type of browser the person is using, and so on. Log-file analyzer programs, such as Statbot, are useful to Webmasters in figuring out peak times of usage, number of hits per day, which other sites are referring visitors to this site, and so on.

mailing list: A discussion group in which the members post messages that a list server relays to them via e-mail. *Open mailing lists* can be joined by anyone; *closed mailing lists* require approval to join.

markup language: A computer programming language that is dedicated to the layout and function of elements on-screen. HTML is the best-known markup language, although there are many others for specialized purposes, such as the Astronomical Markup Language (ASML), the Bioinformatic Sequence Markup Language (BSML), and the Math Markup Language (MATHML), as well as some that hope to compete with HTML to become the new lingua franca of Web-development authors. See also *eXtensible Markup Language, eXtensible HyperText Markup Language,* and *HyperText Markup Language.*

marquee: A scrolling on-screen message resembling the ones that were once common on the signs (marquees) outside theaters.

merchant account: An arrangement with a bank or a bank's sales organization for you to accept credit cards in payment for goods or services.

message board: Similar to a newsgroup but operates on an individual Web site. Message boards, sometimes known as *graffiti walls,* enable site visitors to leave messages for other visitors to read.

metadata: Information beyond what is necessary for the display of a Web page. Common uses of metadata, for example, are the inclusion of the author's name and a content description in the HEAD section of a Web page.

modem (*modulator/demodulator*): Device that enables a computer to send signals over a telephone line.

moderator: Person who controls the content of a mailing list or newsgroup. In extreme cases, this control can amount to censorship, but reasonable moderation simply results in the removal of extraneous material, such as sales pitches for products and services that don't relate to the topic. A moderator may also play peacemaker, attempting to keep tempers in check among the members of the mailing list or newsgroup, thus avoiding flame wars.

Modesty Blaise: Popular adventure character first appearing in a 1962 comic strip and later the subject of about a dozen novels and at least one movie.

netiquette (Inter*net* et*iquette*): A series of customs that enable people to get along while living in cyberspace. Basically, you want to be nice and consider how your actions may affect other people.

newline: A programming instruction — in the form of \n — to move the next bit of text down one line.

Northwest Passage: Channel leading from the Atlantic Ocean to the Pacific Ocean north of North America. Much sought after since the fifteenth century, but not successfully negotiated until 1906.

online service: Sort of a mini-Internet; services such as CompuServe, America Online, and so on provide many of the functions that the Internet does but on a smaller scale. In recent years, the online services have lost much business to the Internet and now provide Internet access as part of their services.

opt-in mailing list: A mailing list that you subscribe to by entering your e-mail address in a form. You then receive a message in your mailbox asking you to confirm the subscription. If you don't reply to that message, your address doesn't go into the system. This sign-up method makes it difficult for anyone else to sign you up for the list.

page-generation program: Software that uses a WYSIWYG (what you see is what you get), point-and-click interface for creating Web pages.

parameter: Information that you add to the HTML code that calls a Java applet. This information sets variable values for the applet's use, and you add it through the PARAM element.

password: Secret word that you use to gain computer access. Sometimes you choose a password; sometimes someone else assigns you one. Two schools of thought on passwords offer contradictory advice. One says to make them so difficult to imagine that no one else can possibly guess yours in a million years. The other school of thought says to make them easy enough that you can remember them.

Pausanias: General of the Greek army in the Battle of Plataea in 479 B.C.

PDF: See *Portable Document Format.*

plug-in: A small program that provides additional functionality to a larger program, such as letting a Web browser use Flash or adding a filter to a graphics program.

podcast: An audio broadcast included as part of an RSS feed.

pop-up: A separate window in which a Web browser displays additional information not found on the Web page that the visitor originally accessed. Pop-up windows are used for a variety of purposes — some are considered legitimate, while others often are not. Pop-up windows, in their best and highest usage, are useful adjuncts to a normal Web page, adding helpful information or additional capabilities. Their common usage as advertising billboards, however, has given them a bad reputation, and programs called *pop-up blockers,* which prevent all pop-up windows from materializing, are increasingly popular. Savvy Web designers should look for ways to avoid using pop-ups.

Portable Document Format (PDF): A proprietary document display format developed by Adobe Systems, Inc. Although it allows people to easily transfer existing documents into a form that's viewable on the Web, visitors need a separate plug-in in order to view those documents.

public domain: The group of all created works that copyright law no longer protects (or never did).

Quimper: French city on the Odet River.

Really Simple Syndication (RSS): A method for providing a continuously updated source of text, images, or audio. Commonly used for news stories and blogs.

reciprocal link: A link to a Web page that also displays a link back to your Web page. Hyperlinking is a common practice for building traffic among Web sites. If you want to establish a reciprocal link with someone else's site, add a link to that site on your own, and then send an e-mail message asking the site's owner to reciprocate.

registrar: A company approved by the Internet Corporation for Assigned Names and Numbers (ICANN) to keep track of domain names on the Internet. A domain name that you register must point to an active Web site. You may also *reserve* or *park* domain names if you have no current site active for that name but still want to prevent anybody else from registering the name. See also ***Domain Name System*** and ***Internet Corporation for Assigned Names and Numbers.***

RGB triplet: A method of defining on-screen colors by specifying the amount of red, green, and blue in the color. Java applets often utilize this method. The possible values range from 0 to 255. Thus, if you want red lettering, you use a value of 255,0,0. This setting tells the applet to use as much red as possible but no green and no blue.

ring: A series of Web sites that connect together through links that lead from one to the other until visitors who follow all the links go full circle and return to their starting place.

robot: A program, also known as a *spider,* that automatically surfs the Web, indexing Web pages and adding information from those pages to a search site's database.

RSS: See ***Really Simple Syndication.***

Runic alphabet: Characters that the Teutonic peoples of early Europe used; also known as *futhark.*

safety paper: The kind of paper on which you print a draft or check.

script: A short program.

search engine optimization (SEO): The process of designing a Web page so it gets the highest possible ranking among the results that a search engine puts on-screen.

Secure Sockets Layer (SSL): An encryption system, originally developed by Netscape, that allows visitors to enter information into online forms and submit that information without allowing anyone else to read it. It's commonly used in processing order forms and other online forms that contain private information.

SEO: See ***search engine optimization.***

server: See ***client/server.***

Server Side Includes (SSI): The capability of a server that processes a CGI script to include data of its own that it sends back to the Web browser.

SGML: See *Standard Generalized Markup Language.*

shopping cart: A program that visitors to your site use to keep track of which items they want to purchase. The shopping cart metaphor extends to the visitor's capability to put items into the cart and remove them before making a final purchasing decision.

sleep: A common practice utterly unknown to authors trying to meet a deadline.

spam: Unsolicited e-mail messages that someone sends in bulk quantities to several addresses; also the same message posted to multiple newsgroups simultaneously.

spider: See *robot.*

SSI: See *Server Side Includes.*

SSL: See *Secure Socket Layers.*

standard: Also known as *specifications.* Generic term for anything that a lot of people agree on. It may apply to a way to transfer files from one system to another, the exact structure and function of a computer language, or a method of compressing video images. If a recognized, organized group develops it, it's known as an *official standard.* If it's just something that the market leader develops, and most of the people in a particular field use it, it's known as a *de facto standard.*

Standard Generalized Markup Language (SGML): The original markup language from which HTML was developed. See also *markup language.*

start tag: See *tag.*

style sheets: See *Cascading Style Sheet.*

subscriber: A member of a mailing list. Also known, amazingly enough, as a list member.

surfing: The act of using a Web browser to visit sites.

syndicate: A content provider that represents several different sources of content, such as comics, opinion columns, horoscopes, and articles.

tag: In HTML, the bracketed name of an element. You indicate the beginning of each element in HTML by placing its name within angle brackets. This part of the element is the *start tag.* You indicate the end of the element by using an *end tag,* which looks just like the start tag except you add a slash before the element's name. The start and end tags for the `TABLE` element, for example, are `<TABLE>` and `</TABLE>`.

telepathy: Ability to transfer thoughts from one mind to another.

text editor: A simple form of word processor that saves text files without formatting.

text file: A file of text. (No kidding. No fancy formatting, either, which is why it's also called a *plaintext* file.) In transferring text files via FTP, you want to be careful to send them as such rather than as binary files because text files often require conversion in transferring between Windows and UNIX systems, which use slightly different text formats. See also *ASCII.*

thread: Hierarchy that shows the relationship of a series of messages on a message board. See also *message board.*

tiling: The repetition of a background image across a Web page until it reaches the edge of the screen. It then begins tiling again in the next available space below the first line of images — and so on until it fills the entire page with multiple copies of the image.

toolbar: An add-on to a Web browser that provides additional functionality, such as easy access to a search engine.

top-level domain (TLD): A domain that contains other domains but is not contained itself, as designated by the final letters (such as .com or .edu) at the end of an Internet address. You consider them *top-level* because you read Internet addresses in steps from right to left, with the part after the last dot on the right being the highest step in a hierarchy that eventually leads down, step by dotted step, to a particular computer. The four most common TLDs are `.com`, `.net`, `.edu`, and `.org`. These TLDs are known as the *generic TLDs* or *gTLDs;* those that specify a country in which a site originates are known as *country-level TLDs* or *CLTLDs.*

traffic: The number of visits to an Internet site, as in, "Our traffic increased by 100,000 visitors last week."

Uncertainty Principle: Fundamental theorem of quantum physics that states that knowing both the direction of travel and the location in space-time of an atomic particle is impossible.

uniform resource locator (URL): The address of a file (or other resource) on the Internet. The URL for a file on a Web server is formed by putting together a series of directions to the file, as in the following example:

```
http://www.someschool.edu/graphics/logo.png
```

Here's a breakdown of the preceding URL:

- ✔ The http:// specifies the HyperText Transfer Protocol (the Web's native method of information exchange).
- ✔ The www tells you that the computer that holds the file is a Web server. Actually, you already know that from the first part — that's why a lot of Web sites don't use the www prefix anymore.
- ✔ The someschool segment gives the *subdomain,* which is what people usually think of as the name of the Web site. The Wiley Web site, for example, is located at www.wiley.com, and its subdomain is wiley.
- ✔ The three-letter extension represents the *top-level domain.* In this case, the subdomain is followed by .edu, meaning that this Web site is in the education domain.
- ✔ The graphics part leads to a particular directory on the specified Web server.
- ✔ The final portion, logo.png, is a file within that directory.

Files located within the same server as a Web page can be referenced in a simpler way by using *relative URLs.* Instead of fully specifying how to find the file from anywhere on the Internet, relative URLs only specify how to find it from the Web page that refers to it. The file in the preceding example could be linked to from the school's home page by using the following relative URL:

```
<IMG src="graphics/logo.png">
```

Because the Web browser that you use to view the home page already knows where it is, it can perform a bit of cutting and pasting to come up with the right URL. The browser "reasons" that it is currently viewing a Web page located at http://www.someschool.edu/index.html. It strips off everything after the final slash to arrive at http://www.someschool.edu/ and then adds graphics/logo.png to that to arrive at http://www.someschool.edu/graphics/logo.png. See also *top-level domain.*

upload: To transfer a file from your computer to another computer. Also the file that you upload. See also *download.*

URL: See *uniform resource locator.*

Van de Graaff generator: A primitive device that generates millions of volts of static electricity.

VBScript: The Visual Basic scripting language from Microsoft. As the name suggests, it is a version of the simple BASIC programming language, but geared to developing Web sites rather than software in general.

virtual server: A directory on a computer that simulates the existence of a separate computer and acts as a server on a network. See also *dedicated server.*

visited link: See *link.*

Webcast: An audio or video presentation offered via a Web site.

Webmaster: The person in control of a Web site. A Webmaster may be an individual with only a single Web page or the manager of a large team of developers who create and maintain Web sites.

Web browser: A program such as Internet Explorer or Firefox that displays Web pages.

Web ring: See *ring.*

Web site: Any presence on the World Wide Web. Usually applies to a collection of Web pages.

William Kidd: Eighteenth-century English privateer who went down in history as the pirate Captain Kidd. He provided documents to political authorities that showed that he'd attacked only ships carrying papers that showed they were at war with England, but the papers were lost until the 1970s.

x-axis: See *axis.*

XHTML: See *eXtensible HyperText Markup Language.*

XML: See *eXtensible Markup Language.*

XSL: See *eXtensible Style Language.*

y-axis: See *axis.*

ytterbium: A rare-earth element that you often find in combination with gadolinite.

z-axis: See *axis.*

zymurgy: The study of the fermentation process.

Index

• X •

• Y •